Dick Goddard's ALMANAC *for* NORTHEAST OHIO

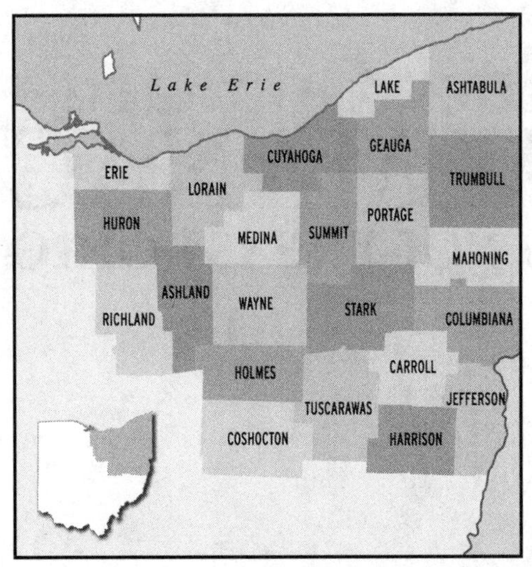

The Counties of Northeast Ohio

Dick Goddard's ALMANAC *for* NORTHEAST OHIO 2005

GRAY & COMPANY, PUBLISHERS
CLEVELAND

A portion of the proceeds from the sale of this book will benefit animal charities in Northeast Ohio.

Gray & Company, Publishers
1588 E. 40th St., Cleveland, OH 44103
(216) 431-2665
www.grayco.com

ISBN 1-886228-92-2

Printed in the United States of America

First printing

CONTENTS

2004–2005 Forecast*

Our pleasant and mild weather of early October will give way in early November to increasingly stronger cold fronts. Winds will become gusty and early snow will often be mixed with rain near Lake Erie. In December we will notice the days are becoming darker earlier and the nights are becoming much longer. The unique phenomenon known as lake-effect snow will develop and continue off and on through January—and February as well—if Lake Erie and Lake Huron remain unfrozen, as they often do. Daylight will become noticeably longer as we reach February, although cold temperatures and occasional snow will continue. March snows will be wet and soggy, and, by month's end, the "gatekeepers" of spring, the tiny cricket frogs known as spring peepers, will be serenading us with their sleighbell chorus. Spring will soon appear, and by early April the Cleveland Indians will be playing baseball at Jacobs Field. During April and May the weather will become warmer and more turbulent, with thunder being heard. Temperatures will continue to steadily rise, becoming very warm to frequently oppressive as we move through the month of June and into the dog days of July and August. By late August and September children will return to school. At this time almanacs will again appear in drug and book stores where nice, but gullible, people will spend countless dollars to find out what the following year will hold. Just as they have for several hundred years.

* *Purists demand that an almanac should forecast the weather for a year in advance. Such extended forecasts are notoriously inaccurate, but after serious consultation with local squirrels, caterpillars, and groundhogs, I offer the above with great confidence. – D.G.*

INTRODUCTION

This is our fifth Almanac and Weather Guide for Northeast Ohio and more than a dozen talented authors have once again contributed an eclectic assortment of essays.

I'm so sure you'll be enlightened and entertained by the 2005 edition that my offer still stands: If you don't find something you really like, I'll buy it back. (In the previous four editions, I've had no takers.)

FOX 8 I-Team sleuth Bill Sheil makes a compassionate appeal on behalf of the Big Brothers and Big Sisters organizations. A true red, white, and blue Cleveland Indians fan, fellow meteorologist Scott Sabol conjures up fond memories of the recently departed Cleveland Stadium. Scott Johnson reveals the secret, albeit squirrelly, aspect to excellent wildlife photography.

Tim Taylor, our golf pro, writes eloquently about his favorite hobby, while Wilma Smith shows her passion for her pooch pals.

The FOX 8 folks are joined by the imaginative and redoubtable Bill Hickey, the former outstanding *Plain Dealer* television critic (what is there to criticize, Bill?),

along with longtime television personality Tom Haley, who teamed with Del Donahoo for a fabulous run on Channel 3's morning show. (Henry, the wakeup rooster, was everybody's favorite.)

Jay Reynolds from the Lake Erie Nature and Science Center in Bay Village guides us on a month-by-month tour around the heavens and advises us on which telescope to buy. Robert Hinkle of the Cleveland Metroparks tells us how to stay out of the poison ivy. Weather guru Ron Hahn recalls what was very likely the most powerful—and least known—tornado ever to strike Ohio.

We couldn't do the Almanac without several uplifting and informative stories about our fuzzy, four-footed friends. Sarah Steiner tells us how to find a lost buddy, and Kate Malarney treats us to some doggone-good stories. Our "Pet of the Year" is Jessie, and Joy Walters has great news on that little lady who was—evidently—purposefully hit by a car.

Of my essays, "The Job of Being God" is my favorite. (I figure God must have a sense of humor or he wouldn't have created us!) Have you wondered where all the black squirrels have come from? I'll let you know the secret.

Enjoy.

JANUARY STATISTICS

(recorded at Cleveland Hopkins Airport)

SUNSHINE %	30
DRIEST MONTH	0.31"/1871
WARMEST MONTH	40.2°/1932
COLDEST MONTH	11.0°/1977
LIQUID PCPN AVG.	2.04"
RAINIEST DAY	2.93"/1995
RAINIEST MONTH	7.01"/1950
THUNDERY DAYS	0
SNOWIEST DAY	10.8"/1996
SNOWIEST MONTH	42.8"/1978
LEAST SNOWFALL	0.5"/1932
DAYS ONE INCH SNOW	5

January is named after the Roman god Janus, the two-faced Keeper of the Gates. Janus usually shows us only his cold and snowy countenance, however. Paradoxically, in early January Planet Earth is three million miles closer to the sun than in July. It is the angle of the incoming solar radiation—acute in winter and more direct in summer—that makes our winter cold and our summer hot. In many Januaries a welcome small reward comes in the form of the legendary January thaw, usually during the third week. The milder weather quickly leaves and Northeast Ohio plunges back into the depths of winter. Another psychological uplift comes as the seed catalogs arrive—like the one that has the guy on the cover holding up an 80-pound rutabaga and saying, "You can imagine my surprise. . . ."

On the 26th day of the month in 1978, Ohio's deepest storm, literally a white hurricane, ravaged the state from south to north. On the 19th day of 1994, Cleveland's temperature fell to an all-time record 20 degrees below zero; temperatures remained below zero for a benchmark string of 56 hours. Our coldest January was in 1977, our warmest in the El Niño year of 1932. Depending on the strength of the cold, the first flower of the year, the snowdrop, will appear by month's end. Mosquitoes are never a problem this month.

DAILY DATA FOR JANUARY

Date	Day	Moon	Day of Year	Days Left	Sunrise	Sunset	Length of Day	Avg. Hi°	Avg. Lo°	Avg. Lake°
1	Sat		1	364	7:53	5:08	9:15	33	20	35
2	Sun		2	363	7:53	5:09	9:16	33	19	34
3	Mon	◑	3	362	7:53	5:10	9:17	33	19	34
4	Tue		4	361	7:53	5:11	9:18	32	19	34
5	Wed		5	360	7:53	5:11	9:18	32	19	34
6	Thu		6	359	7:53	5:12	9:19	32	18	34
7	Fri		7	358	7:53	5:13	9:20	32	18	34
8	Sat		8	357	7:53	5:14	9:21	32	18	34
9	Sun		9	356	7:53	5:15	9:22	32	18	34
10	Mon	●	10	355	7:52	5:17	9:25	32	18	34
11	Tue		11	354	7:52	5:18	9:26	32	18	34
12	Wed		12	353	7:52	5:19	9:27	32	18	34
13	Thu		13	352	7:51	5:20	9:29	32	17	34
14	Fri		14	351	7:51	5:21	9:30	32	17	33
15	Sat		15	350	7:51	5:22	9:31	32	17	33
16	Sun		16	349	7:50	5:23	9:33	32	17	33
17	Mon	◐	17	348	7:50	5:24	9:34	31	17	33
18	Tue		18	347	7:49	5:26	9:37	31	17	33
19	Wed		19	346	7:49	5:27	9:38	31	17	33
20	Thu		20	345	7:48	5:28	9:40	31	17	33
21	Fri		21	344	7:47	5:29	9:42	31	17	33
22	Sat		22	343	7:47	5:30	9:43	31	17	33
23	Sun		23	342	7:46	5:32	9:46	31	17	33
24	Mon		24	341	7:45	5:33	9:48	32	17	33
25	Tue	○	25	340	7:44	5:34	9:50	32	17	33
26	Wed		26	339	7:44	5:35	9:51	32	17	33
27	Thu		27	338	7:43	5:37	9:54	32	17	33
28	Fri		28	337	7:42	5:38	9:56	32	17	33
29	Sat		29	336	7:41	5:39	9:58	32	17	33
30	Sun		30	335	7:40	5:40	10:00	32	17	33
31	Mon		31	334	7:39	5:42	10:03	32	17	33

Rec. Hi°	Rec. Lo°	On This Date . . .
69/1876	-4/1968	Actor Don Novello ("Father Guido Sarducci") born in Ashtabula (1943)
66/1876	-12/1879	Green Bay Packers beat Browns 23-12 in NFL champ. game (1966)
65/1874	-16/1879	Cavaliers retire jersey #34, Austin Carr (1981)
65/1874	-7/1679	Football coach Don Shula born in Grand River (1930)
66/1939	-13/1884	Football coach Chuck Noll born in Cleveland (1932)
66/1946	-9/1884	WKBN TV 27 in Youngstown begins broadcasting (1953)
63/1907	-9/1884	First issue of the Cleveland Plain Dealer published (1842)
66/1937	-10/1968	The State Convention of Baptists in Ohio was formed (1954)
61/1937	-13/1875	-87ºF (-66ºC), Northice Station, Greenland (Greenland record) (1954)
61/1939	-12/1875	Race car driver Bobby Rahal born in Medina (1953)
67/1890	-9/1899	Atlanta, Georgia temperature goes below zeroº F (1982)
65/1916	-9/1886	NFL champion Cleve. Rams given permission to move to L.A. (1946)
69/1890	-10/1977	Congress changes U.S. flag to 15 stars & 15 stripes (1794)
70/1932	-6/1893	Musician Dave Grohl born in Warren (1969)
68/1932	-7/1972	Actor Chad Lowe born in Dayton (1968)
57/1889	-15/1977	18th Amendment (Prohibition) becomes law of the land (1920)
60/1973	-17/1982	Actor Oscar Apfel born in Cleveland (1878)
64/1996	-15/1994	Ghoulardi debuts on "Shock Theater" on WJW TV 8 (1963)
67/1907	-20/1994	Cleveland's WKBF TV, Channel 61, begins broadcasting (1968)
65/1906	-18/1985	Holmes County incorporated (1824)
71/1906	-17/1985	Golfer Jack Nicklaus born in Columbus (1940)
71/1906	-10/1936	Temperature rises 49ºF in 2 minutes in Spearfish, SD (1943)
68/1967	-17/1963	Indians' Bob Feller elected to Baseball Hall of Fame (1962)
65/1909	-19/1963	Cavs' biggest margin of victory, 43 points, vs. Milwaukee 132-89 (1976)
73/1950	-15/1897	Browns' Lou "The Toe" Groza born (1924)
69/1950	-9/1897	Actor Paul Newman born in Cleveland (1925)
69/1916	-6/1966	Browns/Ravens kicker Matt Stover born (1968)
62/2002	-10/1977	25th Space Shuttle (51L)-Challenger 10 explodes (1986)
65/1914	-17/1873	William McKinley born in Niles (1843)
62/1916	-4/1873	The "Lone Ranger" premieres on ABC radio (1933)
62/1989	-5/1971	Coshocton County incorporated (1810)

Flora & Fauna JANUARY

WEEK 1 **BIRDS:** The harshest time of winter has arrived! Fill your feeders each day if you have begun a feeding program. The birds will appreciate your handouts at least through late March. Spill some seed on the ground and watch for white-throated sparrows, white-crowned sparrows, tree sparrows, and mourning doves. **MAMMALS:** Fox squirrels abandon their leaf nests for the relative comfort of tree dens. Many squirrel holes were started by woodpeckers, then enlarged later by crafty squirrels seeking warmer winter homes. After dark, field mice and meadow voles extend their tunnels beneath the snow to take advantage of seeds missed by the squirrels.

WEEK 2 **BIRDS:** Red-tailed hawks begin their courting rituals in the skies over northeastern Ohio. "Would you like this beautiful stick?" he seems to say as he flies by her with a branch longer than he is. "We could build a great nest in the forest." **MAMMALS:** Life goes on rather well under the white snowy blanket. Meadow voles, short-tailed shrews, and deer mice welcome the snows of winter to protect them from predators and keep them insulated from the cold surface air.

WEEK 3 **BIRDS:** It's still winter, but on sunny days you may hear the bright "teakettle-teakettle-teakettle!" of the Carolina wren. Virtually eliminated in the snows of 1978, this more southerly bird is making a comeback along the north shore. **MAMMALS:** Agile coyotes chase white-tailed deer across open meadows when they spot one that seems sick or injured. Most give up the chase in less than a hundred yards if the deer is not caught. Energy conservation is important even to coyotes!

WEEK 4 **BIRDS:** The days grow noticeably longer. Sensing the change in daylight, cardinals cry "cheer-cheer-cheer" and tufted titmice call their plaintive "Peter-Peter-Peter" spring songs. It will be a long time before they see green lawns, however. **MAMMALS:** With no leaves to block your view, deer, foxes, and other mammals become easier to see against the white snows of winter. Tracks in the snow tell stories of predators seen and meadows crossed quickly-and occasionally show evidence of the local food chain. Deer are winter browsers, not grazers, and wander from shrub to shrub nipping off the tender ends of twigs.

Adapted from the Nature Almanac by Robert Hinkle, with permission from Cleveland Metroparks.

FAHRENHEIT/CELSIUS CONVERSION

°F	°C	°F	°C	°F	°C	°F	°C	°F	°C	°F	°C	°F	°C
-20	-29	-2	-19	16	-9	34	1	52	11	70	21	88	31
-19	-28	-1	-18	17	-8	35	2	53	12	71	22	89	32
-18	-28	0	-18	18	-8	36	2	54	12	72	22	90	32
-17	-27	1	-17	19	-7	37	3	55	13	73	23	91	33
-16	-27	2	-17	20	-7	38	3	56	13	74	23	92	33
-15	-26	3	-16	21	-6	39	4	57	14	75	24	93	34
-14	-26	4	-16	22	-6	40	4	58	14	76	24	94	34
-13	-25	5	-15	23	-5	41	5	59	15	77	25	95	35
-12	-24	6	-14	24	-4	42	6	60	16	78	26	96	36
-11	-24	7	-14	25	-4	43	6	61	16	79	26	97	36
-10	-23	8	-13	26	-3	44	7	62	17	80	27	98	37
-9	-23	9	-13	27	-3	45	7	63	17	81	27	99	37
-8	-22	10	-12	28	-2	46	8	64	18	82	28	100	38
-7	-22	11	-12	29	-2	47	8	65	18	83	28	101	38
-6	-21	12	-11	30	-1	48	9	66	19	84	29	102	39
-5	-21	13	-11	31	-1	49	9	67	19	85	29	103	39
-4	-20	14	-10	32	0	50	10	68	20	86	30	104	40
-3	-19	15	-9	33	1	51	11	69	21	87	31		

What to Do If a Pet Disappears

By Sarah Steiner

Before discussing what to do when a cat or dog disappears, let's first discuss prevention. Prevention means always keeping a good buckle collar on your pet with tags on it (license, rabies vaccination, personal I.D.—all tickets home).

Always keep your pet on a leash when it is not inside a fence or indoors. Use an escape-proof collar (slip collar, not a buckle collar) when walking the pet on its leash. If you use the Gentle Leader, run your leash from the buckle collar through the leading ring, in case the Gentle Leader comes off.

Never leave a pet unattended outside. Even cats, in many jurisdictions, are not entitled to roam free, despite being licensed and vaccinated. Dogs are not safe left alone in fenced yards, as boredom sets in quickly, and they have a fabulous sense of exploration. Locks on fence gates do not deter determined thieves. Small children do not constitute guardians. Hire a pet sitter instead of asking a friend or relative to keep an eye on Fido.

Another thing to consider is advance preparation for disappearance by putting information about your pet in an easy-to-find file. Two things to do in advance are (1) put positive identification on the body of the pet, and (2) create some photographic records of the pet.

Positive identification can be a tattoo, which your veterinarian can apply. It also can be a microchip, which a veterinarian, groomer, or breed-specific identification clinic can implant. Tattoos are supplied by two or three companies. These companies can be asked to identify a tattoo. They can tell who tattooed the animal, where and when, what the animal's name is, and usually who the owner is.

Microchips are supplied primarily by two companies. A scanning device is used to show that a chip is present. Even if the device cannot read the particular chip, it can tell which manufacturer's chip it is. Then proper action can be taken to read the chip.

If your pet has positive identification, you can give it to animal control agencies. You will be able to contact the providers of the identification, who may be able to help, to advise them of the pet's disappearance. And you will be able to provide this information to those who help conduct your search. Most important of all, you will be able to prove ownership of the pet when found.

Positive identification enables a public animal control facility, such as a dog pound, or an individual finder to find you. A microchip or tattoo sends a signal to the shelter or finder that an owner is attempting to prevent a loss, and, hopefully, that owner can be located.

Visiting shelters is time-consuming and frustrating, but it must be done.

Photographic records of pets are something most people have. Good, clear photos of pets are helpful in advertising the loss of an animal on flyers or as posters.

Keep a few I.D. photos in an information file where you can find them quickly. Keep basic veterinary information on your pets in the same file. This can help you communicate quickly with your veterinarian about the missing pet. It is surprising how many people don't know, immediately, who their vet is, and how to contact him or her.

If you have a pet that is missing, there is a system that can help you sharpen your focus and narrow the field of places to look.

First, call your local dog warden to report the loss and see if any animal matching your pet's description has arrived in the shelter. If it is after business hours and you get the answering machine, leave a detailed message. Also, after hours, let your local police department or sheriff know. They will probably refer you back to the dog warden, but if a police department knows a pet is missing and they get a found pet call, they may be able to match up the calls immediately.

Second—and this is a little more complicated—imagine yourself in the center of a circle. Give that circle a radius of 20 miles. This will be a big territory, but pets travel, and sometimes they put a lot of miles on. Write down the names of the counties and major towns in the 20-mile radius. Create this list so you won't overlook places to call; it also becomes a checklist for visits and follow-up calls, and helps you stay organized in your search.

Third, make a list of the newspapers in this territory and place ads in the papers, both big and small. When you write an ad, you can offer a reward. Do not state an amount, and keep the ad simple. For example, "Lost—Labrador retriever black male, your phone number, REWARD." It is not necessary, and it may not help, to state where and when the dog was originally lost. This can set false limits and may artificially restrain a reader from considering a dog found in a different location or in a different time frame.

Fourth, call all the local pounds, shelters, police and sheriff offices, and highway patrol posts for the jurisdictions on your list. Animals often cover a surprising amount of territory in their wanderings and may be far from home when found.

When you speak to a shelter, be sure to ask their hours of operation, how long they keep an animal, and how much it costs to redeem a pet.

Fifth, get out those I.D. photos, and make a bunch of copies. Take some to the local animal warden immediately. Then make up some easy-to-read posters and put them up at major intersections in and around your neighborhood. Use large print, preferably black on a white background. Make flyers to put up on bulletin boards in shopping areas and other places where people congregate.

Once you have identified the shelters, visit them. You must go to each targeted shelter. Go daily, or at least every other day, as animals are collected in a variety of locations and come in at different times. Bring along a spare collar and a good leash. Even if your pet was wearing a collar, it may have lost it. Also take the positive identification information. Take I.D. photos to each shelter and ask to post them. Go to the shelters during normal business hours and take cash to redeem your pet.

It is important to go to the shelters for several reasons:

- The person on the phone may not be aware of exactly what animals are in the shelter when you call, or may not know of those brought in recently. Office staff is not obligated to tell you anything. The law requires that you show up and identify your pet.
- The person on the phone may not be able to identify your breed. Even though people work for years in these settings, many of

them are not well trained in breed identification. Only you can be sure.

Visiting shelters is time-consuming and frustrating, but it must be done. Enlist relatives and friends, assigning specific shelters to each person who is willing to help. Each helper can go back to the same places, where they will begin to recognize the shelter workers.

Finally, call the rescue organizations for your pet's breed. It is not unusual for an individual finder of that black male Labrador retriever to call the local area Labrador retriever rescue.

When you find your pet (alive or not), please call the shelters you have talked to and let them know that you are no longer looking. Most shelters keep a list of missing pets as reported by owners. Help the shelters help others by taking found pets off their lists.

When you redeem your pet from a shelter, it may involve buying a new license onsite. Put it on the collar right there in the shelter. This is where the extra collar you brought with you will be worth its weight in gold. Dog or cat, collar and leash will save you a lot of time and effort.

And, to quote a dear friend, "Never give up!"

Directory of Animal Rescue Organizations, Seventh Edition

By the end of 2004, this widely used resource will be available in its newest edition. The book contains more than 70 pages packed with useful information on breed- and species-specific rescues and resources designed to help pet owners solve problems and prevent the need for re-homing a pet. To order, send $25 per copy to Crow Haven Farm, 5405 Hamilton Road, Medina, OH 44256.

Sarah Steiner is the Editor/Publisher of *Directory Of Animal Rescue Organizations*, and the author of *Thinking Of Having Puppies?* Sarah and Jim Steiner live on a small farm in Medina County, where they raise Labrador Retrievers and a flock of sheep producing meat and spinning-quality wool.

According to their website, www.placeapetfoundation.org, the Place-A-Pet Foundation is the **largest non-profit** 501(c)(3) no-kill animal shelter in Cuyahoga County.

NORTHEAST OHIO ANIMAL SHELTERS

ASHLAND COUNTY

Ashland County Animal Shelter
1710 Garfield Ave.,
Ashland, OH 44805
(419) 289-1455
animalshelter@ashlandcounty.org
www.ashlandcounty.org/
animalshelter/

ASHTABULA COUNTY

Animal Protective League
Street address:
5970 Green Rd., Ashtabula,
Mailing address: P.O. Box 367,
Geneva, OH 44041
(440) 224-1222

Ashtabula County Dog Warden
25 W. Jefferson, Jefferson,
(440) 576-3750
www.doglicense.com/counties/
ashtabula/

CARROLL COUNTY

Carroll County Dog Pound/ Dog Warden
2185 Kennsington Rd. NE,
Carrollton, OH 44615
(330) 627-4244

COLUMBIANA COUNTY

Columbiana County Dog Pound
8455 County Home Rd.
Lisbon, OH 44432
(330) 424-6663

COSHOCTON COUNTY

Coshocton County Dog Warden
(740) 622-9741

Coshocton County Animal Shelter
(The Dog Warden also operates out of this office)
217715 Township Rd. 164
Morgan Run Road
Coshocton, OH 43812
(740) 622-9741
www.petfinder.org/shelters/
OH308.html

CUYAHOGA COUNTY

Animal Protective League
1729 Willey Ave., Cleveland, (216) 771-4616
www.clevelandapl.org

Berea Animal Rescue Shelter
400 Barrett Rd., Berea,
(440) 234-2034
www.bereaanimalrescue.com

Stay-Awhile Cat Shelter, Inc.
8800 Akins Rd., North Royalton,
OH 44133 (440) 582-4990
info@stayahilecatshelter.org
www.stayawhilecatshelter.org/

Cleveland City Kennel
2690 W. 7th St.,
Cleveland, OH 44113
(216) 664-3069

Cuyahoga County Animal Shelter
9500 Sweet Valley Dr.,
Valley View,
(216) 525-7877
www.cuyahoga.oh.us/cs/
kennel.htm

Euclid Animal Shelter
25100 Lakeland Blvd., Euclid,
(216) 289-2057
www.euclidanimalshelter.com

Greyhound Adoption of Ohio
7122 Country Ln., Chagrin Falls,
(800) 269-1148
rjrjlp@aol.com
www.greyhoundadoption-ofoh.org

North Coast Humane Society
3615 Cecilia
Cleveland, Ohio 44109
(216) 661 2292

Parma Animal Shelter
6260 State Rd., Parma,
(440) 885-8014
www.parmashelter.org

Place-A-Pet Foundation
P.O. Box 640
Cleveland, OH 44107
216-521-7387
info@placeapetfoundation.com
www.placeapetfoundation.com

Sanctuary for Senior Dogs
P.O. Box 609054, Cleveland,
(216) 485-9233
www.sanctuaryforseniordogs.org/id16.htm

Valley Save-A-Pet
715 Broadway Ave., Bedford,
(440) 232-9124

ERIE COUNTY

Erie County Dog Shelter
2900 Columbus Ave.,
Sandusky, (419) 627-7607
www.erie-county-ohio.net/
dogwarden/dogwarden.htm

Erie County Humane Society
1911 Superior St., Sandusky,
(419) 626-6220
animalsRus@aol.com
www.humanesocietyoferie.org

GEAUGA COUNTY

Geauga Dog Warden
12513 Merritt Rd., Chardon
(440) 286-8135
www.co.geauga.oh.us/
departments/dog_warden.htm
mattgdw@netlink.net

Rescue Village (Geauga County Humane Society)
15463 Chillicothe Rd., Russell
Township, (440) 338-4819
www.geaugahumane.org/

HARRISON COUNTY

Harrison County Dog Pound
100 West Market Street, Cadiz,
(740) 942-4080

HOLMES COUNTY

Holmes County Dog Kennel
5387 County Rd. 349,
Millersburg, (330) 674-6301

HURON COUNTY

Huron County Dog Pound and Dog Warden
130 Shady Ln., Building E,
Norwalk, OH 44857
(419) 668-9773

Huron County Humane Society
246 Woodlawn Ave., Norwalk,
(419) 663-7158
www.hc-humanesociety.org/

JEFFERSON COUNTY

Jefferson County Dog Pound
Fernwood Rd., Wintersville,
(740) 264-6888

NORTHEAST OHIO ANIMAL SHELTERS (continued)

LAKE COUNTY

Lake County Dog Shelter and Warden's Office
49 Fairdale Rd., Painesville,
(440) 350-2640
lcdogs@lakecountyohio.org
www.lakecountyohio.org

Lake County Humane Society
7564 Tyler Blvd., Suite E, Mentor,
(440) 951-6122
LCHS PETS@aol.com

North Coast Humane Society
269 Shoregate Mall, Willowick,
(440) 585-5155

LORAIN COUNTY

Animal Protective League of Lorain County
8303 Murray Ridge Rd., Elyria,
(440) 322-4321
DavidMcClelland@centurytel.net
www.petfinder.org/shelters/OH166.html

Lorain County Dog Pound
301 Hadaway, Elyria,
(440) 326-5995
www.lorcnty.us/dog

Oasis Dog Shelter
P. O. Box 11, Oberlin, OH,
44074-0011
(440) 775-4101
oasisanimal@wmconnect.com
www.oasisanimalshelter.com

MAHONING COUNTY

Mahoning County Kennel and Dog Warden
589 Industrial Rd., Youngstown,
(330) 740-2205
www.doglicense.com

MEDINA COUNTY

Forgotten Animal Shelter
P.O. Box 46, Medina, OH 44258
(330) 723-9918
www.forgottenanimalshelter.org/

Medina County Animal Shelter
6334 Deerview Ln., Medina,
(330) 725-9121
dogcats@brightnet.com
www.co.medina.oh.us/animal/animal.htm

Medina County S.P.C.A.
P.O. Box 135, Medina, OH
44258-0135
(330) 723-7722
mcspca@aol.com
www.medinacountyspca.com

PORTAGE COUNTY

Happy Trails Farm Animal Sanctuary
5623 New Milford Rd., Ravenna,
330-296-5914

Portage County Animal Protective League
8122 Infirmary Rd, Ravenna
(330) 296-4022
portagecountyapl@yahoo.com
www.portagecountyapl.org

Portage County Dog Warden
(330) 297-6924
8120 Infirmary Rd., Ravenna
bkirkhart@portageco.com

RICHLAND COUNTY

Richland County Dog Warden
Street address: 810 N. Home Rd., Mansfield, OH 44906
Mailing: 50 Park Avenue, East, Mansfield,
(419) 774-5892

Richland County Humane Soc.
395 Lantz Rd., Mansfield,
(419) 774-4795
carla@adoptourstrays.com
www.adoptourstrays.com

STARK COUNTY

Stark County Humane Society
5100 Peach St., Louisville,
(330) 453-5529
info@starkhumane.org
www.starkhumane.org/

SUMMIT COUNTY

Friends of Pets
P.O. Box 3034 Cuyahoga Falls,
OH 44223
(330) 571-7387
www.waggingtails.org

Greater Akron Humane Society
4904 Quick Rd.,
Peninsula, OH 44264
(330) 657-2010
www.summithumane.org

Hearts and Paws Rescue Group
P.O. Box 313, Canal Fulton,
(330) 668-9706

Pet Guards Shelter
950 Hardy Road, Cuyahoga Falls
330/849-0635
PetGuardAngels@aol.com

Precious Lives Animal Hospital and Sanctuary
1474 Brittain Rd., Akron,
(330) 633-5959
www.preciouslives.com

South Summit Kitten/ Puppy Rescue
3700 Massillon Rd., Uniontown,
(330) 882-6007
http://www.sskpr.com

Tri-County Adoption Center
1611 Amherst Rd. NE, Massillon,
(330) 833-8479

TRUMBULL COUNTY

Trumbull County Kennel
7501 Anderson, Warren,
(330) 675-2787

TUSCAWARAS COUNTY

Tuscawaras Dog Pound
441 University Dr., Northeast.
New Philadelphia, (330) 339-2616

WAYNE COUNTY

Wayne County Humane Society
1161 Mechanicsburg Road,
Wooster, OH 44691
(330) 262-0152
http://www.wchs.org/

Wayne County Dog Warden
(330) 287-5410
428 W Liberty St, Wooster

Pet Adoption Success Stories

KATE MALARNEY

Sunshine, Star, and More

Rescued animals have been a part of the Boland household for years. No matter where they came from—shelters, farms, friends—they've become members of the family. "We've been blessed with good animals," says Isabelle Boland, who, along with husband Jake, shares her Bainbridge home with dog Star and cats Berkeley and Sunshine, all of whom came from local animal rescue organizations.

Isabelle saw Star's picture on the Cleveland Animal Protective League's website back in 1999, when she was still grieving the death of their dog Bailey, a border collie/sheltie/cocker spaniel mix rescued from the Cleveland APL some 16 years ago.

A frisky blond with eyes rimmed in black, Star was tough to control at first. "When I took her to obedience class I'd come home black and blue from her pulling me so hard," says Isabelle. "I wanted to give up, but the trainer kept me going, and wouldn't you know, she was the best dog in class when it came time for the final exam."

Now, says Isabelle, she couldn't be sweeter. "She doesn't even have the heart to bark when the cats try to eat her food; instead she comes and puts her head on my leg and whines as if to say, "Mom, help!"

Sunshine is usually the one going for Star's gravy. She was just a young mother when the Bolands read an article about her in a local paper. Valley Save-a-Pet was trying to place the nine-month-old cat, who had been found in a field nearly dead from nursing her six kittens. The kittens had all been placed, but Sunshine was still waiting—until Isabelle, her daughter Kelly, and granddaughter Hannah drove to Parkman to bring her home. "I knew she was a great cat when two-year-old Hannah toddled over and put her hands all over her. Sunshine didn't even flinch."

Jake would kill me if he knew I was going to get another animal

At home Sunshine joined calico Berkeley, a rescue from the Lake County Humane Society, who's now 14. "When we heard about Berkeley, I sent my daughter Stacy to go get him because I knew Jake would kill me if he knew I was going to get another animal!" says Isabelle. "That night, dinner was pretty quiet until this little scrapper crawled up Jake's pant leg, got up on the table, and started to lick his ice cream bowl. Jake laughed, and that was that—Berkeley was part of the family."

"All of these animals have just been integral parts of our lives," she says. "They've been there in good times and bad. They're truly gifts from God."

Gray Area

Last January, Linda Perko responded to an SOS call from the director of a greyhound refuge outside of Madrid, Spain. Hundreds of dogs needed help, and people from around the world had funded airfare for folks like Perko, director of Greyhound Adoption of Ohio, to come and save the animals.

Perko could take just eight dogs. Dulce was one of them. "She was just standing there, so quiet amidst many. When I walked over, she put her head under my head." Perko named her Dulce, the Spanish word that described her soft, gentle, agreeable nature.

Bruce and Carol Deehr of Champion, Ohio, are the lucky ones who adopted Dulce in March. Carol said they really did their homework about adopting greyhounds before contacting Perko, who works hard to match a dog's personality to its new family.

"Dulce fits right in with us," says Carol. "We're retired now, and have plenty of time to fuss over her. She's been very pampered."

The Deehrs expected a tough transition when Dulce first arrived, after reading about greyhounds who didn't know how to handle stairs or walks on a leash; instead, they found the black and white pooch to be terrific company right from the start. "She just likes to lay around a lot!" says Carol. "She has her own bedroom, with a pillow she took from our bed. She likes to carry Bruce's slippers around—often when we come home we'll find them in her favorite spot in the living room." She doesn't know how to play with toys, but she will lie down with her paws on top of them, which Carol thinks may be a throwback to her hunting days.

Only once did she take off after a squirrel. "It was a few days after she came to us," says Carol. "We were out on our porch, and she went right through the screen!" Now she waits instead for her walks outside—and gets so excited she tries to put on her own collar. Only once did she try to sneak some food off the counter—the garbage can fell over and scared her away. "She's just so gentle, whatever we do is okay with her," says Carol.

The Deehrs have had such a good experience they are thinking of adopting a second greyhound. They keep in touch with Perko, who likes to follow Dulce's progress. "Linda will see her and say, 'If you only knew where she came from,' with tears in her eyes as she looks at this pampered dog," says Carol.

Come Back, Zack

Living and working on her own after college, Halle Moore desperately wanted a dog. She'd go for walks in the park where other people had dogs and wish for a friendly, loyal canine companion. "I dreamed of an off-leash dog that would be my partner in hiking, and I always pictured a lovable golden retriever or something." Instead, she got Zack.

"He was the cutest thing I'd ever seen," says Halle of the day she found him at the Cuyahoga County Animal Shelter. "He was this wiggly little guy who pushed his snout right out through the gate at me. I totally fell for him." She says she was a sucker for his small head on a big body, for his pancake-sized ears and amber eyes, for his brown tuxedo coat with three white shoes. She loved everything except his name: Beethoven. "Nothing about him said 'classical music,'" says Halle, who changed his name to Zachary.

She calls him a "spreagle," a springer/beagle mix, and over the past seven years they've lived in several different places, including Washington, D.C., before moving to Broadview Heights this year.

She also calls him a "garbivore," for all the times she's found him in her neighbors' garages going through their garbage. And while he does love hiking, the only time he's really good off leash is in the woods, and even then sometimes he just keeps on going. "I used to hide to entice him to come back and find me," she says. He's followed joggers home, climbed up sewer pipes, buried bones in friends' potted plants, and still eats absolutely anything. A few years ago Halle discovered he had seizures; sometimes she wakes up to his middle-of-the-night fits and bouts of incontinence.

I couldn't blame him, I could just take him for who he is.

But she wouldn't trade any of it. "After a few years of struggling with him, I let go and realized this was who Zack was," she says. The vet had always thought he was a little strange, the trainer had called him too tough to teach, the dogwalker blamed his mix of breeds. "I realized that his behavior wasn't necessarily deliberate, it was just his personality. I couldn't blame him, I could just take him for who he is.

"No matter what, whenever I come home, I get that same wiggle from him that I got when I first saw him. That full body wiggle, that's my Zack."

"Hi Norm"

When Jamie Phillips drove to downtown Cleveland to the APL with a friend who wanted to get a cat, she didn't expect to come home with one of her own. Especially since she already had three cats and three dogs at home in South Russell.

But when she went into the cat room at the shelter, a gray kitten just wouldn't stop meowing for her. "Here was this cross-eyed little guy all ready to go home with me," she says. "He sat in my lap on the way home and reached up to suck on my ears and hair like he was nursing!"

When she didn't know what to name him, her brother suggested Norm, after their father who died when Jamie was 20. She thought that might be a little strange, until later that night when she was out for dinner and overheard someone at the next table talking about Norm, the affable character on the TV show *Cheers*, who was always greeted heartily at the bar. She decided it was too big a coincidence, and named the kitten Norm.

"Normie is the most affectionate and playful of all my cats. He likes to sleep practically on top of my head, which was cute at first but can get a little annoying in the middle of the night," Jamie laughs. He still meows a lot, too.

A few months after Norm settled in, Jamie took care over a weekend of the two brother cats her friend had gotten the day they went downtown. "After that, I got the itch again," she says, and made another trip to the APL—this time for a white female kitten she named Lily. "I always wanted a little girl, but I don't see her much! She's not like the boys. She's quiet and reserved, and doesn't 'talk' to me as much as the others. But they all seem to watch out for her, like she's the little sister."

"I like knowing that I saved them," she says of her brood. "It doesn't seem like I have that many animals." Instead, Jamie's house just feels full of love—okay, and a lot of fur.

YOU'D BE AMAZED AT WHAT YOU CAN SEE IN JANUARY

It may be cold outside, but the constellation "Orion the Hunter" burns brightly to the south. With just your eyes, look for the three stars in a row that make up Orion's Belt. If you look at the lowest star in the belt, you may see a smudge of light just below. That light is the Orion nebula, a place where new stars have formed. Binoculars will reveal these new suns and the cloud that surrounds them.

The golden star in the upper left corner is the red supergiant, Betelgeuse. If we replaced our sun with Betelgeuse, its surface would reach beyond Earth nearly to the planet Jupiter!

This month also has Saturn rising brightly in the evening eastern sky.

Courtesy of Jay Reynolds, Schuele Planetarium director, Lake Erie Nature and Science Center.

FIRST & LAST FREEZES IN NORTHEAST OHIO

Location	Average date of first freeze	Average date of last freeze
Akron/Canton	Oct 20	Apr 30
Alliance	Oct 17	May 3
Ashland	Oct 11	May 7
Ashtabula	Nov 2	Apr 22
Canfield	Oct 4	May 15
Chardon	Oct 15	May 10
Chippewa Lake	Oct 6	May 10
Cleveland, inland	Oct 22	May 1
Cleveland, shore	Nov 2	Apr 25
Conneaut	Nov 2	Apr 22
Coshocton	Oct 16	May 1
Dorset	Sep 29	May 19
Elyria	Oct 20	May 1
Fremont	Oct 12	May 1
Geneva	Oct 28	Apr 29
Hiram	Oct 15	May 5
Jefferson	Oct 16	May 5
Kent	Oct 15	May 10
Lima	Oct 11	May 1
Lorain	Oct 17	Apr 29
Mansfield	Oct 10	May 6

Location	Average date of first freeze	Average date of last freeze
Massillon	Oct 20	Apr 30
Medina	Oct 18	May 3
Millersburg	Oct 15	May 3
Millport	Sep 30	May 18
Mineral Ridge	Oct 6	May 11
New Philadelphia	Oct 15	Apr 30
Newcomerstown	Oct 14	Apr 29
Norwalk	Oct 11	May 4
Oberlin	Oct 17	May 3
Painesville	Oct 28	Apr 28
Ravenna	Oct 12	May 15
Steubenville	Oct 18	Apr 29
Warren	Oct 7	May 10
Wooster	Oct 5	May 8
Youngstown	Oct 4	May 15
Other Nearby Cities		
Cincinnati	Oct 25	Apr 15
Columbus	Oct 21	Apr 21
Dayton	Oct 19	Apr 23
Sandusky	Oct 30	Apr 18
Toledo	Oct 20	Apr 27

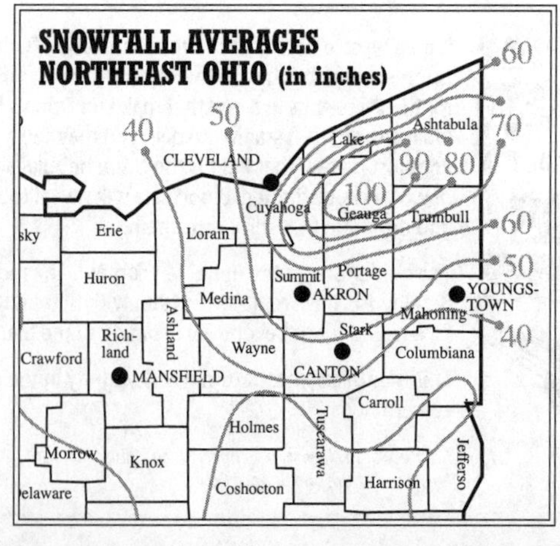

LAST WINTER'S SNOWFALL (2003–2004) in inches

*** = greatest amount of snowfall in Northeast Ohio*
** = least amount of snowfall in Northeast Ohio*

NORTHEAST OHIO

Akron-Canton	50
Alliance *	42
Ashtabula (4S)	104
Burton	102
Canfield	55
Chagrin Falls	98
Chardon	122
Cleveland (Hopkins)	91
Conneaut (inland)	85
Conneaut (town)	66
Eastlake	66
Elyria	62
Euclid	59
Garfield Hts.	97
Hambden	163
Kent	74
Kidron	44
Kipton	44
Lorain	64
Mansfield	60
Medina	62
Monroe Falls	81
Norwalk	45
Painesville	78
Pepper Pike	100
Pierpont	170
Ravenna	67
Russell	114
Thompson (5 SW) **	190
Thompson (town)	152
Vermilion	54
Warren-Youngstown	73
Westlake	64
Wooster	43

OTHER NEARBY CITIES

Columbus	25
Cincinnati	24
Erie, PA	112
Sandusky	38
Toledo	29

WIND CHILL

Wind chill is a "feels-like" number that originated from research done by Ohioan Paul Siple in Antarctica in the 1940s. The formula is based on modern heat-transfer theories, and the wind speed is measured at five feet above ground. Wind chill temperatures of minus 19 and colder can cause frostbite in 15 minutes or less.

Wind chill applies to humans and animals, but not inanimate objects such as automobile radiators.

Temperature (°F) / **Wind (MPH)**

Calm	40	35	30	25	20	15	10	5	0	-5	-10	-15	-20	-25	-30	-35	-40	-45
5	36	31	25	19	13	7	1	-5	-11	-16	-22	-28	-34	-40	-46	-52	-57	-63
10	34	27	21	15	9	3	-4	-10	-16	-22	-28	-35	-41	-47	-53	-59	-66	-72
15	32	25	19	13	6	0	-7	-13	-19	-26	-32	-39	-45	-51	-58	-64	-71	-77
20	30	24	17	11	4	-2	-9	-15	-22	-29	-35	-42	-48	-55	-61	-68	-74	-81
25	29	23	16	9	3	-4	-11	-17	-24	-31	-37	-44	-51	-58	-64	-71	-78	-84
30	28	22	15	8	1	-5	-12	-19	-26	-33	-39	-46	-53	-60	-67	-73	-80	-87
35	28	21	14	7	0	-7	-14	-21	-27	-34	-41	-48	-55	-62	-69	-76	-82	-89
40	27	20	13	6	-1	-8	-15	-22	-29	-36	-43	-50	-57	-64	-71	-78	-84	-91
45	26	19	12	5	-2	-9	-16	-23	-30	-37	-44	-51	-58	-65	-72	-79	-86	-93
50	26	19	12	4	-3	-10	-17	-24	-31	-38	-45	-52	-60	-67	-74	-81	-88	-95
55	25	18	11	4	-3	-11	-18	-25	-32	-39	-46	-54	-61	-68	-75	-82	-89	-97
60	25	17	10	3	-4	-11	-19	-26	-33	-40	-48	-55	-62	-69	-76	-84	-91	-98

Wind Chill (°F) = $35.74 + 0.6215T - 35.75(V^{0.16}) + 0.4275T(V^{0.16})$

T = Air Temperature (°F) V = Wind Speed (mph)

Source: National Weather Service

Frostbite occurs in 15 minutes or less

SNOWFALL IN CLEVELAND . . .

Season	Sep	Oct	Nov	Dec	Jan	Feb	Mar	Apr	May	Total
1954-1955	0	6.4	0.2	11.6	9.4	7.8	3.9	T	0	49.3
1955-1956	0	T	8.7	9.8	14.1	8.9	10.7	2		54.2
1956-1957	0	0	7.4	11.4	12.8	3.1	8.4	13.2	T	56.3
1957-1958	0	2.5	2.5	7.5	4.4	9.4	4.6	0.2	T	31.1
1958-1959	0	T	7.4	9.7	14	5.8	14.6	T	0	51.5
1959-1960	0	T	7.2	5.3	2.8	14.6	19.5	0.5	T	49.9
1960-1961	0	T	4.7	14.1	6	6.8	1.4	5.1	T	38.1
1961-1962	0	T	0.9	4.3	6	16.2	8.9	1	T	37.3
1962-1963	0	8	T	30.3	12.4	13.4	10.4	0.3	0	74.9
1963-1964	0	0	0.1	14.1	16.9	15.7	8.5	0.5	0.1	55.8
1964-1965	0	T	1	8.7	13.6	15.6	12.9	0.4	0	52.2
1965-1966	0	T	1.2	1.2	15.3	10.1	7	2.5	0	37.3
1966-1967	0	0	8.8	10.9	2	18.5	7.3	0.1	T	47.6
1967-1968	0	0.1	9.1	2.8	14.5	8.9	7.7	0.2	0	43.3
1968-1969	0	T	6.8	8.3	5.8	5.6	9	1.5	T	37
1969-1970	0	0.6	6.6	17.4	10.5	6.6	11.5	0.2	T	53.4
1970-1971	T	T	5.2	6	8.6	14.3	16.6	0.7	T	51.4
1971-1972	0	0	5.3	1.9	15	14.8	6.3	2.3	0	45.6
1972-1973	0	5.5	7.8	15.2	9.8	20.4	8.3	0.9	0	68.5
1973-1974	0	T	3.3	13.8	8.9	16.9	7.1	6.4	0.6	58.5
1974-1975	0	1.6	5.3	24.1	9.7	9.9	15.2	1.2	2.1	67
1975-1976	0	0	5.6	13.1	21.5	6.8	5.8	1.6	0	54.4
1976-1977	T	1.6	8.9	16.3	21.1	9.6	4.2	1.7	T	63.4
1977-1978	0	T	9.7	23.1	42.8	10.8	3.5	0.2	0	90.1
1978-1979	0	0	1.9	2.5	15.1	16	2.4	0.4	0	38.3
1979-1980	0	0.2	0.5	4	11.3	19.2	3.5	T	0	38.7
1980-1981	0	T	5.4	13.5	15	9.7	16.9	T	T	60.5
1981-1982	0	4	2.9	27.1	28.1	7.6	17.6	13.2	0	100.5
1982-1983	0	0	2.2	6.3	6.5	8.3	11.3	3.4	0	38
1983-1984	0	0	7.1	13	12.9	27.1	19.3	T	0	79.4
1984-1985	0	0	4	8.9	25.5	18.2	1.2	5.9	0	63.7
1985-1986	0	0	T	23.4	17.2	10.8	6.7	0.2	0	58.3
1986-1987	0	T	3.1	1.1	16.4	5	26.2	4	0	55.8
1987-1988	0	T	1	16.4	8.7	22.9	20.4	1.9	0	71.3
1988-1989	0	T	1.7	17.9	6.6	13.8	9.9	4.9	T	54.8

. . . LAST 50 YEARS (in inches)

Season	Sep	Oct	Nov	Dec	Jan	Feb	Mar	Apr	May	Total
1989-1990	0	T	9.1	24	10.5	9.9	4.4	4.7	0	62.6
1990-1991	0	0	T	7.4	16.6	18.9	4.2	T	0	47.1
1991-1992	0	0	3.5	9.4	23.8	6.2	18.4	4.4	0	65.7
1992-1993	0	T	7.1	7.1	8.7	39.1	25.4	1.1	0	88.5
1993-1994	0	0.2	3	19	27.4	12.3	7	3.6	0	72.5
1994-1995	0	0	T	1	23.4	14.7	4.3	0.2	0	43.6
1995-1996	0	0	9.9	29.6	21.9	10.1	19.4	10.2	0	101.1
1996-1997	0	0	23.4	5	13	8.4	5.3	0.8	0	55.9
1997-1998	0	T	8.6	10.7	5	0.2	9.5	0	0	34
1998-1999	0	0	0.1	6.9	29.6	14.2	11.6	0	0	62.4
1999-2000	0	0	1.6	10.3	24.7	13.9	8	1.2	0	60.1
2000-2001	0	0.1	11	21.9	14.9	3.2	16.7	0.3	0	78.1
2001-2002	0	1	T	3.7	6.3	16.9	15.9	2.2	T	46
2002-2003	0	T	6.1	22.4	30.3	30.1	0.1	0	0	95.7
2003-2004	0	0.3	4.5	26.6	39.2	5.5	18.6	2.6	0	91.2

T = Trace amounts

"REMEMBER, IF WE'RE NOT SCARING THE HELL OUT OF OUR VIEWERS WE'RE NOT DOING OUR JOB!"

{DICK'S INSECT OF THE YEAR}

MONARCH OF THE SKIES

BY DICK GODDARD

A melancholy sight here in September is the annual migration of the big orange, black, and white butterfly known as the monarch. Aside from the green darner dragonfly, I know of no other insect that migrates.

The monarchs flutter some 3,000 miles in autumn, headed for the Sierra Madre Mountains of Mexico, a destination they have never seen. Monarchs, with a favorable tailwind, can travel 50 miles a day.

Monarchs in Ohio and the eastern United States are joined by their Canadian cousins, while monarch butterflies that live west of the Rocky Mountains migrate to the California coast from just north of San Francisco to just south of Los Angeles.

The monarchs that depart Ohio in autumn will live about eight months and are the great-great-grandchildren of the monarchs that left Mexico the previous spring. Using a mysterious (to humans) compass, they will return to the same nesting site that their parents used.

Monarchs often arrive on tattered wings in Mexico and they crawl from one Oyamel fir tree to another while laying their eggs.

There are four stages in the life of the monarch: egg (green,

oval shaped), larva (orange, black, and yellow striped caterpillars), pupa (bright green), and adult butterflies (wings of orange with black stripes and white dots). The male monarch sports a black spot on each of his rear wings.

During summer the female monarch will lay up to 400 eggs on the underside of her favorite food, the common milkweed plant. Because of their main diet of milkweed, which is toxic, the monarch butterfly has few predators. A bird who decides to have a monarch meal will soon vomit, guaranteeing there will not be another monarch sandwich.

Hatching from an egg, the monarch caterpillar will in two weeks spin a silky cocoon. The pupa stage follows, from which a butterfly emerges in just five days. As an adult butterfly, the monarch will snack on nectar from flowers, sap, and dew.

With highway departments destroying so much milkweed through mowing and spraying, you can help monarchs by actually planting milkweed in your yard and garden next spring.

It was in 1930 that entomologists concluded that monarch butterflies, just like many birds, migrate southward in autumn and northward in spring. But to where? A search organized in 1940 failed to solve the puzzle.

The monarchs' over-wintering place was not discovered until 36 years later. Rumors had spread that monarchs could be found from November to March above the 8,000-foot level in the chilly, misty fir forests of Mexico. In January of 1976, Lincoln Brower, an entomologist from the University of Florida, went hiking in the Sierra Chinuca Mountains just west of Mexico City. It was there that Brower suddenly stumbled upon what he said was "a massive wall of orange!" Brower had found the Holy Grail of insect lore.

Further studies have concluded that this site is annually the winter home to about four million monarchs per acre within a 20-mile by 40-mile corridor.

NORTHEAST OHIO'S WARMEST AND COLDEST WINTERS

(by Median Temp)

WARMEST

Cleveland: 38.7° / 1931–32

Akron/Canton: 38.2° / 1889–90

COLDEST

Cleveland: 19.8° / 1976–77

Akron/Canton: 20.7° / 1976–77

INDUCTED INTO NORTHEAST OHIO HALLS OF FAME

PRO-FOOTBALL HALL OF FAME

2004 INDUCTEES:

Bob (Boomer) Brown, *Tackle*, 1964–1968 Philadelphia Eagles, 1969–1970 Los Angeles Rams, 1971–1973 Oakland Raiders

Carl Eller, *Defensive End*, 1964–1978 Minnesota Vikings, 1979 Seattle Seahawks

John Elway, *Quarterback*, 1983–1998 Denver Broncos

Barry Sanders, *Running Back*, 1989–1998 Detroit Lions

2004 FINALISTS:

Harry Carson, *Linebacker*, 1976–1988 New York Giants

Richard Dent, *Defensive End*, 1983–1993, 1995 Chicago Bears, 1994 San Francisco 49ers, 1996 Indianapolis Colts, 1997 Philadelphia Eagles

Cliff Harris, *Safety*, 1970–1979 Dallas Cowboys

Bob Hayes, *Wide Receiver*, 1965–1974 Dallas Cowboys, 1975 San Francisco 49ers

Lester Hayes, *Cornerback*, 1977–1986 Oakland/ Los Angeles Raiders

Bob Kuechenberg, *Guard*, 1970–1984 Miami Dolphins

Jim Marshall, *Defensive End*, 1960 Cleveland Browns, 1961–1979 Minnesota Vikings

Art Monk, *Wide Receiver*, 1980–1993 Washington Redskins, 1994 New York Jets, 1995 Philadelphia Eagles

Rayfield Wright, *Tackle*, 1967–1979 Dallas Cowboys

George Young, *General Manager/Administrator*, 1968–1974 Baltimore Colts, 1974–1978 Miami Dolphins, 1979–1997 New York Giants, 1998–2001 National Football League

Gary Zimmerman, *Tackle*, 1986–1992 Minnesota Vikings, 1993–1997 Denver Broncos

ROCK AND ROLL HALL OF FAME AND MUSEUM

2004 INDUCTEES:

Performers:

Jackson Browne, The Dells, George Harrison, Prince, Bob Seger, Traffic, ZZ Top

Lifetime Achievement in the non-performer category: **Jann Wenner** *(launched Rolling Stone magazine)*

INVENTORS HALL OF FAME

2004 INDUCTEES:

Frederick Banting *(1891–1941)*, **Charles Best** *(1899–1978)*, and **James Collip** *(1892–1965)*, for purified insulin

Vannevar Bush *(1890–1974)*, for the Differential Analyzer

Harry Coover *(1919–)* for Superglue

Wallace Coulter *(1913–1998)*, for the Coulter Principle

Ray Dolby *(1933–)*, for Dolby Noise Reduction

Edith Flanigen *(1929–)*, for molecular sieves

Robert Gallo *(1937–)* and **Luc Montagnier** *(1932–)*, for HIV Isolation and Identification

Ivan Getting *(1912–2003)* and **Bradford Parkinson** *(1935–)* for the Global Positioning System (GPS)

John Gibbon *(1903–1973)*, for the heart-lung machine

Lloyd Hall *(1894–1971)*, for food preservatives

Elias Howe *(1819–1867)*, for the sewing machine

Charles D. Kelman *(1930–)*, for cataract surgery

Bernard Oliver *(1916–1995)* and **Claude Shannon** *(1916–2001)*, for pulse code modulation

Norbert Rillieux *(1806–1894)*, for automated sugar refining

John Roebling *(1806–1869)*, for the suspension bridge

POLKA HALL OF FAME

2003 AWARDEES:

Cultural/Heritage Award: **Penn-Ohio Polka Pal Boosters**

Support/Promotion: **Ken Zalar**

Best Musician (Individual): **Eddie Rodick**

Sideman of the Year: **Wayne Habat, Eddie Klancnik, Ron Sluga**

Greatest All-Time Hits: **Zapula Waltz, Simcic's Waltz**

Best Vocalist: **Christine Hibbs**

Button Box (Individual): **Kathy Hlad**

Button Box (Group): **Captain's Crew**

Recording of the Year: **Greatest Slovenian Hits**, *Dick Tady*

Band of the Year: **George Staiduhar and the Revue**

Trustees Honor Roll: **John Habat, Don Kotnik, Don Krance, Benzy Rathbone, Eddie Vallus, Paul Wilcox**

Lifetime Achievement: **Sam Pugliano, Roman Possedi**

FEBRUARY STATISTICS

(recorded at Cleveland Hopkins Airport)

SUNSHINE %	37
DRIEST MONTH	0.18"/1877
WARMEST MONTH	37.5°/1930
COLDEST MONTH	15.8°/1875
LIQUID PCPN AVG.	2.19"
RAINIEST DAY	2.33"/1959
RAINIEST MONTH	7.73"/1887
THUNDERY DAYS	1
SNOWIEST DAY	14.8"/1993
SNOWIEST MONTH	39.1"/1993
LEAST SNOWFALL	0.2"/1998
DAYS ONE INCH SNOW	4

The first two weeks of February are often the coldest of winter. King Winter is on his throne and Northeast Ohio is a still-life painting, a study in frozen motion. On the second day of the month, Ohio's official state groundhog, Buckeye Chuck (he lives in a heated burrow at a radio station in Marion), makes his end-of-winter forecast. No self-respecting meteorological marmot would be above ground at this time of the year; if it were, it would be an amorous boy groundhog looking for you-know-what. Ohio's lowest official temperature came on February 10, 1899, at Milligan, near Zanesville; the temperature may even have been under the observed -39°F reading, since the mercury probably froze (for temperatures that cold, alcohol thermometers are required).

Naturalists tell us that spring in the eastern United States begins during early February deep in the Florida Everglades, then moves northward at a rate of about 15 miles each day. As the frostline moves by, insects emerge from their winter hibernation places and migrant birds follow the movable feast northward. Each day the sun rides a little higher in the sky, and stays a little longer. Insects known as snow fleas (springtails) can be seen doing their circus act in the snow near the base of trees.

DAILY DATA FOR FEBRUARY

Date	Day	Moon	Day of Year	Days Left	Sunrise	Sunset	Length of Day	Avg. Hi°	Avg. Lo°	Avg. Lake°
1	Tue		32	333	7:38	5:43	10:05	32	17	33
2	Wed	◑	33	332	7:37	5:44	10:07	32	17	33
3	Thu		34	331	7:36	5:46	10:10	32	17	33
4	Fri		35	330	7:35	5:47	10:12	32	17	33
5	Sat		36	329	7:34	5:48	10:14	33	17	33
6	Sun		37	328	7:33	5:49	10:16	33	18	33
7	Mon		38	327	7:32	5:51	10:19	33	18	33
8	Tue	●	39	326	7:30	5:52	10:22	33	18	33
9	Wed		40	325	7:29	5:53	10:24	33	18	33
10	Thu		41	324	7:28	5:54	10:26	34	18	33
11	Fri		42	323	7:27	5:56	10:29	34	18	33
12	Sat		43	322	7:25	5:57	10:32	34	18	33
13	Sun		44	321	7:24	5:58	10:34	34	19	33
14	Mon		45	320	7:23	5:59	10:36	34	19	33
15	Tue		46	319	7:21	6:01	10:40	35	19	33
16	Wed	◐	47	318	7:20	6:02	10:42	35	19	33
17	Thu		48	317	7:19	6:03	10:44	35	20	33
18	Fri		49	316	7:17	6:04	10:47	36	20	33
19	Sat		50	315	7:16	6:06	10:50	36	20	33
20	Sun		51	314	7:15	6:07	10:52	36	20	33
21	Mon		52	313	7:13	6:08	10:55	37	21	33
22	Tue		53	312	7:12	6:09	10:57	37	21	33
23	Wed		54	311	7:10	6:10	11:00	37	21	33
24	Thu	○	55	310	7:09	6:12	11:03	38	21	33
25	Fri		56	309	7:07	6:13	11:06	38	22	33
26	Sat		57	308	7:06	6:14	11:08	39	22	33
27	Sun		58	307	7:04	6:15	11:11	39	22	33
28	Mon		59	306	7:03	6:16	11:13	39	22	33

NORTHEAST OHIO'S WETTEST AND DRIEST WINTERS *(Liquid)*

WETTEST: Cleveland: 14.95" / 1949–50 • Akron/Canton: 15.09" / 1949–50

DRIEST: Cleveland: 3.27" / 1900–01 • Akron/Canton: 2.86" / 1905–06

Rec. Hi°	Rec. Lo°	On This Date . . .
59/1989	-6/1971	Actor William Clark Gable born in Cadiz (1901)
61/1903	-7/1971	Smallest crowd at Cleveland Arena, Cavs vs Golden State: 1,641 (1974)
57/1890	-8/1996	Charles Follis, 1st black US football player, born in Shelby, OH (1879)
65/1874	-10/1996	Woody Hayes born (1913)
61/1938	-13/1918	Cleveland Rockers guard Adrienne Johnson born (1974)
61/1938	-6/1895	NBA expands to include Cleveland Cavaliers (1970)
60/1925	-5/1988	Cleveland's WVIZ TV channel 25 (PBS) begins broadcasting (1965)
69/1937	-8/1977	Largest crowd at Cleve. Coliseum, Cavs vs Wash.: 21,130 (1976)
63/2001	-14/1899	47th NBA All-Star Game; East beats West 132–120 at Cleveland (1997)
66/1932	-16/1899	-39ºF, Milligan, OH (state lowest temperature record) (1899)
73/1932	-15/1885	73ºF highest temperature ever recorded in Cleveland in Feb. (1932)
68/1999	-9/1917	Actor Arsenio Hall born in Cleveland (1959)
68/1938	-9/1995	Stark County incorporated (1808)
62/1918	-11/1905	Broadcaster Hugh Downs born in Akron (1921)
67/1954	-4/1963	1st adhesive postage stamp in U.S. (1842)
72/1883	-8/1904	Cavs guard Mark Price born (1964)
62/1911	-7/1885	Cleveland Public Library established (1869)
62/1981	-5/1936	Author Toni Morrison born in Lorain (1931)
68/1939	-4/1936	Congress accepts Ohio's constitution (1856)
69/1930	-3/1968	Total eclipse of the Moon (1989)
68/1930	-3/1885	WHK-AM in Cleveland OH begins radio transmissions (1922)
72/1930	-8/1963	Cleveland Metroparks Zoo's Primate & Cat Building is dedicated (1979)
66/2000	-4/1873	Louis Stokes born (1925)
69/1961	-7/1889	Dick Goddard born in Akron (1931)
70/1930	-5/1993	Actor Jim Backus born in Cleveland (1913)
74/2000	-15/1963	Michael Owens of Toledo patents a glass-blowing machine (1895)
66/1996	-10/1863	People magazine begins sales (1974)
67/1939	0/1884	1st commercial railroad in U.S., Baltimore & Ohio, chartered (1827)

NORTHEAST OHIO'S SNOWIEST AND LEAST SNOWY WINTERS

SNOWIEST: 101.1", 1995–96 • Akron/Canton: 82.0", 1977–78

LEAST SNOWY: Cleveland: 8.8", 1918–19 • Akron/Canton: 10.8", 1932–33

Flora & Fauna FEBRUARY

WEEK 1 **BIRDS:** The bright whistling calls of "Spring's here!" signal that chickadees are sensing the longer days too. Goldfinches return to winter thistle feeders in large flocks. Great horned owls are already nesting in stolen hawks' nests atop high forest canopies. **MAMMALS:** The January thaw brings portly woodchucks and skinny skunks out to rediscover their worlds. Only male woodchucks appear in early February. Did Brecksville Ben see his shadow this year?

WEEK 2 **BIRDS:** In winter, bald eagles often travel widely in search of food and potential nesting sites. They have become a common sight along the Lake Erie shoreline and down the valleys of the Grand, Chagrin, Cuyahoga, Rocky River, and Black Rivers. **MAMMALS:** Chipmunks begin to appear if the snow is mostly melted. They have been active all winter but stay underground eating from their plentiful storehouses of nuts and seeds carefully stashed away last summer and fall. Beavers venture out of holes in their icy ponds and streams in search of fresh bark to eat. **TREES:** The reddish buds of red maple are nearly ready to burst open. Not far away, groves of sugar maples begin to yield their sweet sap.

WEEK 3 **BIRDS:** "Oka-reee!" Red-winged blackbirds arrive around Valentine's Day. Their annual reappearance marks one of the first and surest signs of spring. Spring migrating ducks begin to reappear at inland lakes and along the Erie lakeshore. They are among the first of the waterfowl to follow spring northward. **MAMMALS:** Breeding seasons for squirrels, raccoons, and skunks begin. Their pups will be born in only a few weeks. The timing of spring is critical to the survival of the young. **INSECTS:** Mourning cloak butterflies, which overwinter as adults, may reappear on any warm day this month. Their velvety-brown wings tipped with yellow and small blue spots surprise winter-weary hikers.

WEEK 4 **BIRDS:** Forlorn-looking red-winged blackbirds huddle on snow-covered branches. Look for the red and yellow shoulder patches against the dark black body that distinguish the males from all other blackbirds. **TREES:** The maple sugaring season should be in full swing. Branches broken by ice and snow attract flying squirrels and fox squirrels who hunger for the tasty sap that drips from the end of the broken branches.

Adapted from the Nature Almanac by Robert Hinkle, with permission from Cleveland Metroparks.

STORM SAFETY: Ice

Be wary of a lake or pond with heavy snow cover, as the ice underneath could be weak. New ice is stronger than old, and ice that turns to a darker shade of gray is thinning. Always test before you step onto ice. Toss a large rock onto the ice surface to determine support. Eskimos carry ice chisels and thump the ice frequently, remembering that "when ice cracks it will bear, when ice bends it will break."

ICE SAFETY TIPS:

1. Pond ice one or two inches thick is not considered safe for skating or winter sports. A three-inch layer of clear, firm ice is safe for one person.
2. Four inches will support a small group of people placed several feet apart. This thickness will also support snowmobiles, if spaced at 33-foot intervals.

The Making of a News Desk HEAVYWEIGHT

By Bill Hickey

When I was a little boy growing up, I wanted to be a television star like Dick Goddard. He was my hero and I watched him every night my parents allowed me to stay up. I am now 77, so I can only imagine how old Goddard really is. But that's beside the point because I could have become a star on the tube during a newspaper strike in 1974 if my professorial looks, outstanding intellect, and delightful persona hadn't threatened the egos of a local television news crew.

Don't get me wrong. I'm not saying the people involved, then appearing nightly on WEWS Channel 5 newscasts, resembled troglodytes, were stupid, and had vapid personalities. It's just that they were bound to suffer greatly by comparison. I can almost hear the question you're asking—if you were so handsome, smart, and charming, why didn't you become a television star instead of remaining a newspaper hack who merely covered the doings of local television stations?

The reason is a simple. The entire on-air crew at Channel 5, upon hearing I had been hired to do man-about-town pieces on the six and eleven o'clock newscasts, rattled their jealous bones, enviously circled their wagons, so to speak, and hatched an evil plot to make sure that I didn't succeed. In short, they were scared that a multi-talented person like myself just might take over the evening and nightly newscasts, and they had every right to feel that way.

Sad to say, Dorothy Fuldheim was also in on the conspiracy.

An explanation is in order. Don Perris, then president of the Scripps Howard Broadcasting Company and one of the keenest minds ever to illuminate the television industry, saw the newspaper strike as a blessing in disguise, one so great he doubted that even he deserved it. The strike was called at midnight, and at 12:30 a.m. he was begging me to add a touch of class to the nightly newscasts at Scripps Howard's local outlet and willing to pay me big bucks.

The woebegone on-air Channel 5 personalities were coanchors John Hambrick and Dave Patterson, weatherman Don Webster, and sportscaster Gib Shanley. Although Perris did not come right out and say it in so many words, I got the distinct impression that he considered them a rather ill-mannered, déclassé lot that desperately needed touches of my smooth savoir faire.

I almost forgot. There was also an elderly woman named Dorothy Fuldheim, who daily walked about the station and sometimes forced her way on camera to the dismay of the aforementioned quarter. Her on-air intrusions, I was told, were to demonstrate proper decorum when disseminating news to the viewing public, but her real job was to serve as a den mother to the four adolescents and curtail their nightly antics. Sad to say, she also was in on the conspiracy.

While I fully expected a certain amount of fear and resentment to make their presence known among the on-air foursome plus one, I was shocked to discover that they had managed to convince the behind-the-scenes news editor that I was a threat to the normal newsroom order. The man in question was Gary Ritchie. Remember that name, for it will live in infamy, as we shall see. I must confess that he was very clever in performing his underhanded duties, and it took me several hours to discover that his fatherly role was merely a part of the dirty-trick scheme.

He had me report to him at noon so that he could teach me a few ways to appear at ease on camera, especially how he wanted me to smile while delivering my lightweight items. Then he dropped the bomb—I would have a paltry 60 seconds for my man-about-town piece at six o'clock but a whopping 90 seconds at 11, since the latter newscast had been expanded to serve the public better during the newspaper blackout. Then he told me to write my pieces and report back to him.

Since I had an inordinate amount of daily space in the *Plain Dealer*, I was not used to writing "tight," as they say in the newspaper business. Accordingly, I brought about five minutes' worth of material to my first run-through. It seemed as if I had just opened my mouth when he shook his head from side to side, evinced a sad little smile, and said, "Time's up, you've got to do much better, get the words out, be more positive, more dynamic." What he didn't say, of course, is that there is no way you can physically say five minutes' worth of material in 60 seconds.

There is no way you can phsically say five minutes worth of material in 60 seconds.

As the run-through progressed, I became more and more panicky. So much so that I began to sound the way Rush Limbaugh does when he becomes excited about some nefarious deed pulled off by a left-wing, radical liberal. The man becomes excited to the point where one hopes he's wearing Depends because his words race up the backs of preceding ones and he is unable to finish a solitary thought, so anxious is he to get to his next great thought.

Anyway, I could see that Ritchie was immensely pleased when I began running out of breath in the middle of a word. Not a sentence, mind you, but a word, which was police. All I managed to eke out was "po." By 5:30, I was a basket case and would have sold my soul for a martini, anything to calm my nerves. Then he took me into the studio, where the other on-camera types were horsing around without so much as a nervous tic on any of their faces.

Ritchie then seated me at a small desk opposite John Hambrick, who enjoyed watching my nervous death throes. He smiled and said, "Buddy, how about a cigarette? It will help calm your nerves." He kept up a patter about how unhinged I appeared and kept urging me to smoke one of his Marlboros. I had not touched a cigarette in 10 years, but I couldn't stand the tension as the clock edged closer to six. I stuffed one in my mouth and began puffing away furiously. If you can remember how dizzy you became upon smoking your first cigarette, you know how I felt then.

At two minutes to six, Ritchie escorted me to an oversized chair on the set, informing me that I was to share it with the den mother, Miss Fuldheim. I bumped her slightly upon sitting down and she glared at me, muttering something about having to put up with one King Farouk is enough in anyone's lifetime. Perhaps I should have revealed earlier in this piece that I was somewhat reluctant about accepting Perris's offer to lend class to his newsroom because after quitting smoking a decade before, I had put on a little weight. When I moaned about my sudden surge in avoirdupois to around 250 or so, my friends assured me that I could handle the extra pounds because I was tall, and I believed them. Unfortunately, my seatmate didn't.

I tried to smile and look intelligent at her insistence.

The red light on the camera directly in front of me went on and Miss Fuldheim came on. I tried to smile and look intelligent at her insistence, but all I could manage was a defeated wrinkle where my mouth usually is, the kind of look a guy gets when told that his wife is having an affair with the milkman, his daughter has run away to join the carnival that has just passed through town, and his son was expelled from school for getting his lips tattooed. Mercifully, the light went off and the two anchors began chatting breezily about a fire at a vacant house that not even the owner gave a damn about. I sagged in the chair upon Miss Fuldheim's departure.

I did manage to sit upright as my time on camera neared, but I could do nothing as far as unfreezing my face was concerned. Rather than taking pity on me, the conspirators readied another bit of trickery for which I was ill prepared. Upon introducing me to the half million viewers in northeastern Ohio as a gentleman should, Hambrick said, "And now we have William Hickey, the flower of the *Plain Dealer*, to help us with our expanded newscast."

That really steamed me and I turned to him and said, "John, are you calling me a pansy?" I would have really laid into him, but out of the corner of my eye, I noticed that lines were slowly slipping from my teleprompter into oblivion. The conspirators had even stooped so low as to corrupt an innocent young woman working her way through college by handling one of the station's teleprompters. Her job was to roll the lines off the machine as I spoke them and not a second before. My head was now swimming in a sea of brain-numbing terror and sinking fast. Even though I had written the disappearing lines only an hour or two before, I couldn't remember them. Someone told me later that he liked my first piece because he had never before heard of rioters arresting a group of unruly police somewhere on the near West Side.

Of course, my next item was every bit as incoherent, something about Pope Paul VI chastising his good friend Nick Mileti for building another Coliseum to torture Christians. My third item never made it out of my mouth for I was now totally breathless. I simply stared sullenly at the red light until my 60-second allotment was ignominious history and the camera switched to Webster, whose weather report was almost as fun-filled as Shanley's sports roundup.

I sneaked back into the newsroom, copping Hambrick's pack of Marlboros on the way, and began smoking and wheezing as befits anyone weighing over 300 pounds. I was just about to waddle off into the night, intending to drown my sorrows at the Headliner Café, when Ritchie—there's that man again—hurried me back into the studio because the entire ensemble had to appear as their cheery selves at the end of each newscast, for reasons known only to God.

Ah, but the conspirators weren't through with me yet.

Ah, but the conspirators weren't through with me yet. What they did to me, a hefty type edging the scale around the 400-pound mark, was unconscionable. There was no Miss Fuldheim to share the seat to which I was assigned, but in her place sat a button-bright young man named Mark Koontz, plucked fresh from a college campus. He was handsome and stylishly slender, all 150 pounds of him. The contrast between us was something to behold. After nearly stupefying a friend with eight martinis in order to get an unbiased appraisal of how I looked sitting next to Koontz, he said that I looked something like Orson Welles, only a much bigger version, but that he thought I carried my 457 pounds quite well, all things considered.

Needless to say, the evildoers at Channel 5, on-camera and off-camera, destroyed all my hopes of becoming a television star in an instant, or should I say 60 instants? I had to face the bitter fact that dreadful night: I would never be like my hero Dick Goddard. I would never attain celebrity status and all that goes with it, the adulation, the money, the limos, the groupies.

I could have been a somebody, and I have spent countless sleepless nights thinking about how close I came to becoming one, which causes me to cry often. Trust me, I can hear what you're saying—don't ever forgive those people that did you in. Don't worry. I never will, because they prevented me from fulfilling my childhood dream.

The only consolation I've managed to squeeze out of my terrible time at Channel 5 over the past three decades was that my on-camera appearance led to an offer from the Cleveland Sumo Wrestling Club to become a member, which I did, and managed to become a celebrity of sorts when I became the club's heavyweight champion, but then, that's another story.

Bill Hickey had many assignments during his 37-year career with the *Plain Dealer*, but is most likely remembered for his award-winning critiques of the television industry.

YOU'D BE AMAZED AT WHAT YOU CAN SEE IN FEBRUARY

The brightest star (besides our sun) is Sirius, the dog star, which lies directly in the south at about 9 p.m. You may notice it has a blue color to it. Darker locations may show the outline of our best friend "the dog," as having a rather beagle-like shape to it. While looking, slowly move your eyes upward to the two brighter stars almost directly above it, Castor and Pollux (blue and orange), the brightest stars in the constellation Gemini ("the twins"). Saturn will be the yellow object to the right and on the lower side.

Late this month, Saturn really displays some of its best early evening views. This planet is by far the most marveled at by the public. (One woman actually thought I had painted it in my telescope!) To see the majestic ringed planet, you will need access to at least a small telescope of 60X magnification. Everyone should see Saturn in a telescope at least once in his or her life; it is something you truly will never forget!

Courtesy of Jay Reynolds, Schuele Planetarium director, Lake Erie Nature and Science Center.

Animal Groupies

By Dick Goddard

When animals congregate they are given group names. We've all heard of a school of fish and a flock of birds, but how about a clowder of cats, or a leap of leopards? A festival of caterpillars?

At a barristers' convention, would this be a litigation of lawyers? How about a meeting of meteorologists? I would suggest a "guess" of weathermen.

The following knowledge could be of great help to you if you are ever a contestant on *Jeopardy!*:

BALE of turkeys

BED of snakes

BEVY of quail

BOUQUET of pheasants (in flight)

CHARM of finches

COLONY of ants, badgers, frogs

COVEY of partridges, pheasants, or quail (on the ground)

EXALTATION of larks

GAGGLE of geese (on the ground)

GAM of whales

GANG of elk

HIVE of bees

HOST of sparrows

HUSK of hares

KNOT of toads

LABOR of moles

MURDER of crows

MURMURATION of starlings

NEST of rabbits, wasps, or vipers

PACE of asses

PARLIAMENT of owls

PLAGUE of locusts

POD of seals or whales

SHREWDNESS of apes

SKEIN of geese (in the air)

SKULK of foxes

SLOTH of bears

SWARM of insects, especially bees

TROOP of monkeys

WATCH of nightingales

NORTHEAST OHIO WEATHER YEAR IN REVIEW–2003

CLEVELAND HOPKINS AIRPORT:

Average high: 58.3°, which is 0.2° above normal

Average low: 41.7°, 0.5° above normal

Average temperature: 50.0°, 0.4° above normal

Warmest day: 92° on Jul 4 and Aug 21

Coldest day: -4° on Jan 27

Record highs: 82° on Apr 15, 77° on Nov 2, 79° on Nov 4

Record lows: 2° on Mar 3, 28° on Apr 24, 34° on Oct 6

Precipitation: 42.51", 3.80" above normal

Peak wind: 61 MPH from the southwest on July 7

HIGHLIGHTS:

5th warmest Nov on record at 47.8°. The warmest is 51.2° in 1931.

5th wettest May on record at 6.49". The wettest is 9.14" in 1989.

2nd snowiest Jan on record at 30.3". The snowiest is 42.8" in 1978.

4th snowiest Feb on record at 30.1". The snowiest is 39.1" in 1993.

6th snowiest Dec on record at 26.6". The snowiest is 30.3" in 1962.

Earliest measurable snowfall of 0.2" on Oct 2.

AKRON-CANTON AIRPORT:

Average high: 57.5°, which is 1.4° below normal

Average low: 40.1°, 0.1° above normal

Average temperature: 48.8°, 0.7° below normal

Warmest day: 89° on July 4

Coldest day: -8° on Jan 27

Record highs: 81° on Apr 15, 76° on Nov 4

Record lows: 38° on Jun 2

Precipitation: total 51.11", 12.64" above normal

Peak wind: 58 MPH from the west on Nov 12

HIGHLIGHTS:

9th snowiest Feb on record at 17.13". The snowiest is 25.3" in 1910.

4th wettest May on record at 8.16". The wettest is 9.60" in 1956.

Wettest July on record at 12.55".

5th wettest Sep on record at 7.48". The wettest is 11.98" in 1926.

3rd wettest year on record at 51.11". The wettest is 65.70" in 1990.

3rd wettest summer on record at 18.15". The wettest is 20.28" in 1892.

7th wettest autumn on record at 13.14". The wettest is 19.59" in 1926.

9th snowiest Dec on record at 18.6". The snowiest is 29.4" in 1974.

10th coldest winter on record at 23.4°. The coldest is 20.7° in 1976/77.

MANSFIELD AIRPORT:

Average high: 57.2°, which is 1.3° below normal

Average low: 39.0°, 0.1° above normal

Average temperature: 48.1°, 0.6° above normal

Warmest day: 89° on July 4

Coldest day: -10° on Jan 27

Record highs: 70° on Mar 17, 80° on Apr 15, 83° on May 1, 76° on Nov 4

Record lows: -2° on Jan 26, -10° on Jan 27, 0 on Mar 3, 26° on Apr 13, 37° on Jun 1, 37° on Jun 2, 46° Jun 19, 44° on Jun 20, 34° Oct 1, 30° Oct 2, 30° on Oct 3

Precipitation: total 41.58", 1.66" below normal

Peak wind: 52 mph from the west on Jul 8

HIGHLIGHTS:

7th coldest Jan on record at 18.7°. The coldest is 8.7° in 1977.

5th coldest Feb on record at 22.6°. The coldest is 15.4° in 1978.

10th coldest Sep on record at 61.1°. The coldest is 58.7° in 1975.

8th coldest Oct on record at 49.5°. The coldest is 45.1° in 1988.

7th warmest Nov on record at 44.5°. The warmest is 47.6° in 2001.

6th wettest Jul on record at 6.01". The wettest is 13.23" in 1992.

3rd wettest Sep on record at 6.54". The wettest is 7.76" in 1986.

3rd snowiest Feb on record with 16.5". The snowiest is 19.1" in 1984.

2nd snowiest Dec on record with 23.3". The snowiest is 23.4" in 1995.

YOUNGSTOWN AIRPORT:

Average high: 57.1°, which is 1.1° below normal

Average low: 38.6°, 0.2° below normal

Average temperature: 47.9°, 0.6° below normal

Warmest day: 88° on Aug 21

Coldest day: -5° on Jan 27

Record highs: 71° on Mar 17, 75° on Apr 14, 82° on Apr 5, 77° on Nov 4

Record lows: -5° on Jan 27, 0° on Mar 3, 26° on Apr 24, 48° on Jul 19, 19° on Nov 9

Precipitation: total 46.01", which is 7.99" above normal.

Peak wind: 53 mph from the west on Nov 13.

HIGHLIGHTS:

9th coldest Jan on record at 19.3°. The coldest is 10.3° in 1977.

9th coldest Feb on record at 22.7°. The coldest is 15.6° in 1978.

8th coldest Oct on record at 48.9°. The coldest is 45.1° in 1988.

7th warmest Nov on record at 44.9°. The warmest is 47.7° in 2001.

2nd wettest May on record at 6.84". The wettest is 9.87" in 1946.

Wettest Jul on record at 10.40".

5th wettest Sep on record at 5.62". The wettest is 6.35" in 1996.

5th wettest year on record at 46.01". The wettest is 48.58" in 1956.

5th snowiest Jan on record at 25.6". The snowiest is 36.4" in 1999.

Snowiest Feb on record at 26.4".

9th snowiest Dec on record at 19.2". The snowiest is 29.5" in 1987.

Earliest measurable snowfall is 0.1" on Oct 2.

According to a 2002 study of **Northeast Ohio retail development** in seven counties (Cuyahoga, Geauga, Lake, Lorain, Medina and Portage Counties, and a portion of Summit County), the region has more than 27,000 stores and 135 million square feet of retail floor space, and shopping trips in this area currently generate an estimated 5.6 billion vehicle miles annually. The study states: "While the population of suburban Cuyahoga County decreased by 9.2% between 1968 and 1998, the amount of retail floor space increased by 90.9%." *[source:www.asu.edu/caed/proceedings02/KASTEL/kastel.htm]*

Stargazing in Northeast Ohio

The following locations offer informative and entertaining programs on astronomy and general sky watching in Northeast Ohio. (Dates, times, and costs for programs vary, so please call ahead for information.)

Lake Erie Nature and Science Center
Schuele Planetarium
28728 Wolf Rd. • Bay Village, Ohio
440-871-2900 • www.LENSC.org

Schuele Planetarium (at Cleveland Metroparks' Huntington Reservation) offers weekly public programming on the night sky and "What's News in Space." Twinkle Tots (15 minutes long) is for the youngest members of the audience; they can even practice not being afraid of the dark! Year-round telescope viewing is open to the public the first and third Saturday of every month, with an early planetarium presentation to get you ready. Appropriate for ages 5 and over. Special programs for holidays and astronomical events.

Cleveland Museum of Natural History
Shafran Planetarium
1 Wade Oval Dr. • Cleveland, Ohio
216-231-4600 • www.cmnh.org

Shafran Planetarium offers weekend public programming throughout the year. The observatory is open on Wednesday evenings, with planetarium presentations from September through May.

Cuyahoga Astronomical Association
(meets at Rocky River Nature Center)
24000 Valley Pky. • North Olmsted, Ohio
440-779-9779 • www.geocities.com/cuyastro/

Monthly meetings on the second Monday of every month at 7:30 p.m. at the Rocky River Nature Center. Each session consists of a brief business meeting followed by a social break with refreshments when members can discuss astronomical issues. Then a CAA member or invited guest presents a lecture on an astronomy-related topic. The CAA also sponsors programs open to the general public. Programs are usually held at their observatory outside Spencer, Ohio (weather permitting).

Courtesy of Jay Reynolds,
Schuele Planetarium director,
Lake Erie Nature and Science Center.

The Chagrin Valley Astronomical Society
Contact: stevef@en.com
www.chagrinvalleyastronomy.org

This is a group of dedicated amateurs whose goals are promotion of public education in astronomy, the continuation of useful research, and the preservation of unpolluted skies in the interests of both the astronomer and the general public. The group offers public observing programs at Indian Hill Observatory.

Black River Astronomical Society
Contact: davelengyel@amherst.k12.oh.us

Serves Lorain County and the surrounding area. Meetings are free and open to the public, on the first Wednesday of each month at 7 p.m. at the Lorain County Metroparks Visitors Center on Nickel Plate-Diagonal Road in Carlisle Township. Public star parties are held at the nearby Nielsen Observatory, at the Lorain County Metro Parks Equestrian Center.

Astronomy Club of Akron
Portage Lakes State Park
5301 Manchester Rd. • Akron, Ohio
330-658-3125 (after 5 p.m.) • www.acaoh.org

Operates out of the ACA Observatory. Indoor and outdoor programs are coordinated to astronomical events. Biweekly programs are held during the summer. The observatory also holds a monthly open house in the wintertime. All events are free and open to the public.

Penitentiary Glen Reservation
8668 Kirtland-Chardon Rd. • Kirtland, Ohio
440-256-1404 • http://www.lakemetroparks.com/HTML/PG/penitentiaryglen.html

This is the site of the annual "Super Star Party," which will next be held August 6, 2005. With activities for the kids, animals on display, great exhibits, and great views through many different types of telescopes, these star parties live up to their name and are very well attended.

MARCH STATISTICS

(recorded at Cleveland Hopkins Airport)

SUNSHINE %	45
DRIEST MONTH	0.41"/1910
WARMEST MONTH	49.5°/1946
COLDEST MONTH	24.0°/1960
LIQUID PCPN AVG.	2.91"
RAINIEST DAY	2.76"/1848
RAINIEST MONTH	8.31"/1913
THUNDERY DAYS	2
SNOWIEST DAY	16.4"/1987
SNOWIEST MONTH	26.3"/1954
LEAST SNOWFALL	TRACE/1927
DAYS ONE INCH SNOW	3

NORTHEAST OHIO'S WARMEST AND COLDEST SPRINGS

(by Median Temp)

WARMEST

Cleveland: 53.4° / 1991

Akron/Canton: 55.1° / 1991

COLDEST

Cleveland: 41.3° / 1885

Akron/Canton: 43.5° / 1926

The winds of March that make your heart a dancer have occasionally brought record amounts of snow with them. On March 30–31, 1987, Cleveland received its second-heaviest 24-hour snowfall, 16.4 inches. Several days later the Akron/Canton area was buried under a record 20.6 inches. Curiously, many of Northeast Ohio's monumental snowfalls have come in November and March, on either side of what is officially winter. Snows in March are usually very wet and hard to shovel, but the crystals melt quickly. March is the month of reawakening, and on mild nights the tiny tree frogs known as spring peepers begin their vernal concerts.

Spring, the vernal equinox, arrives on the 20th of the month; this is one of only two times each year that our sun rises due east and sets due west. We now enjoy three more hours of daylight than we did in dark December, and we'll gain another three hours by the summer solstice in June.

DAILY DATA FOR MARCH

Date	Day	Moon	Day of Year	Days Left	Sunrise	Sunset	Length of Day	Avg. Hi°	Avg. Lo°	Avg. Lake°
1	Tue		60	305	7:01	6:17	11:16	46	23	34
2	Wed		61	304	6:59	6:19	11:20	40	24	34
3	Thu	◑	62	303	6:58	6:20	11:22	41	24	34
4	Fri		63	302	6:56	6:21	11:25	41	24	34
5	Sat		64	301	6:55	6:22	11:27	42	25	34
6	Sun		65	300	6:53	6:23	11:30	42	25	34
7	Mon		66	299	6:51	6:24	11:33	43	25	34
8	Tue		67	298	6:50	6:26	11:36	43	26	34
9	Wed		68	297	6:48	6:27	11:39	43	26	34
10	Thu	●	69	296	6:46	6:28	11:42	44	26	34
11	Fri		70	295	6:45	6:29	11:44	44	27	34
12	Sat		71	294	6:43	6:30	11:47	45	27	34
13	Sun		72	293	6:42	6:31	11:49	45	27	34
14	Mon		73	292	6:40	6:32	11:52	46	28	34
15	Tue		74	291	6:38	6:34	11:56	46	28	35
16	Wed		75	290	6:36	6:35	11:59	46	28	35
17	Thu	◐	76	289	6:35	6:36	12:01	47	29	35
18	Fri		77	288	6:33	6:37	12:04	47	29	35
19	Sat		78	287	6:31	6:38	12:07	48	29	35
20	Sun		79	286	6:30	6:39	12:09	48	30	35
21	Mon		80	285	6:28	6:40	12:12	48	30	35
22	Tue		81	284	6:26	6:41	12:15	49	30	36
23	Wed		82	283	6:25	6:42	12:17	49	30	36
24	Thu		83	282	6:23	6:43	12:20	50	31	36
25	Fri	○	84	281	6:21	6:45	12:24	50	31	36
26	Sat		85	280	6:20	6:46	12:26	50	31	36
27	Sun		86	279	6:18	6:47	12:29	51	32	36
28	Mon		87	278	6:16	6:48	12:32	51	32	36
29	Tue		88	277	6:14	6:49	12:35	52	32	36
30	Wed		89	276	6:13	6:50	12:37	52	32	37
31	Thu		90	275	6:11	6:51	12:40	52	33	37

Rec. Hi°	Rec. Lo°	On This Date . . .
69/1912	-2/1984	Ohio becomes 17th state (1803)
64/1991	-4/1978	Cavaliers win 22nd straight home game (1989)
74/1974	2/2003	Summit County incorporated (1840)
76/1983	2/1943	Collinwood School fire (1908)
81/1983	-2/1873	U.S. rocket flies record 4800 KPH to 126k height (1948)
74/1973	-2/1960	Lake County incorporated (1840)
76/2000	3/1960	Huron County incorporated (1809)
79/2000	-1/1960	WFMJ TV 21 in Youngstown OH (NBC) begins broadcasting (1953)
73/1878	-5/1984	Cleveland Spiders sign Louis Sockalexis (1897)
72/1973	5/1983	Harry Gammeter of Cleve. patents multigraph duplicating machine (1903)
73/1973	-3/1983	President & Chief Justice William Taft buried in Arlington (1930)
75/1990	-5/1948	1st branch of Cleveland Public Library system opens on Pearl St. (1892)
76/1990	3/1960	Band leader Sammy Kaye born in Cleveland (1913)
79/1990	6/1993	1st American town meeting (1743)
80/1990	3/1993	Buzzards first appear at Hinckley (1881)
78/1945	7/1885	Erie County incorporated (1838)
72/1945	0/1900	It is announced there is no smoking in Jacobs Field (1994)
75/1903	0/1877	WGSF TV channel 31 in Newark OH (PBS) begins broadcasting (1963)
76/1903	7/1885	Indians reject Boston's offer of $1 million for Herb Score (1957)
76/1995	0/1885	Harriet Beecher Stowe's Uncle Tom's Cabin published (1852)
76/1938	-4/1885	Moon Dog Coronation Ball (1st rock and roll concert) (1952)
83/1938	0/1885	Indians players Steve Olin and Tim Crews killed in accident (1993)
77/1966	5/1885	Draper takes 1st successful photo of the Moon (daguerrotype) (1840)
83/1910	8/1888	83°F highest temperature ever recorded in Cleveland in March (1910)
83/1945	8/1888	Musician Michael Stanley born (1948)
80/1967	14/2001	Dayton almost destroyed by flood (1913)
80/1989	12/1982	Morman temple at Kirtland dedicated (1836)
80/1945	9/1982	Ohio passed law restricting movement of blacks (1804)
81/1910	11/1887	Notorious gangster Alex "Shondor" Birns blown up in his car (1975)
82/1986	16/1987	15th Amendment passes, guarantees right to vote regardless of race (1870)
77/1943	11/1923	Cavaliers clinch their 1st ever NBA playoff berth (1976)

Flora & Fauna MARCH

WEEK 1

BIRDS: Bluebirds may have returned if winter has not been too harsh and cold. In mild winters, some actually stay all winter long and mix with a few resident American robins feeding on berries and crab apples in yards and fields. **MAMMALS:** Most male white-tailed deer have lost their antlers by now. Deer, moose, and elk drop their antlers and regrow them each year. It is not possible to tell the age of the deer by the number of points, but an antler's age makes little difference to mice, squirrels, and woodchucks, which gnaw on the calcium-rich prizes left in the mud and snow of March. **WILDFLOWERS:** Pungent skunk cabbage begins to bloom in low wet places on forest edges. The rhubarb-like leaves continue to grow for months after the flower has produced seeds. The flower head, which produces its own heat, grows slowly though the ice and snow each winter to become the first blooming plant each spring.

WEEK 2

BIRDS: Great blue herons and kingfishers become common sights as soon as open water makes fish available to them. Where open water persists, and the winter is not too harsh, some may stay all winter. Song sparrows begin to reappear under bird feeders this week. Watch for their streaked breast with a central chocolate spot. The male's calls begin with three sharp notes, then blur into a melodious trill. **AMPHIBIANS:** Spring peepers begin to fill evening twilight with their sharp "perreep-perreep" calls. As the evening cools, the little frogs sing less often, until finally the cold shuts their song down for the night.

WEEK 3

BIRDS: March brings the first of the migrating woodcocks to perform their spring mating flights in brushy pasture and fields this week. Their celebrated "sky dance" each evening is one of the first sure signs that spring has truly arrived. The buzzards are back! On March 15, turkey vultures return like clockwork to the village of Hinckley, Ohio. Visit Cleveland Metroparks' famous "buzzard roost" on the first Sunday after March 15 and take part in a day of songs, stories, and fun. **MAMMALS:** It's the season for woodchuck love! The females have finally awakened to greet the males, who awakened in February. Spring comes quickly and summer is only a few weeks away! The rapid changes of April give way to a slower and more stately procession of nature as May begins.

WEEK 4

BIRDS: The phoebe's raspy "fee-bree" call reassures forest hikers that spring is truly here. These shy birds nest under bridges and eaves. The flocks of male goldfinches, who seem to progressively grow a more brilliant yellow each week, are another sign of impending spring. Set out fresh thistle seed for them! For a few weeks golden-crowned kinglets pass through on their way to Canada. Only half the size of chickadees, they flit continuously from branch to branch in search of food. **AMPHIBIANS:** Spring peepers "peep" and wood frogs "quack" as their spring mating cycle begins. Shallow temporary ponds in or near forests are preferred breeding places for these small frogs as mates are found and eggs are laid each spring. Chorus frogs, sounding like a comb being stroked with your thumb, will appear in a week or so. **SHRUBS:** By month's end pussy willows begin to bloom in low wet places as the days grow longer. The fuzzy part is the flower of this shrubby willow, which quickly produces yellow pollen and is replaced with newly growing leaves.

Adapted from the Nature Almanac by Robert Hinkle, with permission from Cleveland Metroparks.

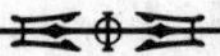

fun facts NORTHEAST OHIO

Food Network's Rachael Ray came to Cleveland to film her show *$40 a Day* in April of 2004. She visited Tommy's in Cleveland Heights, the Rock and Roll Hall of Fame and Slyman's in downtown Cleveland, and Trattoria Roman Gardens in Little Italy. *Source: www.foodnetwork.com*

·THE· Burlington Tornado

BY RON HAHN

On Wednesday, May 18, 1825, severe weather broke out across Ohio, Indiana, and Pennsylvania. Ohio was hardest hit with several strong tornadoes striking the central and northern sections of the state. The most violent of all these twisters, with winds most probably in excess of 300 miles per hour, was the storm that wiped the settlement of Burlington (now known as Homer, in Licking County) off the map.

First touchdown of the tornado funnel was in eastern Delaware County, and it traveled northeasterly into Licking County. At its widest, the tornado was between two-thirds of a mile and a mile in width. Two men near Burlington were plowing when they suddenly noticed trees flying in the air. As the outer edge of the funnel overtook them, one man was carried a short distance until he grasped a bush. He clung to the bush until it was torn out of the ground, but he finally managed to cling to another bush until the storm passed. His companion found refuge beside a large fallen tree. There he remained safe from the storm, but so many other trees had fallen over his spot that he could not get out until his friend cut through the limbs with his axe.

The citizens of Burlington itself heard a "loud, rolling wind" that alarmed them and saw the "dark, black cloud" approaching. They saw trees being thrown in every direction, and they raced to their houses, most of which were made of logs, but the storm took even the lowest logs of all forty log houses away. Amazingly, only three people were killed.

One man's brick home was totally destroyed. His wife and children managed to save themselves by going into the cellar. The whirling funnel was so powerful that huge trees were torn out of the ground by their roots and carried some distance through the air. One tree was three to four feet in diameter, but it was taken out by the roots and carried for distances of twenty or thirty miles. Destruction was so complete that on farms of 200 to 300 acres, there was not one tree left standing. Nearly all the animals in the path of the tornado funnel were killed.

Horses, cattle, and oxen were lifted and carried between 550 and 1,100 yards through the air. A creek over which the tornado passed was running full of water from recent heavy rains but was only a trickle after the twister's passage. Soggy roads and fields over which the storm swept were left "almost dusty." Debris of all kinds, including trees and logs, was taken high into the sky by the powerful funnel, making the sky look as through it were full of large birds. Even the ground was said to tremble as the tornado passed.

Shelby and Logan counties were hit by an equally violent twister that day, although this one was only about one-fourth of a mile wide at its widest. One man's brick house was totally leveled, and the upper floor and joists, which were spiked together, could not be found. This funnel even tore tree stumps out of the ground and cleared away everything in its path so completely that the path "had the appearance of a state road." Ponds were emptied almost completely of their water, and geese were dashed to death against trees by the violence of the wind.

While spring is usually our prime tornado season here in the Buckeye state, tornadoes have occurred in every month of the year in Ohio. During the thirty years from 1971 to 2000, approximately 80 percent of all Ohio tornadoes occurred during the months of April through July. Within this same period, January and December had one tornado each, February had 2, October and November had 5 apiece, March had 16, and September had 17. Lorain County had the dubious distinction of being visited most often by tornadoes from 1971 to 2000. That county was struck 18 times. Huron County was a close second with 17 hits. Franklin and Richland counties saw twisters 16 times during this period, while Medina and Trumbull counties were traversed by twisters 13 times. Believe it or not, Greene County (where Xenia is located) was visited by tornadoes just 7 times in the thirty years from 1971 to 2000.

There is no known photo of the Burlington Tornado. This photo, taken in Columbus in 1973, shows a common tornado form. *Courtesy of Jim Fry.*

Because the thunderstorms from which tornadoes come need heat to thrive, the majority of Ohio tornadoes come to earth during the afternoon or evening hours. During the period 1971–2000, more than 90 percent of all May tornadoes and more than 95 percent of all June tornadoes formed between the hours of noon and midnight, and the majority of these touched down between noon and 6 p.m.

Of course, there are always exceptions. A strong tornado swept through Knox, Tuscarawas, and Carroll counties on January 20, 1854. Houses directly in its path were either destroyed or unroofed, and just before it hit the air was said to have grown very warm. Another "out of season" tornado struck Mayfield, Kirtland, and Painesville in Cuyahoga and Lake counties on February 4, 1842. One barn filled with several tons of hay and some horses was lifted in its entirety off the ground and carried a few feet before the bottom fell out of it. Beams from this barn were carried a considerable distance further.

Holmes County was visited by a tornado on March 7, 1903. This storm carried a piece of lumber one-half mile and then threw it into a barn with such force that several rafters were broken. Slate roofing was carried four miles by the twister. Cattle, chickens, horses, and sheep were killed by this violent storm. However, one barn filled with animals was entirely carried away except for the floor-not one of the animals there was touched!

Such "tornado freaks," if we may call them that, have not been uncommon in Ohio. A March 11, 1917, tornado in Fayette County drove shingles, straws, and a piece of tin into trees. In addition, this powerful tornado took the roof off one house and sucked all the furniture out, but left the walls standing by themselves. A brick house with its chimney was lifted totally off its foundation and then dumped in rubble 100 feet away. The twister that hit north of Orrville in Wayne County on April 10, 1922, carried away a barn but left a cow untouched, still tied to her stall. Clermont and Brown counties were visited by a tornado on June 2, 1916. Those people who lived through the storm escaped without so much as a speck of clothing left on them. Then there was the Tiffin (Seneca County) funnel of June 24, 1930, which picked up a large tile, carried it 200 feet through the air, tossed it through a window, and placed it gently on a table without breaking either the tile or the table.

How can such freak events be explained? Within many tornado funnels, there are what are known as suction vortices—almost like mini-tornadoes whirling around inside the main funnel. Where these suction vortices hit, everything may be swept away, but in between them even frail, delicate objects can be left untouched.

Tornadoes frequently pick up light objects and carry them high into the clouds, where these objects are carried along by the winds until they come to earth perhaps a hundred or more miles away. The Xenia (Green County) storm of April 3, 1974, picked up checks and other papers, some of which were dropped more than 130 miles away in Wayne County. A picture from Cardington (Morrow County) was picked up by the June 13, 1981, tornado there and deposited 70 miles away in Wayne County. On June 27, 1812, a tornado moved northwest to southeast through Darke, Montgomery, and Greene counties. Sheaves of grain, laurel tree branches, chestnut tree branches, and tree leaves rained from the sky along the sides of the tornado's path. There were no such trees within 100 miles of the tornado track in Ohio, and many of the tree branches and leaves were either covered with ice or had icicles on them.

Ice and snow are to be found in the cumulonimbus (thunderhead) clouds from which tornadoes come, even during the hottest weather, for these clouds build high into the sky where temperatures go well below zero. In fact, temperatures of some thunderstorm cloud tops that produced tornadoes have been recorded by satellite sensors at temperatures below -100° F. This fact was demonstrated well by a funnel cloud that did not touch down but passed overhead near Wabash, Indiana, on June 2, 1924. It deposited 8 inches of snow over 20 square feet of ground!

Sometimes, the level of electrical activity (lightning flashes) in a thunderstorm can be a tip as to when a tornado is about to touch down. However, there have been tornadoes that have not been accompanied by any lightning. Such a storm hit Morgan County on June 19, 1823. This storm struck at approximately 9:30 in the evening, and the entire tornado funnel was said to be illuminated like "a glowing oven," with the light from it being greater than that made by a full moon. No lightning or thunder and no hail or rain accompanied the passage of the funnel, but there was a continuous roar, and the brilliant glow of the tornado enabled a man to read by its light for ten minutes after its passage! However, the tornado that struck near Mt. Vernon, Knox County, on January 20, 1854, was said to look like a "black pillar" but was lit up by "blinding flashes of lightning."

As the description of the Knox County tornado shows, these storms do not always have the classic funnel shape. A tornado that struck Hardin, Hancock, and Wyandot counties on May 14, 1886, at 11:30 p.m. was said to resemble "an immense balloon." This balloon-shaped twister also had an extremely fast forward speed, covering ground at about 80 miles per hour. The Fulton County tornado of June 24, 1886, was called a "blue ball," while the twister that swept through St. Clairsville and Martins Ferry in Belmont County on April 15, 1887, was said to look like a "whirling cloud of dense smoke." Stark County was hit on August 13, 1943, by an umbrella-shaped tornado.

No matter what their shape, tornadoes are hard to beat for an exhibition of power and mystery. The April 11, 1965, Palm Sunday tornado outbreak was a good example. The whirling tornado funnel that swept through Shelby County on that day derailed 53 cars of a 68-car train and carried an automobile 200 yards through the air. On the same date, a very powerful storm hit the northern edge of Toledo. While that tornado was on the ground, two columns of light were seen in the sky in that area. They may have been glowing twin tornado funnels, but no one really knows.

Ron Hahn has been a weather observer in Kidron (Wayne County) since 1963. Ron's "Ohio Weather Past" column has appeared in the Ohio Weather Journal (OWON newsletter) since 1993.

The Strangest Storm in the World

By Dick Goddard

Shortly after midnight on the morning of June 15, 1960, under clear skies and otherwise normal conditions, a damaging, scorching northwest wind inflicted terror and near disaster on a 25-mile stretch across the northwest side of Lake Whitney, northwest of Waco, Texas, for nearly three hours.

It was like any other Texas night in mid-June. The temperature was in the 70s, the stars were out, and a light breeze was blowing. There had been some lightning earlier, but no one paid much attention to it. Then, without warning . . . it struck! A searing, blowtorch-like wind hit with speeds estimated at 80 to 100 miles per hour, and the temperature jumped from near 70 to 140 degrees.

The Mooney Village Store lost its roof and was badly damaged; the interior was smashed and loaves of bread and canned goods blown from the shelves. The strong winds smashed down a huge tree at the home of Mrs. Vergie Moon, near the damaged store. She said it took three people to keep the wind from blowing down her front door. The D. L. Downeys took refuge in their storm cellar, which soon was filled with neighbors seeking shelter from this unusual and frightening storm.

The heat and searing wind were stifling. Mothers wrapped their crying babies in wet sheets and towels to protect them from the intense heat. Fire sprinkler systems were set off, car radiators boiled over, and panic-stricken women were crying, thinking the end of the world had come.

The cotton field of rancher Pete Burns was scorched by the hot wind. It was an average stand of cotton, which he had plowed on Tuesday. The wind and the heat carbonized it, leaving only a few burnt stalks standing. Cornfields in the area, green when the sun went down Tuesday, were scorched and wilted at sunup Wednesday.

No one knows for sure how hot it was, but the thermometer outside the Charley Riddle Bait and Tackle Shop in Kopperl jumped from near 80 degrees about midnight to 100 degrees in just a few minutes, reaching a high of 140 degrees. There was nothing wrong with the thermometer; it was working all right the next day and, if anything, was reading a little low.

The event would have gone undocumented except for veteran cameraman Floyd Bright, who, hearing of the incident, recorded it on film.

Several attempts have been made to explain the phenomenon, but this probably is what happened. Scattered thunderstorms had earlier been detected in the area by Fort Worth radar, but they disappeared off the scope shortly before midnight. The weather observations at Waco showed a high overcast, with light southwest winds and a temperature at midnight of 87 degrees.

Characteristic of all thunderstorms is the rain shaft falling from the center or forward portion of the storm, bringing cooler rain and air from the cold temperatures of the higher portions of the cloud. This cold rush of air and rain evaporating moisture into the air as it descends offsets the usual heating effect of descending air. The rain shafts were seen on the Fort Worth Radar until near midnight, and then they disappeared.

It may be that the downward thrust of air continued even after the rain ended. In so doing, it would have heated at the rate of 5.5° F for every 1,000 feet of fall.

The downward force of this air from the old dried-up thunderstorm must have been fierce, for heated air tends to rise, not fall. The bases of the thunderstorms that night were 8,000 to 10,000 feet above the ground. If the air temperature in the dissipating cloud at a height of 20,000 feet was 20° to 25° F, then the falling air would be heated another 110 degrees by compression by the time it reached the ground, and this, added to the initial temperature, would be close to the 140 degrees observed on the thermometer at the bait shop. ■

"BEFORE I GO I WANT YOU TO BEG, SIT AND ROLL OVER."

African-American Firsts in Cleveland

Three years prior to the Civil War, Robert Boyd Leach, the first African-American physician in Cleveland, set up shop.

The first African-American in Cleveland to be elected to public office was John P. Green, who was elected in 1873 as a justice of the peace on the Republican ticket.

AT WHAT YOU CAN

March 11, at about 6:30, Mercury will be joined in the western sky by our crescent moon.

March 15, a nearly first-quarter moon will be in the western sky; just a little lower and slightly to the right will be the Pleiades, better known as "the Seven Sisters." Easily seen with naked eyes, these are very young, hot, blue stars, the "open cluster" of stars closest to Earth.

Courtesy of Jay Reynolds, Schuele Planetarium director, Lake Erie Nature and Science Center.

APRIL STATISTICS

(recorded at Cleveland Hopkins Airport)

SUNSHINE %	51
DRIEST MONTH	0.65"/1915
WARMEST MONTH	55.9°/1955
COLDEST MONTH	39.6°/1874
LIQUID PCPN AVG.	3.14"
RAINIEST DAY	2.24"/1961
RAINIEST MONTH	6.61"/1961
THUNDERY DAYS	4
SNOWIEST DAY	11.6"/1982
SNOWIEST MONTH	14.3"/1943
LEAST SNOWFALL	TRACE *(most recently in 1991)*
DAYS ONE INCH SNOW	1

April is also known as the month of fools. It's foolish, indeed, to set out any tender-plants during this month. April marks the beginning of the tornado season in Northeast Ohio, and April tornadoes are often strong, accounting for the highest monthly death toll from twisters in the United States. The April 11, 1965, Palm Sunday tornado killed 19 at Pittsfield in Lorain County. The massive F5 twister that struck Xenia, Ohio, on the 3rd of April in 1974 killed 35. (That tornado was part of the greatest "family outbreak" of tornadoes in American weather history.) Thanks to Ben Franklin, who came up with the idea, we revert to Daylight Savings Time on the first Sunday of April. At 2 a.m. we'll lose an hour's sleep by setting our clocks ahead to 3 a.m. Raucous and cunning crows are returning from the depths of the winter woods. Juncos (snow birds) have returned and bluebirds often arrive by the third week in April.

Woollybear caterpillars, who spent all winter in their larval stage, will be munching on dandelion and plantain weed before spinning cocoons out of their body hair. In a few weeks a beige, purple-spotted tiger moth will emerge and flit away in the spring sunshine. Each moth lays thousands of eggs, which will become the woollybears of autumn. If snow should cover your flowers, don't bother to brush it away; snow acts as a protective, insulating blanket.

DAILY DATA FOR APRIL

Date	Day	Moon	Day of Year	Days Left	Sunrise	Sunset	Length of Day	Avg. Hi°	Avg. Lo°	Avg. Lake°
1	Fri		91	274	6:09	6:52	12:43	53	33	37
2	Sat	◑	92	273	6:08	6:53	12:45	53	33	37
3	Sun		93	272	7:06	7:54	12:48	53	34	38
4	Mon		94	271	7:04	7:55	12:51	54	34	38
5	Tue		95	270	7:03	7:56	12:53	54	34	38
6	Wed		96	269	7:01	7:58	12:57	55	34	38
7	Thu		97	268	6:59	7:59	13:00	55	35	39
8	Fri	●	98	267	6:58	8:00	13:02	55	35	39
9	Sat		99	266	6:56	8:01	13:05	56	35	39
10	Sun		100	265	6:55	8:02	13:07	56	36	39
11	Mon		101	264	6:53	8:03	13:10	56	36	40
12	Tue		102	263	6:51	8:04	13:13	57	36	40
13	Wed		103	262	6:50	8:05	13:15	57	36	40
14	Thu		104	261	6:48	8:06	13:18	57	37	41
15	Fri		105	260	6:47	8:07	13:20	58	37	41
16	Sat	◐	106	259	6:45	8:08	13:23	58	37	41
17	Sun		107	258	6:44	8:09	13:25	58	38	41
18	Mon		108	257	6:42	8:11	13:29	59	38	42
19	Tue		109	256	6:41	8:12	13:31	59	38	42
20	Wed		110	255	6:39	8:13	13:34	60	39	42
21	Thu		111	254	6:38	8:14	13:36	60	39	42
22	Fri		112	253	6:36	8:15	13:39	60	39	43
23	Sat		113	252	6:35	8:16	13:41	61	40	43
24	Sun	○	114	251	6:33	8:17	13:44	61	40	44
25	Mon		115	250	6:32	8:18	13:46	61	40	44
26	Tue		116	249	6:30	8:19	13:49	62	41	44
27	Wed		117	248	6:29	8:20	13:51	62	41	45
28	Thu		118	247	6:27	8:21	13:54	62	41	45
29	Fri		119	246	6:26	8:22	13:56	63	41	45
30	Sat		120	245	6:25	8:23	13:58	63	42	46

Rec. Hi°	Rec. Lo°	On This Date . . .
80/1986	10/1964	Baseball Hall of Fame opens in Cooperstown, NY (1938)
81/1963	19/1883	Record wind speed 450 kph in tornado, Wichita Falls, TX (1958)
78/1999	19/1954	ICC transfers Ohio to Eastern time zone (1927)
77/1882	19/1971	Cleveland Society for Prevention of Cruelty to Animals founded (1873)
81/1988	17/1881	World Trade Center opens in NYC (1974)
84/1929	21/1982	George D. Forbes elected 1st black pres. of Cleve. City Council (1973)
83/1929	17/1982	1st settlement in Ohio, at Marietta (1788)
80/2001	11/1982	House of Representives 1st meeting (1789)
81/1931	17/1972	General Lee surrenders to General Grant (1865)
83/1978	20/1997	Cleve Cavaliers win their 1st NBA Central Division title (1976)
82/1945	22/1982	Actor Joel Grey born in Cleveland (1932)
82/2001	21/1874	Highest wind velocity recorded–231 mph, Mt Washington, NH (1934)
85/1941	20/1950	Best view of Halley's Comet in 2000 years (1837)
85/1883	20/1950	John Wilkes Booth shoots Abraham Lincoln (1865)
82/2003	22/1935	Titanic sinks (1912)
85/2002	18/1875	Bob Feller pitches opening-day no-hitter (1940)
84/1896	15/1875	Benjamin Franklin dies at 84 (1790)
85/1896	17/1875	Paul Revere's famous ride (1775)
84/1941	22/1887	Eliot Ness born (1903)
83/1985	23/1904	86% of black students boycott Cleveland schools (1964)
86/1942	24/1875	Fire at Ohio State Penitentiary kills 320 (1930)
84/1985	23/1875	Actor Ralph Byrd born in Dayton (1909)
86/1985	27/1994	Hank Aaron hits 1st of his 755 homers (1954)
88/1925	28/2003	1st AL game, White Sox beat Indians 8-2 (1901)
87/1990	27/1888	US declares war on Spain (1898)
87/1948	26/1972	Charles Richter, earthquakes seismologist born in Ohio (1900)
86/1990	27/1971	NFL officially recognizes Hall of Fame in Canton (1961)
88/1986	25/1947	Chernobyl nuclear power plant disaster (1986)
84/1899	25/1977	Cleve Indian Wes Ferrell no-hits St Louis Browns, 9-0 (1931)
88/1942	28/1969	Brightest supernova in recorded history is observed (1006)

Flora & Fauna APRIL

WEEK 1 **BIRDS:** White-throated sparrows, singing their plaintive "old Sam Peabody-Peabody-Peabody" songs, continue to pour through Ohio on their way to Canada. Rufus-sided towhees and pine warblers return this week. Killdeer return to the North Coast in large numbers, the vanguard of a major invasion of migrating birds to come in the next 30 days. **WILDFLOWERS:** White petals of bloodroot mingle with bluebells and trout lilies in damp forests this week. Spring beauty and hepatica join them as well. Many wildflowers bloom and fade before we begin to think of taking spring hikes to look for them. Some years the wildflowers from Cleveland to Ashtabula and a few miles beyond bloom almost a week late due to the "lake effect."

WEEK 2 **BIRDS:** The male woodcock's spectacular "sky dance" is in full swing each morning and each evening at twilight through mid-May, in hopes of attracting a female. Watch open fields with some shrub cover and discover the spectacle for yourself. Canada geese are incubating eggs throughout our region. Protective males nearby may bite if the nests are approached too closely-be careful! **WILDFLOWERS:** Violets, Virginia bluebells, rue anemone, and cut-leaf toothwort should be in bloom this week in area woodlots. Please remember-enjoy, but don't take any of these woodland beauties, now becoming scarce. **AMPHIBIANS:** On warm, wet rainy evenings in Brecksville, Rangers close Valley Parkway as hundreds of salamanders wriggle across roads to their ancestral breeding ponds. Naturalists present each evening explain the migration and help protect the salamanders. American toads' long trilling calls can be heard in wet spots this week as their short breeding cycle begins.

WEEK 3 **BIRDS:** If south winds prevail this week, this may be the week of the big migration. Look for Swainson's and hermit thrushes, sandpipers, and some of these warblers: yellow-throated, yellow-rumped, black-throated, green, and hooded. House wrens also return this week. Get your wren houses emptied and ready! **WILDFLOWERS:** Three-petaled, three-leafed white trilliums should be up but not quite yet blooming in most of the region's forests. Marsh marigolds add their butter-yellow hues to low wet places this week. **SHRUBS:** Spicebush and shadbush (serviceberry) are blooming. Their soft whites and pinks still provide a contrast with the emerging forest canopy overhead. **REPTILES:** Garter snakes should be seen frequently as they leave their winter dens and soak up the warm spring sunshine.

WEEK 4 **BIRDS:** Migratory bluebirds should be back in force this week. Is your bluebird house cleaned out and ready for this year's visitors? More birds of the deep forest such as the Baltimore oriole, scarlet tanager, and rose-breasted grosbeak should have returned from their winter haunts in tropical rainforests. **WILDFLOWERS:** Grassy open places are carpeted with tiny four-petaled bluets. So many bloom that they resemble a pale-blue snowdrift in the spring woods. Snowy white trilliums now dot most of our region's deep woodlands. Look around them for the last of the Virginia bluebells, Dutchman's breeches, and squirrel corn flowers.

Adapted from the Nature Almanac by Robert Hinkle, with permission from Cleveland Metroparks.

YOU'D BE AMAZED AT WHAT YOU CAN SEE IN APRIL

All this month, look to the eastern sky and see "Leo the Lion." The backwards question mark or sickle is actually Leo's head and mane.

On April 15, if you are mailing your taxes this evening, you can see a beautiful "first-quarter moon" with yellow Saturn next to it.

Courtesy of Jay Reynolds, Schuele Planetarium director, Lake Erie Nature and Science Center.

BEST OF POLICE BLOTTER

FROM SUN NEWSPAPERS

Each year, *Sun Newspapers* editors round up the more unusual items from their police blotters. These are some of their favorites from 2002 and 2003.

SOLON—A 34-year-old woman showed up drunk at the Solon Police station on the evening of Nov. 22. She wanted police to return her necklace. She said she had lost the necklace during a previous stay in jail.

When officers told her they didn't have the necklace, the woman became angry. She said the city's corrections officers were thieves, among other things. She said the jail's supervisor and administrator were incompetent.

The woman calmed down and presented officers with a "peace offering"—a donut with a dollar bill in the middle. However, she still wanted her necklace.

Police tried to convince the woman to leave the station. She began to walk away, but turned around and attacked a Christmas tree outside the station door. She swung her fists at the tree and started to pull the lights off before the officers arrested her.

LAKEWOOD—File this one under "Only in Lakewood," or "Beam Me Up, Scottie." On Jan. 9, employees of Bobson's Hardware on Detroit Avenue called police after two individuals wearing only tinfoil and black capes were making shooting motions at each other. Officers checked out the scene and found no weapons involved.

MEDINA—A 25-year-old Wadsworth man went to the Medina Police station Oct. 26 and wanted to know if he had to listen to his mother, who keeps telling him what to do. Police told the man he was an adult and didn't have to listen to her if he didn't want to. The man does not live with his mother.

RICHFIELD—An Alger Rd. resident called Richfield police

on July 24 after discovering that someone had stolen a Big Wheel toy car from her property. Police later discovered that a small child entrepreneur had sold it to a woman for $1.

STRONGSVILLE—A husband and wife from Cambridge, Ohio, were charged after they filled their cars with gas at a Strongsville service station and left without paying. The clue that led to their arrest? Both previously worked at the station and were recognized by employees.

OLMSTED FALLS—When a woman stole a case of beer from a truck making a delivery to a gas station, no one got her license plate number. But police had something better—an employment application the woman had filled out just before taking the beer. Olmsted Falls officers simply looked up her address, went to the house, and found the stolen alcohol. She was arrested, and just may have hurt her chances of getting hired.

OLMSTED FALLS—An Olmsted Falls woman called police to report a suspicious man in the neighborhood—he was wearing a long black robe and going door to door with shopping bags. Turns out, he was a priest collecting food for the needy. Likely story, Padre. Next thing you know, the guy in blue carrying envelopes will claim he's a mailman.

NORTH ROYALTON—A Canton man asking for directions to Lake Erie apparently didn't like the answers he got—he yelled at the people until North Royalton police carted him off to the detox unit. Police said he stood outside a gas station asking customers for directions, but when they'd tell him, he'd shout at them and complain about women.

MIDDLEBURG HTS.—Don't you hate when this happens? A man accused of stealing chicken wings by putting them down the front of his pants told Middleburg Heights police he was simply holding the packages against his stomach to see if they were cold when an employee startled him, causing them to fall down his pants. He told police he checks his beer the same way.

PARMA—A would-be burglar in Parma gets points for quick thinking, if nothing else. When police caught him kneeling in front of a door after a homeowner heard noises, he told officers he wasn't trying to break in—he just needed the rubber strip at the bottom of the door.

■

Our Greatest President

By Dick Goddard

This year marks the 140th anniversary of the death of the person who saved the Union and, to many, symbolized what is great about this country.

In all national surveys by presidential historians, the American president considered the greatest of them all was Abraham Lincoln. More than 100,000 books have been written about our 16th president, more than all others combined.

To many, Lincoln is America. He represents all that is good about our nation and is the exemplar of greatness and decency in an era when many other countries believe, rightly or wrongly, that the U.S. has lost its way,

Abraham Lincoln was born dirt-poor on February 12, 1809, in a log cabin three miles south of Hodgenville, Kentucky. Lincoln was our tallest president, standing 6 feet, 4 inches tall, and weighing 180 pounds, with long, gangling limbs. His eyes were gray; he had a wart on his right cheek just above the corner of his mouth. Swinging an ax in his youth had given him muscular arms and shoulders. The scar over his right eye came from a brawl with a gang of robbers.

Considered homely by many, Lincoln was very self-deprecating and often poked fun at himself. Although given to periods of melancholy, the man known by the sobriquet "Honest Abe" had a wonderful sense of humor and a rollicking, high-pitched laugh.

His physical appearance suggests that Lincoln suffered from Marfan's syndrome, and he was probably dying of heart disease at the time of his death.

Abraham Lincoln's father, Tom, was illiterate and never out of debt. Abe had no formal education, and late in life he reckoned that he never had more than one year of schooling. He was an avid reader and became a self-taught lawyer in Springfield, Illinois.

There is no doubt that Abraham Lincoln was an extremely kind man and treasured all life. In his youth he wrote an essay on the merits of the lowly ant and its right to live. In an era when every boy hunted, Abe would not. At age eight he had shot and killed a wild turkey. He vowed he would never kill again.

In 1829, when Abe was 20, the Lincoln family was headed westward in a covered wagon from Indiana to Illinois. They became temporarily stranded on a sandbar in the Wabash River. Finally becoming unstuck, the wagon began to move again, when Abe's little mongrel dog hopped off the wagon and began to run away. Tom Lincoln said to his son, "Let the dog go," but Abe jumped off the wagon, caught up with his little friend, and brought him back on the wagon. On another occasion, he rescued a pig that had become hopelessly mired in mud.

At the age of 23, in 1832, Abe Lincoln volunteered in the Illinois militia and was given the rank of captain, an honor he said he treasured more than his nomination for president years later. In 1832 he ran for the Illinois state legislature, placing eighth in a field of 13 candidates. Two years later he was elected to the state legislature, becoming a Whig congressman in 1947. Lincoln's intense opposition to slavery caused him to bolt the Whig party for the more antislavery Republican Party in 1856.

To be technically correct, the Republican Party was not against slavery in the southern states, but was against its spreading into the more northern states. On this platform, Stephen Douglas defeated Lincoln in an election for the U.S. Senate.

In May of 1860 the Republican Party chose Abraham Lincoln for president over frontrunner William Seward of New York against the Democrats' Douglas. Lincoln won handily over Douglas and two other opponents.

Lincoln's stance as an opponent of slavery drove the southern states to secede from the Union. The Confederate attack on Fort Sumter, South Carolina, in 1861 started the Civil War. This four-year war was the bloodiest in our nation's history and resulted in the deaths of an estimated 800,000.

The Civil War ended on April 9, 1865, when Confederate general Robert E. Lee surrendered to the Union forces commanded by Union general Ulysses S. Grant.

Five days after the Civil War ended, President Lincoln and his wife, Mary Todd Lincoln, went to Ford's Theatre in Washington, D.C., to watch the poplar stage comedy Our American Cousin. As the last act began, the president's bodyguard, John Parker, stepped out of the presidential box. At that point, John Wilkes Booth, a Confederate sympathizer from a prominent theatrical family, easily entered the box where Lincoln was seated.

Onstage, the character called Asa Trenchard spoke the last words that President Lincoln ever heard, "You sockdologizing old man-trap!" That line was always a big laugh-getter, and as the audience roared, the deranged 27-year-old Booth, from a distance of two feet, shot the president in the back of the head with a .44 single-shot derringer. The bullet, made from an alloy of tin, copper, and antimony, split in two, with one piece stopping in the middle of the brain and the other going through the brain and lodging in the bone of the right eye socket.

Dr. Charles Leale, who was in the audience, immediately ran to the presidential box and pronounced the wound fatal.

Booth, who had broken his leg while leaping onto the stage, shouted, "Sic semper tyrannis!" ("thus always to tyrants") and escaped.

Booth was subsequently tracked down at a tobacco farm at Bowling Green, Virginia, where he was shot and killed. (It is unclear if the fatal wound was self-inflicted.)

The dying Lincoln was carried to the Peterson boardinghouse across the street from Ford's

Theatre. President Lincoln died without regaining consciousness.

Since the assassination occurred on Good Friday, a Washington minister chided anyone who would attend the theater for entertainment on such a special Christian day, saying they should expect to confront "the very gates of hell."

Concerning Abraham Lincoln's religion, his closest friends and associates said he was truly a Doubting Thomas. Contrary to what is popularly thought—and wished—Lincoln was not a religious man and never belonged to a church. Lincoln, like Thomas Jefferson, had no use for members of the clergy and professed no belief in biblical tradition or prophecy.

Lincoln's closest friend and colleague for the last 22 years of his life was fellow lawyer William Herndon. While members of the clergy claimed that they had personally made a miraculous last-minute deathbed convert of the president (as was the case with Thomas Jefferson), Herndon called them all opportunists and liars. The pragmatic Lincoln, said Herndon, was a "scientific materialist and fatalist." Lincoln believed in providence (fate) but not in any higher power. Lincoln was truly a beloved infidel.

Abraham Lincoln appeared twice in Cleveland, both times on gray, rainy days. The Great Emancipator was in Cleveland on February of 1861 while president-elect and on his way to Washington. Four years later, on April 28, 1865, more than 100,000 mourners filed past the president's coffin as it lay in state for 12 hours in Cleveland's Public Square.

Some of Lincoln's favorite sayings:

- *You cannot bring about prosperity by discouraging thrift.*
- *You cannot strengthen the weak by weakening the strong.*
- *You cannot help the wage earner by pulling down the wage payer.*
- *You cannot further the brotherhood of man by encouraging class hatred.*
- *You cannot keep out of trouble by spending more than you earn.*
- *You cannot build character and courage by taking away man's initiative and independence*
- *You cannot help men permanently by doing for them what they could and should do for themselves.*
- *It has been my experience that men who have no vices have very few virtues.*
- *Honor is better than honors.*

So, you want to buy a telescope?

BY JAY REYNOLDS

One of the most frequent questions asked of me is "I'd like to buy my child a telescope, what should I buy?"

This cannot be answered in five seconds. Like any frying pan or screwdriver, if you purchase the wrong tool, you will find it nearly useless!

Telescopes are tools to help you see what you can't see with your naked eyes. Human eyes are best adapted for daytime use and are small (just compare your eyes to those of a cat or owl). A telescope actually is an extension of your eye, effectively making your eye as large as your telescope (Superman would be envious).

Telescopes are actually quite simple. They work by gathering as much light as they can. The wider they are, the more light they gather. It's NOT about the degree of power or magnification. Most telescopes effectively operate at 80 to 250 power . . . that's it. Even those in most large observatories don't operate at a much higher level than that because Earth's atmosphere distorts the image (it's like looking at the bottom of a moving stream—every so often, you can see very clearly).

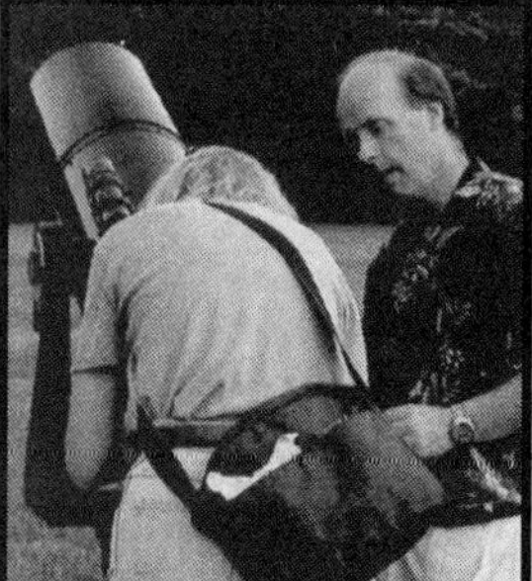

If you own binoculars, start with them: they're not just for daytime anymore. You can easily see craters on the moon, our Milky Way galaxy with actual blue, yellow, and red stars, and Jupiter's moons and satellites in orbit around our Earth. If you don't own binoculars, you don't have to spend a lot. It is a good way to start out, and if it turns out stargazing isn't for you, you can use them for bird-watching instead. Most camera or department stores will have a good range to choose from. A good starting size is either 7x35, 7x50, or 10x50. You'd be surprised what you can see.

If you still would like to own a telescope, keep in mind these simple guidelines:

What would you like to see? Different telescopes have different purposes. Some capture galaxies and nebulas well, others are great for viewing planets. You will not really see a lot of color either. The color photos you see in magazines were taken with long-exposure photography.

Portability: Most backyard telescopes weigh 10 to 125 pounds. If you buy something too large, you may think twice about setting it up for a short, marginal viewing session (as we have many marginal nights here in Ohio).

- Buy a telescope that you will use!
- Select a scope that you can easily lift, move, and store.
- Ask yourself, will this fit in my car?

Size (aperture): Remember, the wider the scope, the more you see, but the more it can cost and the heavier it becomes! You have to find a happy balance.

Recommended Apertures:

- Anything less than 70 millimeters is usually poor.
- 90 millimeters (3-6 inches) will offer good viewing.
- 8-12 inches will provide great views but can be heavy (20-60 pounds).

Budget: A reasonable telescope will cost $250 and up. Whatever you budget, plan on 60 percent for the scope and the rest on accessories that you will need, in addition to extra eyepieces, star charts, and perhaps a subscription to a monthly periodical. (You may want to take your understanding spouse out to dinner as well.) If taken care of, quality telescope equipment will retain usually 80-90 percent of its value when new. Avoid any thoughts of astrophotography for now.

Computer or manual? A great feature you will see offered is a computerized telescope. Some of these calculate and align nearly every aspect of the scope for use. They then point the telescope to objects that you may not have thought to look at (it's like inviting me over for dinner, then telescoping). The only drawback is that you are paying for computers and motors and getting less telescope. Some astronomers despise these, as you are less likely to learn where the object really is in the sky.

Computerized: Easier to find faint objects, costs more, less telescope, more to go wrong

Manual: More scope for the money, less to go wrong. Can be challenging to find faint objects

- Seek advice (you don't have to go it alone).
- Contact a planetarium, as they may have telescopes available to examine and practical advice.

- Contact one of the many astronomical clubs in our area, as they are always willing to help and may have loaner scopes for members.
- Research on the Internet.
- Ask someone knowledgeable before you purchase!

Jay Reynolds is currently the Director of the Schuele Planetarium at Lake Erie Nature and Science Center in Bay Village. He is a member of the NASA Glenn Research Speakers Bureau, serves as a "Solar System Ambassador," and teaches at both Cleveland State University and Cuyahoga Community College.

24-HOUR RAINFALL RECORDS

CITY	AMOUNT	DATE
Toledo	5.98"	September 4, 1918
Akron/Canton	5.96"	July 7, 1943
Cincinnati	5.22"	March 12, 1907
Mansfield	5.06"	July 4, 1969
Cleveland	4.97"	September 1, 1901
Columbus	4.81"	January 20, 1959
Dayton	4.75"	April 12, 1886
Youngstown	4.31"	October 15, 1954

NORTHEAST OHIO'S WETTEST AND DRIEST SPRINGS

(Rainfall)

WETTEST

Cleveland: 16.33" / 1989

Akron/Canton: 18.18" / 1964

DRIEST

Cleveland: 4.45" / 1895

Akron/Canton: 4.19" / 1915

JAN FEB MAR APR MAY JUN JUL AUG SEP OCT NOV DEC

ROBOTS TO EXPLORE OUR SOLAR SYSTEM

There is a small fleet of robotic space probes roaming all over our solar system. One is heading for Mercury, there are four at Mars and one at Saturn, one is about to land on a moon of Saturn, and there are four leaving the solar system. They all are managed at the Jet Propulsion Laboratory (JPL) in California. Thanks to our own NASA Glenn Research Center, some of those missions have their roots right here in northeastern Ohio. Here is an overview of a few missions to look at or to listen for news of in the coming months:

NASA GLENN RESEARCH CENTER VISITOR CENTER

A great place to see an overview of current and past missions, as well as technology that has made it into our everyday lives.

www.grc.nasa.gov

CASSINI-HUYGENS MISSION TO SATURN

We've already seen dazzling photos of Saturn. On January 15, 2005, a second, smaller probe will land on the "early Earth-like" surface of Titan, a moon of Saturn.

www.saturn.jpl.nasa.gov

MARS EXPLORATION ROVERS

At the time of this writing, our two intrepid rovers, Spirit and Opportunity, continue to send back photos on a daily basis. Both rovers have shown us that Mars once had large bodies of salt water and now the planet is a desert! While these rovers are not designed to discover life, they are setting the stage for that future objective. We expect both rovers will survive the Martian winter and continue on well into 2005.

www.marsrovers.jpl.gov

DEEP IMPACT SPACE PROBE TO SAMPLE DEEPLY BELOW THE SURFACE OF A COMET.

Starting July 4, 2005, a space probe called "Deep Impact" will send back photos and launch a 700- pound copper probe into Comet Tempel. Deep Impact will yield a dramatic breakthrough in our understanding of comets with the first experiment to sample deeply below the surface of a comet.

http://deepimpact.jpl.nasa.gov/science/cratering.html

MARS RECONNAISSANCE ORBITER (MRO)

In 2005, NASA/JPL will launch the Mars Reconnaisance Orbiter (MRO) to track changes in the water and dust in Mars's atmosphere. The orbiter will carry a powerful camera capable of taking sharp images of surface features the size of a beach ball. The spacecraft will also serve as a relay station for future missions. It will arrive at its destination in March 2006.

http://mars.jpl.nasa.gov/missions/future/2005-plus.html

Courtesy of Jay Reynolds, Schuele Planetarium director, Lake Erie Nature and Science Center.

Lake Erie is the southernmost, the shallowest (average depth just 62 feet),the warmest, and the most biologically productive of the Great Lakes. More fish are produced each year for human consumption from Lake Erie than from the other four Great Lakes combined. *Source: www.ecocitycleveland.org*

MAY STATISTICS

(recorded at Cleveland Hopkins Airport)

SUNSHINE %	58
DRIEST MONTH	0.58"/1934
WARMEST MONTH	66.9°/1991
COLDEST MONTH	51.1°/1907
LIQUID PCPN AVG.	3.49"
RAINIEST DAY	3.37"/1995
RAINIEST MONTH	9.14"/1989
THUNDERY DAYS	5
SNOWIEST DAY	2.1"/1974
SNOWIEST MONTH	2.1"/1974
LEAST SNOWFALL	TRACE *(most recently in 1986)*
DAYS ONE INCH SNOW	0

The emerald month can be a cool and sometimes cruel jewel. This month is notorious for claiming prematurely planted flowers and vegetables. May 20 is a safe date for most plantings, but some veteran Northeast Ohio gardeners wait until the Memorial Day weekend before digging in. A tip: When you slip on the gardening gloves that have spent all winter in the dark recesses of your garage, be sure to squeeze each finger vigorously. That's because spiders (the brown recluse and black widow are especially venomous) often use the fingers of gloves for cozy winter headquarters. Colorful woodland wildflowers dominate the month of May in Northeast Ohio before the spreading canopy of leaves shuts off the springtime sunlight. Ohio's only hummingbird—the ruby-throated—usually makes its first darting appearance about midmonth. Towards the end of May and into early June, those pesky non-stinging insects called muckleheads (also known as midges) move inland from Lake Erie, joined by mayflies (a.k.a. Canadian soldiers).

On Memorial Day Northeast Ohioans are often reminded that the reason three-day weekends were created is because it's impossible to cram all the bad weather into only two days. Beware during those early-season picnics—strong thunderstorms that can spawn deadly tornadoes can happen at any time during May.

DAILY DATA FOR MAY

Date	Day	Moon	Day of Year	Days Left	Sunrise	Sunset	Length of Day	Avg. Hi°	Avg. Lo°	Avg. Lake°
1	Sun	◑	121	244	6:23	8:25	14:02	63	42	46
2	Mon		122	243	6:22	8:26	14:04	64	42	47
3	Tue		123	242	6:21	8:27	14:06	64	43	47
4	Wed		124	241	6:20	8:28	14:08	64	43	47
5	Thu		125	240	6:18	8:29	14:11	65	44	48
6	Fri		126	239	6:17	8:30	14:13	65	44	48
7	Sat		127	238	6:16	8:31	14:15	65	44	48
8	Sun	●	128	237	6:15	8:32	14:17	66	45	49
9	Mon		129	236	6:14	8:33	14:19	66	45	49
10	Tue		130	235	6:13	8:34	14:21	67	45	49
11	Wed		131	234	6:11	8:35	14:24	67	46	50
12	Thu		132	233	6:10	8:36	14:26	67	46	50
13	Fri		133	232	6:09	8:37	14:28	68	46	50
14	Sat		134	231	6:08	8:38	14:30	68	47	51
15	Sun		135	230	6:07	8:39	14:32	68	47	51
16	Mon	◐	136	229	6:06	8:40	14:34	69	47	52
17	Tue		137	228	6:06	8:41	14:35	69	48	52
18	Wed		138	227	6:05	8:42	14:37	69	48	52
19	Thu		139	226	6:04	8:43	14:39	70	48	53
20	Fri		140	225	6:03	8:44	14:41	70	48	53
21	Sat		141	224	6:02	8:45	14:43	70	49	53
22	Sun		142	223	6:01	8:46	14:45	71	49	53
23	Mon	○	143	222	6:01	8:47	14:46	71	50	54
24	Tue		144	221	6:00	8:48	14:48	71	50	54
25	Wed		145	220	5:59	8:49	14:50	72	50	54
26	Thu		146	219	5:58	8:49	14:51	72	51	54
27	Fri		147	218	5:58	8:50	14:52	72	51	54
28	Sat		148	217	5:57	8:51	14:54	73	51	54
29	Sun		149	216	5:57	8:52	14:55	73	52	55
30	Mon	◑	150	215	5:56	8:53	14:57	74	52	55
31	Tue		151	214	5:56	8:53	14:57	74	52	56

Rec. Hi°	Rec. Lo°	On This Date . . .
88/1942	28/1876	TV host Jack Paar born in Canton (1918)
86/1951	26/1963	Olympic baseball pitcher Mark Johnson born in Dayton (1975)
85/1949	27/1986	David Bell debuts for the Indians; 3rd generation player, Gus & Buddy (1995)
89/1949	23/1971	Four killed in antiwar protest at Kent State University (1970)
89/1949	30/1968	Charles Nagy born in Fairfield CT (1967)
92/1959	26/1968	Representative Eric D. Fingerhut born (1959)
87/1936	28/1970	Actress Traci Lords born in Steubenville (1968)
88/1889	30/1976	Former U.S. representative James A. Traficant Jr. born (1941)
88/1979	29/1983	WJW-AM in Cleveland OH begins radio transmissions (1929)
90/1953	25/1966	25ºF lowest temperature ever recorded in Cleveland in May (1966)
87/1881	33/1977	BF Goodrich manufactures 1st tubeless tire, Akron (1947)
89/1881	32/1976	Philadelphia A's Chief Bender no-hits Cleveland Indians, 4-0 (1910)
86/1991	32/1895	Pachyderm Building at Cleveland Metroparks Zoo opens (1956)
91/1962	33/1994	Indians' Stan Coveleski sets club record for most innings pitched–19 (1918)
89/1962	35/1977	Cleveland Clinic fire kills 129 people (1929)
89/1991	29/1984	Actress Debra Winger born in Cleveland (1955)
90/1962	33/1979	Cleveland Indian Tris Speaker gets his 3,000th hit (1925)
91/1962	36/1985	Tropical Butterfly Garden at Cleveland Metroparks Zoo opens (1994)
89/1911	33/1976	George II grants charter to Ohio Company to settle Ohio Valley (1749)
91/1962	34/1981	Cleveland Indians tie AL record of 18 walks (beat Red Sox 13-4) (1948)
90/1941	32/1895	Humphrey Bogart and Lauren Bacall married in Mansfield (1959)
90/1941	35/2002	Indians' pitcher Jose Mesa born (1966)
90/1991	34/1961	Actor/comedian Drew Carey born (1958)
89/1950	32/1963	Astronaut Ronald A. Parise born in Warren (1951)
89/1914	35/1956	Actress Ann Heche born in Aurora (1969)
89/1914	34/1969	Actor Philip Michael Thomas born in Columbus (1949)
90/1967	35/1969	Golden Gate Bridge is completed and open to pedestrian traffic (1937)
91/1941	37/1971	White Sox beat Indians, 6-3, in 21 innings; game started 5/26 (1973)
91/1991	38/1949	Patriot Patrick Henry born in Studley, VA (1736)
92/1879	32/1961	92º F highest temperature ever recorded in Cleveland OH in May (1972)
92/1944	39/1984	The Arcade opens (1917)

Flora & Fauna MAY

WEEK 1 **BIRDS:** In safe ponds, newly hatched wood ducklings, mallard duckling, and goslings follow their parents in fuzzy yellow armadas. Canada geese raising their young display a behavior called "gang-brooding," where a single pair may watch as many as 30 goslings. Fortunately for the frazzled geese, the responsibility is soon shifted to another pair. **MAMMALS:** Woodchucks seem to be everywhere along parkways and all-purpose trail edges, already stuffing themselves with tender young grasses. Young woodchucks will venture forth with their mothers next month. Cleveland marks the boundary between the central (silver-bellied) and eastern (red-bellied) species of woodchucks. Are yours red- or silver-bellied? **WILDFLOWERS:** May apple flowers should be blooming under their umbrella-shaped leaves by this weekend. Their applelike fruit is poisonous through most of its growing period. **SHRUBS:** Redbud is in bloom.

WEEK 2 **BIRDS:** Hummingbirds, rose-breasted grosbeaks, nighthawks, and chimney swifts should all be arriving this week or next. The peak of warbler migration is likely to occur this week. Bird walks in the forests and fields are likely to turn up more birds than you ever knew existed! Many will soon be gone as they continue their migration, while others "disappear" in the newly unfolding leaves of the treetops. Visit the Crane Creek Wildlife Refuge near Huron to see warblers in migration at eye level.

WEEK 3 **BIRDS:** Wood thrushes and veeries return to fill our forests with their haunting flutelike calls each evening through the summer months. Baltimore orioles begin to look for elms to build their hanging nests. **TREES:** The tall white flowers of the Ohio buckeye stand in sharp contrast to the new green leaves in many places this week. Apple trees and wild lilacs now in bloom may mark locations of old farmsteads long abandoned in the countryside. **AMPHIBIANS:** Green frogs call at midday. Their banjolike "gunk-gunk" calls are easy to tell from the "jug-o-rum" calls of the larger, look-alike bullfrog.

WEEK 4 **BIRDS:** Many birds are in their courtship phase and some have begun nest building and incubating eggs. Get up early this weekend and listen to the early morning chorus. Naturalists and Audubon groups lead free bird walks throughout our region and offer free and friendly advice in identification. Bluebird houses are sometimes appropriated by tree swallows, house wrens, or chickadees. Though they're not bluebirds, each species is a beautiful addition to the world. **WILDFLOWERS:** Daisy fleabane, first and smallest of the summer daisies, begins to open its white blossoms this week. It's rumored that they have been used as an insect repellent, with their petals crushed or burned. Dame's rocket, also called "soapwort," adds its lavender and pink flowers to roadsides and stream banks.

Adapted from the Nature Almanac by Robert Hinkle, with permission from Cleveland Metroparks.

YOU'D BE AMAZED AT WHAT YOU CAN SEE IN MAY

Starting this month, early evening will have Saturn in the west and Jupiter in the east. The largest planet in our solar system, Jupiter really puts on a show. In a telescope, you can actually watch its moons revolve around this gas giant!

Also in May, the Big Dipper is directly overhead. Count the stars in the handle; the second to last is actually two stars called Mizar and Alcor. If you can see both, that means you have fairly good vision. With the Big Dipper upside down, it actually seems to be pouring straight down into the Little Dipper.

Courtesy of Jay Reynolds, Schuele Planetarium director, Lake Erie Nature and Science Center.

Cleveland Stadium

By Scott Sabol

Ask anyone who has known me for a long time what my favorite interests are and they'll name two subjects: weather and baseball. Broadcasting the weather on WJW FOX 8 is my day job, but baseball has always evoked a childhood fantasy. It starts with me at the plate during the seventh game of the World Series at the old Cleveland Stadium with a full count, game tied, bases loaded in the bottom of the ninth inning. It culminates with me hitting an upper-deck homer to left field to win the game. As I round the bases, fireworks go off beyond the scoreboard . . .

Of course, as with all great dreams, reality invariably resurfaces and I am back to scanning box scores on the Internet in the comfort of my computer room, still waiting for that elusive championship. Yes, Cleveland Stadium for me is the nexus of my baseball life.

The history of Cleveland Stadium baseball runs congruent with the history of my family living in greater Cleveland. My grandfather went to old League Park in the late '20s and '30s and made the transition to the Stadium in the late '30s. He was an usher during the Indians' heyday of the late '40s and early '50s. My father practically lived at the stadium as a youngster. He idolized Bobby Avila, Vic Wertz, and Rocky Colavito and even obtained one of Colavito's broken bats from my grandfather. For the Sabols, baseball is synonymous with Cleveland Stadium.

On September 30, 1980, I made my first trip to Cleveland Stadium with my dad. For weeks, I knew we had tickets and, being only six years old, I was a bit overwhelmed at the thought of going to downtown Cleveland.

The walk from the car to Gate A across the stadium parking lot was filled with anticipation of the world that lay beyond the vast outer wall of the ballpark. My dad held my hand as our seemingly endless trek took us to the turnstile. Once through, I could hear the drone of cheers emanating from the inside, which seemed a mile away. Back then, the Indians were the basement dwellers of the American League, or pretty close to it, with attendance averaging around 12,000 per game. However, this day was different. They were playing the New York Yankees, who had the best record in baseball, and the stadium was packed! Before we started up the tunnel toward our section, all I had seen was concrete, old weathered windows, and steel beams. But once we reached the end of the tunnel, my eyes widened as the antiseptic gray of concrete was replaced with bright, lush grass and a beautifully manicured infield with not a speck of dirt out of place. It was an oasis of beauty among the concrete behemoths of the city. At that infinitesimal yet seemingly eternal moment in my life, I saw perfection.

During the game, my eyes were glued to the field. Even though we were in the upper deck on the right field side, I could see *everything*! While my memories of the game itself are fragmented, I remember other elements of the experience with fantastic detail. I fixated on the groundskeepers dragging the field, watering the dirt, painting the foul lines, and changing the bases in the fifth inning. I was stunned by the grandstands that rose up for what seemed like a mile above the field. It was like nothing I had ever seen. I sat with my dad, awestruck for the entire nine innings, eating a hotdog lathered in the famous brown mustard that only Cleveland Stadium could offer. When the game was over, I went home happy from having gone to the old ballpark on the lake for the first time, but also because we beat the hated Yankees 12-9!

My love of Cleveland Stadium grew as I witnessed more games, as the Indians got better. I remember the home opener in 1992 as if it were yesterday. Attendance was almost 70,000, which was common for a home season opener. But this game was different. A buddy of mine and I had seats behind the left field foul pole, which we hoped would increase our odds of getting a home run ball. Sure enough, nothing happened. In fact, the game was tied 5-5 in the ninth inning and stayed tied for *ten more* innings. Six hours and five hotdogs later, with only 10,000 people remaining, the game was decided with a two-run home run, which landed only two rows away from our seats. The Red Sox won 7-5. In fact, I almost went to the game the following day. Unfortunately, history eluded me. The Red Sox starting pitcher threw a no-hitter but *lost the game!* The Indians won 2-1 without garnering a single hit!

By 1996, Cleveland Stadium's days were numbered. It had been nearly three years since the Indians moved to Jacobs Field and almost a year since the Browns marched downfield toward the dawg pound. It was a cold, cloudy, and damp October evening. I had heard that stadium seats were up for sale, so I drove downtown without hesitation. As I entered the maintenance opening outside the bleachers, I felt as if I had stepped on sacred ground. I remembered the first time I had entered the stadium as a youngster feeling all of the excitement with my dad. On that October day, I looked out onto the field through grown-up eyes and felt a chill overtake my body. As I peered down on the faded goal line and dismantled advertisements along the upper deck, I thought back to all the history that took place here in sports and in my family. It was like stepping into the house that you grew up in shortly before it was to be demolished.

On that day, I felt a sense of closure. My grandfather, who had now passed on, was here in the '30s for many firsts. In those moments, I became the final link to the past. Although Cleveland Stadium now belongs to the depths of Lake Erie, a part of me will always stand at home plate amidst 70,000 fans during an imaginary playoff game. Odds are, the two stadium seats displayed in my house are seats my grandfather wiped down as an usher back in the day. For me, my Cleveland Stadium memories live on forever.

Scott Sabol is a meteorologist for the weekend and noon editions of FOX 8 NEWS.

City-by-City Weather Statistics

Temperature and Precipitation Averages, last 30 years

AKRON/CANTON (Elev. 1,209 ft.)

Month	Max(°)	Min(°)	Pcpn(")	Snow(")
Jan	33	17	2.16	12
Feb	36	19	2.23	10
Mar	47	29	3.33	9
Apr	59	38	3.16	3
May	70	48	3.73	T
Jun	79	57	3.18	0
Jul	82	62	4.08	0
Aug	80	60	3.32	0
Sep	74	54	3.32	0
Oct	62	43	2.35	1
Nov	50	34	3.01	5
Dec	38	24	2.95	10

ASHLAND (Elev. 1,050 ft.)

Month	Max(°)	Min(°)	Pcpn(")	Snow(")
Jan	30	14	2.12	10
Feb	33	15	1.88	8
Mar	44	25	2.95	7
Apr	55	36	3.23	1
May	69	46	3.86	0
Jun	78	55	3.40	0
Jul	83	59	3.56	0
Aug	80	57	3.63	0
Sep	73	51	2.96	0
Oct	61	39	2.06	T
Nov	48	31	3.10	3
Dec	34	20	2.70	8

ASHTABULA (Elev. 690 ft.)

Month	Max(°)	Min(°)	Pcpn(")	Snow(")
Jan	31	17	2.35	20
Feb	53	19	1.78	15
Mar	43	27	2.40	11
Apr	55	36	2.98	3
May	68	48	3.41	0
Jun	78	57	3.52	0
Jul	81	61	4.07	0
Aug	80	60	3.81	0
Sep	74	54	3.63	0
Oct	63	44	3.29	T
Nov	50	25	3.48	7
Dec	38	25	2.85	17

CHARDON (Elev. 1,210 ft.)

Month	Max(°)	Min(°)	Pcpn(")	Snow(")
Jan	30	13	2.64	29
Feb	33	14	2.51	21
Mar	43	24	3.33	17
Apr	56	34	3.55	5
May	68	44	3.57	T
Jun	77	53	4.18	0
July	81	58	3.53	0
Aug	79	57	3.61	0
Sep	72	50	3.75	0
Oct	60	40	3.75	2
Nov	48	32	4.05	12
Dec	35	21	3.79	27

ELYRIA (Elev. 730 ft.)

Month	Max(°)	Min(°)	Pcpn(")	Snow(")
Jan	36	20	1.83	11
Feb	39	21	1.85	10
Mar	50	31	2.80	8
Apr	62	41	2.82	1
May	73	50	3.51	T
Jun	82	59	3.76	0
Jul	86	63	3.39	0
Aug	84	62	3.00	0
Sep	78	56	3.03	0
Oct	67	45	2.30	0
Nov	53	37	3.14	4
Dec	40	26	3.05	10

IRONTON (Elev. 555 ft.)

Month	Max(°)	Min(°)	Pcpn(")	Snow(")
Jan	41	21	2.55	7
Feb	46	24	2.78	5
Mar	58	33	3.06	3
Apr	67	42	3.50	0
May	78	51	3.98	0
Jun	85	60	3.57	0
Jul	88	64	4.58	0
Aug	87	63	3.77	0
Sep	81	56	2.59	0
Oct	70	44	2.80	0
Nov	58	35	2.93	1
Dec	46	27	3.13	3

KENT/RAVENNA (Elev. 1,150 ft.)

Month	Max(°)	Min(°)	Pcpn(")	Snow(")
Jan	34	17	2.30	12
Feb	38	18	2.15	11
Mar	48	28	3.21	9
Apr	59	38	3.20	2
May	71	48	3.42	T
Jun	80	57	3.33	0
Jul	82	62	3.88	0
Aug	81	60	3.38	0
Sep	75	54	3.14	0
Oct	63	43	2.39	1
Nov	49	33	2.92	5
Dec	39	24	2.59	10

LIMA (Elev. 860 ft.)

Month	Max(°)	Min(°)	Pcpn(")	Snow(")
Jan	31	15	1.75	7
Feb	34	17	1.59	6
Mar	45	27	2.65	5
Apr	58	37	3.03	T
May	72	49	3.79	0
Jun	81	58	3.09	0
Jul	85	63	3.44	0
Aug	82	60	2.67	0
Sep	76	54	2.95	0
Oct	63	42	1.95	0
Nov	49	33	2.51	2
Dec	37	22	2.50	4

MANSFIELD (Elev. 1,295 ft.)

Month	Max(°)	Min(°)	Pcpn(")	Snow(")
Jan	32	17	1.65	10
Feb	35	19	1.66	9
Mar	47	29	2.88	7
Apr	59	38	3.43	2
May	69	48	4.15	0
Jun	78	57	3.68	0
Jul	82	62	3.67	0
Aug	80	60	4.00	0
Sep	74	54	3.25	0
Oct	62	43	2.08	T
Nov	49	34	3.12	2
Dec	37	23	2.82	9

MARIETTA (Elev. 580 ft.)

Month	*Max(°)*	*Min(°)*	*Pcpn(")*	*Snow(")*
Jan	39	21	2.36	8
Feb	43	22	2.49	5
Mar	54	32	3.11	4
Apr	65	40	2.84	T
May	75	50	3.62	0
Jun	83	59	3.64	0
Jul	86	63	3.90	0
Aug	84	62	3.33	0
Sep	78	55	3.01	0
Oct	67	43	2.69	0
Nov	55	35	2.77	2
Dec	44	26	2.91	4

MEDINA (Elev. 1,192 ft.)

Month	*Max(°)*	*Min(°)*	*Pcpn(")*	*Snow(")*
Jan	31	14	2.01	12
Feb	35	15	2.13	10
Mar	46	25	3.12	7
Apr	58	35	3.25	3
May	69	46	3.86	0
Jun	78	55	3.61	0
Jul	82	59	3.86	0
Aug	80	57	3.24	0
Sep	74	51	3.39	0
Oct	62	39	2.29	1
Nov	49	31	3.33	4
Dec	36	21	3.00	10

NEW PHILA/DOVER (Elev. 890 ft.)

Month	*Max(°)*	*Min(°)*	*Pcpn(")*	*Snow(")*
Jan	34	16	2.37	9
Feb	38	17	2.46	7
Mar	49	27	3.49	5
Apr	61	36	3.52	1
May	72	46	3.93	T
Jun	81	55	4.06	0
Jul	85	59	4.28	0
Aug	83	58	3.35	0
Sep	76	51	3.06	0
Oct	64	39	2.48	T
Nov	51	32	2.55	2
Dec	39	23	2.94	6

NORWALK (Elev. 670 ft.)

Month	*Max(°)*	*Min(°)*	*Pcpn(")*	*Snow(")*
Jan	31	15	1.46	9
Feb	34	17	1.83	7
Mar	44	27	2.69	6
Apr	58	36	3.28	1
May	70	47	3.76	0
Jun	79	56	3.84	0
Jul	83	61	3.37	0
Aug	81	59	3.25	0
Sep	75	52	2.90	0
Oct	62	41	1.83	0
Nov	50	33	2.56	2
Dec	36	22	2.77	7

PAINESVILLE (Elev. 600 ft.)

Month	*Max(°)*	*Min(°)*	*Pcpn(")*	*Snow(")*
Jan	34	20	2.33	15
Feb	36	21	1.82	13
Mar	46	29	2.62	9
Apr	57	38	3.20	1
May	68	48	3.06	0
Jun	77	58	3.37	0
Jul	81	62	3.31	0
Aug	80	61	3.44	0
Sep	75	53	3.30	0
Oct	64	46	3.04	T
Nov	51	36	3.44	5
Dec	40	26	2.77	15

SANDUSKY (Elev. 606 ft.

Month	*Max(°)*	*Min(°)*	*Pcpn(")*	*Snow(")*
Jan	31	17	1.29	9
Feb	33	19	1.71	7
Mar	43	29	2.18	S
Apr	55	39	2.80	T
May	68	50	3.68	0
Jun	78	60	3.26	0
Jul	83	65	3.27	0
Aug	80	63	3.17	0
Sep	74	56	2.53	0
Oct	61	45	2.01	0
Nov	49	35	2.50	2
Dec	37	24	2.82	7

STEUBENVILLE (Elev. 992 ft.)

Month	*Max(°)*	*Min(°)*	*Pcpn(")*	*Snow(")*
Jan	37	19	2.97	12
Feb	40	21	2.47	10
Mar	50	29	3.87	7
Apr	63	39	3.58	2
May	73	49	3.88	0
Jun	81	58	4.16	0
Jul	84	62	3.97	0
Aug	83	61	3.43	0
Sep	77	55	2.84	0
Oct	65	43	2.65	T
Nov	52	34	2.64	3
Dec	41	25	2.87	8

TIFFIN (Elev. 760 ft.)

Month	*Max(°)*	*Min(°)*	*Pcpn(")*	*Snow(")*
Jan	33	18	2.44	8
Feb	36	20	1.98	6
Mar	47	29	3.12	5
Apr	61	39	3.54	1
May	72	49	3.55	0
Jun	81	59	3.46	0
Jul	84	62	3.88	0
Aug	82	61	3.22	0
Sep	76	54	2.74	0
Oct	65	44	2.05	0
Nov	50	34	2.65	2
Dec	38	29	2.62	7

WOOSTER (Elev. 1,020 ft.)

Month	*Max(°)*	*Min(°)*	*Pcpn(")*	*Snow(")*
Jan	32	17	1.60	9
Feb	35	19	2.01	8
Mar	47	28	2.60	6
Apr	59	37	3.00	1
May	69	47	3.73	0
Jun	78	56	3.37	0
Jul	82	60	3.97	0
Aug	80	58	3.58	0
Sep	73	52	2.78	0
Oct	62	41	1.78	T
Nov	49	33	2.72	3
Dec	37	23	2.50	7

Northeast Ohio possesses the **most concentrated dairy area** in Ohio in Wayne County, with 473 dairy farms, and in adjoining Holmes County, with 506 dairy farms.

YOUNGSTOWN (Elev. 1,178 ft.)

Month	Max(°)	Min(°)	Pcpn(")	Snow(")
Jan	31	16	2.13	13
Feb	34	18	2.03	11
Mar	45	27	3.11	11
Apr	58	37	3.06	3
May	69	46	3.52	T
Jun	77	55	3.94	0
Jul	81	59	4.07	0
Aug	80	58	3.32	0
Sep	73	52	3.48	0
Oct	61	42	2.62	1
Nov	48	34	3.11	6
Dec	36	23	2.93	12

Cities outside Northeast Ohio:

CINCINNATI (Elev. 869 ft.)

Month	Max(°)	Min(°)	Pcpn(")	Snow(")
Jan	37	20	2.59	7
Feb	41	23	2.69	5
Mar	53	33	4.24	4
Apr	64	42	3.75	1
May	74	52	4.28	T
Jun	82	60	3.84	0
Jul	86	65	4.24	0
Aug	84	63	3.35	0
Sep	78	57	2.88	0
Oct	66	44	2.86	T
Nov	53	35	3.46	2
Dec	42	25	3.15	4

COLUMBUS (Elev. 813 ft.)

Month	Max(°)	Min(°)	Pcpn(")	Snow(")
Jan	34	19	2.18	8
Feb	38	21	2.24	6
Mar	51	31	3.27	5
Apr	62	40	3.21	1
May	72	50	3.93	T
Jun	80	58	4.04	0
Jul	84	63	4.31	0
Aug	82	61	3.72	0
Sep	76	55	2.96	0
Oct	65	43	2.15	T
Nov	51	34	3.22	2
Dec	39	25	2.86	5

DAYTON (Elev. 995 ft.)

Month	Max(°)	Min(°)	Pcpn(")	Snow(")
Jan	34	18	2.13	8
Feb	33	21	2.17	6
Mar	50	31	3.42	5
Apr	62	41	3.46	1
May	73	51	3.88	T
Jun	82	59	3.82	0
Jul	85	63	3.54	0
Aug	83	61	3.20	0
Sep	77	55	2.54	0
Oct	65	44	2.48	T
Nov	51	34	3.07	2
Dec	39	24	2.93	6

ERIE, PA (Elev. 731 ft.)

Month	Max(°)	Min(°)	Pcpn(")	Snow(")
Jan	33	18	2.22	23
Feb	34	18	2.28	16
Mar	44	28	3.00	11
Apr	55	38	3.24	3
May	66	48	3.44	T
Jun	75	58	4.09	0
Jul	80	63	3.43	0
Aug	79	62	4.06	0
Sep	72	56	4.39	T
Oct	61	46	3.77	1
Nov	49	37	4.02	10
Dec	38	25	3.59	22

TOLEDO (Elev. 669 ft.)

Month	Max(°)	Min(°)	Pcpn(")	Snow(")
Jan	30	15	1.75	10
Feb	33	17	1.73	8
Mar	46	27	2.66	6
Apr	59	36	2.96	2
May	71	47	2.91	T
Jun	80	56	3.75	0
Jul	83	61	3.27	0
Aug	81	58	3.25	0
Sep	74	52	2.85	0
Oct	62	40	2.10	T
Nov	49	32	2.81	3
Dec	35	21	2.93	8

STORM SAFETY *Tornado*

It is estimated that 75 percent of all tornadoes occur in the conterminous U.S. and nearly all the F5 super twisters strike within our borders. Most tornadoes develop during the months of April, May, and June, but when conditions are right, they can drop from the sky in any month at any time. In the U.S. an average of 818 tornadoes are reported each year, with Ohio averaging about one dozen annually.

TORNADO SAFETY RULES:

1. When a tornado watch has been issued, conditions are right for a tornado. Be prepared to take shelter and keep informed of the latest storm conditions. A tornado warning means that a tornado has been sighted and confirmed in the area. When a warning is issued, take cover immediately.
2. Take a flashlight and transistor radio with you to the area that will provide the most shelter.
3. Go to the center of the basement, taking cover under heavy tables or a workbench, if possible. If no basement is available, take shelter under heavy furniture or in a closet, near the center of the house. In any case, stay clear of large windows or any other glass.
4. If caught in the open, lie flat in the nearest ditch or depression. A culvert offers good protection. Abandon your car for a ditch if you cannot outrun the storm.

"THAT 'UN WAS 7 MINUTES EARLY!"

The Cyclones of Codell

By Dick Goddard

It has now been ninety years since the first of the tornadoes ripped through the tiny north-central Kansas town of Codell. In those days the storms we now call tornadoes were called, inaccurately, "cyclones." (Which, meteorologically speaking, are simply the low-pressure centers designated by the letter *L* on weather maps.)

The story began on May 20, 1915, when a twister appeared on the Codell horizon late in the afternoon and veered away into the Kansas prairie. Residents could not recall any such storm coming that close to their small community.

Exactly one year later, at precisely the same time, a tornado dropped like an elephant's trunk from a yellow, green, and black sky and tore through Rooks County, damaging much of Codell. The May 20, 1916, cyclone made it two in a row; one hit, one miss.

Those who were in Codell as May 20, 1917, approached made a few lame jokes about the cyclone that was due later that day. They were not disappointed. As the sky steadily blackened, the terrified residents of Codell scrambled into their underground storm cellars. The tornado destroyed some of the buildings that the earlier twisters had somehow overlooked. That made it three in a row.

Up to this point, although damage was heavy, none of the

tornadoes had caused deaths within the Codell community. This would change one year later. On the same day, at the same time.

Those who were in Codell on May 20, 1918, knew that the previous cyclones were just an incredible coincidence. There was no visible panic among those who remained in Codell, but all were aware of the date and time.

"We didn't spend that day in our storm cellars," recalled one Codell resident. For ten people who didn't, May 20, 1918, became their last day on earth.

As the hours went by that sultry spring day, there was every reason to believe that the May 20th jinx had been broken.

But darkness came early to Codell later that afternoon as the sun's rays were suddenly blotted out by a towering anvil cloud that reared over the southwestern horizon.

This tornado was the longest and most devastating of them all. Starting in Ellis County, the twister gouged northeastward into Rooks County and tore directly over tiny Codell before dissipating many miles away in Osborne County.

A 1912 publication had called Codell "a thriving little town of Paradise Township, Rooks County, and a station on the Union Pacific Railroad about 20 miles southeast of Stockton, the county seat." The population of Codell at the time was 175.

The May 20, 1918, tornado took away the town's hotel, the harness shop, the Methodist church and its parsonage, and almost everything else that was above ground.

It also took away Codell's future as a growing prairie community. Very little of Codell was rebuilt after the last twister, and all new business gravitated to the nearby towns of Plainville and Hays.

Today, 90 years later, the population of Codell is little more than 100. Just off Kansas Highway 18, Codell still has railroad service, but only on an "as needed" basis.

The odds of a tornado striking any one square mile in Kansas in any one year are roughly 1,000 to 1. The odds against a tornado striking approximately the same spot, on the same date, at the same time for three years in a row are astronomical.

Although other communities and towns have been struck by tornadoes on several occasions, none have been victimized like Codell, Kansas.

Codell has never seen another tornado. ■

JUNE STATISTICS

(recorded at Cleveland Hopkins Airport)

SUNSHINE %	65
DRIEST MONTH	0.39"/1933
WARMEST MONTH	73.9°/1949
COLDEST MONTH	62.2°/1903
LIQUID PCPN AVG.	3.70"
RAINIEST DAY	4.00"/1972
RAINIEST MONTH	9.77"/1902
THUNDERY DAYS	7
SNOWIEST DAY	TRACE/1907
DAYS ONE INCH SNOW	0

As the song says, "June is bustin' out all over." The first consistently warm—even hot—weather often delays until this month. Mid- to late June can sometimes be a blazer here. At 4:37 p.m. on June 25, 1988, Cleveland's temperature rocketed to an all-time high of 104° F. (Bone-dry and very windy thunderstorms added a meteorological exclamation point that evening.)

Thunderstorms are common here in June and tornadoes are not strangers. The great Sandusky-Lorain tornado hit on June 28, 1924. The tornado that killed 9 in Cuyahoga County (20 in Ohio) on June 8, 1953, passed very close to Cleveland's Public Square before exiting over Lake Erie around East 40th Street. In 1959, heavy rains caused severe flooding on Cleveland's East Side, submerging many vehicles; passengers on a transit bus in University Circle were rescued by motorboats. The latest Cleveland snow—only a trace—fell on June 5, 1907. Summer arrives with the solstice occurring around the 21st (leap year can make it vary).

Sun worshipers should be aware of the strengthening sunshine, especially powerful between the hours of 10 a.m. and 2 p.m. On warm, moist evenings fireflies (glowworms) will jet across the grass, eternally followed by small children carrying glass mason-jar prisons.

DAILY DATA FOR JUNE

Date	Day	Moon	Day of Year	Days Left	Sunrise	Sunset	Length of Day	Avg. Hi°	Avg. Lo°	Avg. Lake°
1	Wed		152	213	5:55	8:54	14:59	74	53	57
2	Thu		153	212	5:55	8:55	15:00	75	53	57
3	Fri		154	211	5:54	8:56	15:02	75	53	58
4	Sat		155	210	5:54	8:56	15:02	75	54	58
5	Sun		156	209	5:54	8:57	15:03	76	54	59
6	Mon	●	157	208	5:53	8:58	15:05	76	54	59
7	Tue		158	207	5:53	8:58	15:05	76	55	59
8	Wed		159	206	5:53	8:59	15:06	77	55	60
9	Thu		160	205	5:53	8:59	15:06	77	55	60
10	Fri		161	204	5:53	9:00	15:07	77	56	60
11	Sat		162	203	5:52	9:00	15:08	77	56	61
12	Sun		163	202	5:52	9:01	15:09	78	56	61
13	Mon		164	201	5:52	9:01	15:09	78	56	62
14	Tue		165	200	5:52	9:02	15:10	78	57	62
15	Wed	◐	166	199	5:52	9:02	15:10	78	57	62
16	Thu		167	198	5:52	9:03	15:11	79	57	62
17	Fri		168	197	5:52	9:03	15:11	79	57	63
18	Sat		169	196	5:53	9:03	15:10	79	58	63
19	Sun		170	195	5:53	9:03	15:10	79	58	63
20	Mon		171	194	5:53	9:04	15:11	79	58	64
21	Tue		172	193	5:53	9:04	15:11	80	58	64
22	Wed	○	173	192	5:53	9:04	15:11	80	59	64
23	Thu		174	191	5:54	9:04	15:10	80	59	65
24	Fri		175	190	5:54	9:04	15:10	80	59	65
25	Sat		176	189	5:54	9:04	15:10	81	59	65
26	Sun		177	188	5:55	9:04	15:09	81	59	65
27	Mon		178	187	5:55	9:04	15:09	81	59	65
28	Tue	◑	179	186	5:55	9:04	15:09	81	60	66
29	Wed		180	185	5:56	9:04	15:08	81	60	66
30	Thu		181	184	5:56	9:04	15:08	81	60	66

Rec. Hi°	Rec. Lo°	On This Date . . .
95/1934	40/1981	Superman Comics launched (1938)
94/1934	39/1966	Congress grants citizenship to Native Americans (1924)
91/1925	35/1977	Alexander Graham Bell transmits first wireless message (1880)
93/1925	40/1947	10-cent beer night riot at Municipal Stadium (1974)
93/1925	38/1990	Browns' Marion Motley born (1920)
92/1988	38/1945	Cleveland Museum of Art opens (1916)
91/1999	39/1977	Actor Dean Martin born in Steubenville (1917)
98/1933	39/1977	Tornadoes kill 110 in Michigan & Ohio (1953)
92/1914	41/1949	Donald Duck debuts (1934)
92/1999	31/1972	Rocky Colavito homers in 4 consecutive at-bats for Indians (1959)
93/1933	31/1972	WJW-AM/TV in Cleveland changes call letters to WRMR (1985)
92/1954	42/1980	Race riot in Cincinnati (300 arrested) (1967)
93/1954	43/1979	Comedian Paul Lynde born in Mt. Vernon, OH (1926)
95/1988	43/1978	U.S. Army founded (1775)
97/1954	43/1997	1 inch of snow falls in northern Pennsylvania (1918)
96/1952	39/1961	1st Father's Day celebrated in Spokane, WA (1010)
93/1994	38/1980	Final edition of Cleveland Press published (1982)
96/1944	41/1950	Challenger launched; Sally Ride 1st U.S. woman in space (1983)
95/1995	46/1965	KYW-AM in Cleveland Ohio returns call letters to Philadelphia (1965)
96/1988	46/2003	Joe Dimaggio's 2,000th hit, Yanks beat Indians 8-2 (1950)
95/1941	45/1897	Carl Stokes, first black mayor of major U.S. city, born in Cleve. (1927)
98/1988	39/1992	Last (?) of the Cuyahoga River fires rages (1969)
94/1948	41/1963	U.S. Secret Service created (1860)
96/1952	44/1915	Picasso's first exhibit (1901)
104/1988	41/1979	Custer's last stand (1876)
99/1952	47/1984	U.N. Charter signed (1945)
98/1944	44/1981	Browns' Don Rogers dies of cocaine poisoning (1986)
101/1944	49/1988	Lorain-Sandusky tornado kills 72 (1924)
94/1952	51/1985	Statesman Henry Clay dies at age 72 (1852)
95/1941	41/1988	Battle of Fort Recovery, Ohio (1794)

JAN FEB MAR APR MAY JUN JUL AUG SEP OCT NOV DEC

Flora & Fauna JUNE

WEEK 1 **BIRDS:** Adult chickadees and tufted titmice grow scarce at bird feeders as they busily tend to their young. June evenings bring the flutelike calls of wood thrushes and veeries as twilight settles on the land. **WILDFLOWERS:** Summer flowers begin to dot the open meadows with the oranges and yellows of hawkweed, and the yellows of cinquefoil. Ox-eye daisy adds its tall white blossoms to the colorful mix.

WEEK 2 **BIRDS:** Nighthawks (not true hawks but relatives of whippoorwills) grace the evening skies throughout the region as they hunt for their insect prey. Listen for the "b-z-z-z-t" sound made by their wings as they dive for food. **MAMMALS:** Young woodchucks now emerge to learn the ways of the woodchuck world with their ever-watchful mothers. **WILDFLOWERS:** Yellow iris adds a touch of bright color to the green of marsh edges. Cow parsnip as tall as a person appears along stream banks and marsh edges, with its umbrella-shaped white blossoms. A look-alike plant, water hemlock, is poisonous if eaten. Fortunately its distinctive mouselike odor keeps most people away. **TREES:** Is it snowing in June? No, it's just the cottonwood tree's countless millions of seeds drifting about in the summer breeze.

WEEK 3 **BIRDS:** Fledgling chickadees begin to appear at bird feeders with their tired parents. Watch the parents' tattered and worn feathers as they are gradually molted and replaced over the summer. **WILDFLOWERS:** By tradition, St. John's wort first blooms on June 21 to ward away evil spirits on midsummer night's eve. Tiny but delicious wild strawberries ripen in this third week of the "strawberry moon." Watch open fields and roadsides for the first of the pale-blue flowers of chicory, sometimes called blue sailors. **FISH:** Carp begin to thrash along shorelines of local lakes and slow-moving rivers as they spawn and lay eggs in warm shallow water.

WEEK 4 **WILDFLOWERS:** Common milkweed unfolds fragrant purple flowers beginning this week and continuing through July. The flowers turn into green dill-pickle-sized pods and are a prized "wild edible" in some parts of the country. Queen Anne's lace begins to bloom. Yellow-and-orange-spotted jewelweed is blooming on moist sites. Later in summer, its "exploding" seed pods delight hikers brave enough to touch! **AMPHIBIANS:** American toadlets finish their metamorphosis and emerge to live new lives on land. As small as a pencil eraser, they are perfect miniatures of their warty parents.

Adapted from the Nature Almanac by Robert Hinkle, with permission from Cleveland Metroparks.

HOW A CAR CAN TURN QUICKLY INTO AN OVEN

Temperatures rise in a closed car in varying weather conditions. Researchers placed sensors in a dark blue 2000 Honda Accord and recorded these results:

Outside Temp.	Temperature inside closed automobile after . . . 10 min.	20 min.	30 min.	40 min.	50 min.
72°	94°	99°	104°	108°	111°
75°	97°	104°	111°	115°	118°
79°	100°	106°	110°	114°	116°
84°	109°	119°	125°	128°	130°
88°	105°	117°	125°	130°	133°

Reprinted from the Plain Dealer.
Source: San Francisco State University

HALEY'S COMMENT:

Little Memories from a Big Life in Television

BY TOM HALEY

In the early forties, I was a page boy at NBC in Radio City. A year later, I became a rookie announcer at a 250-watt station in Allentown, PA (did everything but sweep out the place). NBC in Washington was next. I wasn't quite ready for the big time, so I came west to Cleveland. I tried WJW for a few months, got fired, and decided to go back east. Then WTAM offered me a job. Figured I would give it a short try and then go back. Almost 50 years later, I hadn't left yet. It was a great ride!

Some memories are more vivid than others:

WTAM added a TV station, WNBK. Those who knew our voices from radio were now able to see what we looked like. Many had been sure I was a little fat guy.

No one knew much about this new medium, so we improvised. I created one of the first TV talk shows, *Haley's Daily*—an hour, five days a week. Guests Hume Cronyn and Jessica Tandy asked Pat Weaver to take a look at me. He's Sigourney's dad, and the genius behind *Today*, *The Home Show*, and *The Tonight Show*. He sent me a note promising to keep an eye on me. Never heard from him again.

I'll never forget the night I introduced Bob Hope on a special TV show for the March of Dimes. He strode onto the stage, waved to the crowd with one hand, and pushed me aside with the other. That was reality TV before it had a name!

I remember when Dick Goddard came up from the weather bureau in Akron to audition for a TV weather spot. Most of us watching were sure he wouldn't make it. The rest is history.

One interview was with old-time comic Joe E. Brown. My boss wanted to know if I had asked all of the questions I had prepared. I wasn't sure. He also wanted to know if I had heard the answers. I learned that day that listening is the most important part of interviewing.

To add some news time, WKYC-TV put Del Donahoo and I together for an early-morning half hour. They left us alone and it worked . . . for 18 years.

Can't forget the day a viewer sent Del a cool western Stetson. He admired himself on camera and said: "I love the way it sits on my head," only it didn't come out that way!

They left us alone and it worked . . . for 18 years.

Shortly after that I found out the station was going in a different direction, and I wasn't going with 'em. I had a plan. I would hold up a huge sign at the Emmys, where Del and I were to be co-presenters, and Al Roker was the host: "WILL WORK FOR FOOD." It would have brought down the house. Still regret I didn't do it!

Haven't forgotten how John Erlichman, from Watergate, surprised me when I asked him why anyone would want to be president. His total answer: "Power"!

Once Al Roker, our weatherman, told me he was going to the top and nobody could stop him. Nobody could!

Got goose pimples talking to Jimmy Cagney, and listening to Barbra Streisand before anyone knew who she was.

Like to think that *Dialogue*, an interfaith talk show I hosted for 20 years, brought the different religious denominations closer. Walsh College thought so and made me the commencement speaker—gave me the right to be called doctor!

There is life after TV. You just have to live it. For me it is aerobics, walking, golf, speaking to groups, even narrating "Holy Cleveland" for WVIZ, plus doing an occasional benefit for the Cleveland Christian Home for children and, of course, having time for my grandchildren!

Retirees lose it when I open with: "the golden years, my a_ _!!"

Let me leave you with "a little old passing thought" (had a different one every morning on the Tom and Del show):

"What lies behind us and what lies before us are tiny matters, compared to what lies within us" (Emerson).

Have a good life filled with lots of love and some peace, too.

Tom Haley, now retired from WKYC-TV, Channel 3. He is likely remembered as the co-host of the "Today in Cleveland" show with Del Donahoo and "Sunday Magazine" with Mona Scott.

NORTHEAST OHIO'S WARMEST AND COLDEST SUMMERS

(by Median Temp)

WARMEST: Cleveland: 75.0° / 1949 • Akron/Canton: 73.9° / 1931

COLDEST: Cleveland: 66.7° / 1927 • Akron/Canton: 67.3° / 1992

Cleveland's **African American Museum**, the only one of its kind in Northeast Ohio, is also the oldest African American Museum in the United States. For more information, visit www.aamcleveland.org.

AT WHAT YOU CAN

Early this month, Saturn and Venus will be visible in the early evening, very low in the western sky.

On June 16 our beautiful crescent moon will pass very close to Jupiter. This is a great time for close-up views of those craters.

The week of the 25th, at 9:30 p.m., look to the western sky to see Saturn, Venus, and Mercury bunched tightly together.

Courtesy of Jay Reynolds, Schuele Planetarium director, Lake Erie Nature and Science Center.

The Man Who Invented Television

By Dick Goddard

The popularity of those unrealistic "reality" programs on television is a phenomenon that many feel is proof that God never meant for pictures to fly through the air. Today in the United States there are 180 million homes with television, and cable or satellite service is in 88 percent of those homes.

Only one in 50 people claim they never watch television.

But whom should we honor—or blame—for the electronic invention that glues millions of Americans to flickering images in a box for an average of four and one-half hours every day of the year?

Did Thomas Edison invent television? No.

How about Albert Einstein? No.

Guglielmo Marconi? No.

In spite of claims by the Radio Corporation of America (RCA) and its former egomaniacal president, David Sarnoff—who founded the National Broadcasting Network—the first television image was created by a humble Dagwood Bumstead-type farm boy character named Philo T. Farnsworth. Philo (Phil to friends and family) has never received proper recognition for his genius and intellect.

Phil Farnsworth was born in

a log cabin to a dirt-poor family at Beaver, Utah, on August 19, 1906. There was no electricity in his home and Phil rode to school on horseback in the hardscrabble days of his youth.

When he was 11 his family loaded all of their meager possessions into three covered wagons and headed northward into the Snake River Valley at Rigby, Idaho. They moved into the home of Phil's uncle, Albert Farnsworth, on a 240-acre farm with electricity that was supplied by a Delco generator.

Seldom smiling, with a slight build and bright blue eyes, Phil had a sandy-brown shock of hair that surmounted a larger-than-ordinary head and a prominent forehead.

The young man developed an intense interest in science very early in life, devouring every radio and electronics magazine he could find. By age 14 he had memorized Einstein's photoelectric theories and at that point he decided that he would be the one to invent what would become known as television.

It was in early spring in 1921, when he was 14, that the epiphany of how television could work came like a lightning bolt out of the blue. Phil had been plowing a potato field on a horse-drawn harrow. As he gazed at the freshly plowed rows of soil, Phil imagined that electrons (negatively charged elementary particles) could be lined up in the same way in order to scan a picture.

Phil jumped from his seat on the harrow and shouted to his startled father, "Papa, papa, I've got it!"

Lewis Farnsworth realized that his son had an unusual imagination when at the age of 12 Phil had said he could repair the failed electric generator that was so important to the farm operation.

"THE DAMNED THING WORKS!" EXCLAIMED HIS FATHER

Phil understood that electricity can be produced by passing a strong magnet along a wire. That puts electrons into motion and electricity results. He knew that magnetism and electricity were companions, and that streams of electrons could be manipulated by magnets.

When young Farnsworth told his dad that he thought he could fix the generator, several of his cousins gathered around to laugh and mock their "Einstein" relative. After dismantling and cleaning the generator, Phil made a few adjustments and pressed the "on" button.

"The damned thing works!" exclaimed his father.

His son's esoteric and deep thinking amazed the elder Farnsworth so much that he made Phil promise to keep his arcane abilities secret. "People think you are a bit odd," said his father, "and this will remove all doubt."

Radio was exploding across the country in the 1920s, and building your own radio crystal set was a very popular subject in science and electronic magazines. Phil knew that the next giant step would be putting moving pictures with the sound. It was from a Sears Roebuck catalog that Phil ordered his first crystal set (the Sears catalog was a young man's treasure, since it gave him his first exposure to such forbidden things as ladies' undergarments). By selling his baby lambs Phil had earned enough money to also order a violin from the catalog. He became so proficient with the fiddle that his father imagined him as a concert violinist. Phil collected five bucks every Friday night for playing in the band at the high school gymnasium ("Down by the Old Mill Stream" was a favorite tune).

In 1926, at age 20, Phil Farnsworth continued his dream of inventing television, applying for two basic patents, one for a television camera and the other for the reception of television signals. He called his device an "image dissector." Phil was not alone in his quest, because there were hundreds of scientists working in laboratories around the United States, all pursuing the holy grail of broadcasting.

Enter a Goliath named David, a five-foot-eight-inch Napoleon with steel-blue eyes.

David Sarnoff had also come from poor and humble beginnings in his native province of Minsk in Russia. His family fled to the United States in the cargo section of a steamship and they landed in the slums of New York City on the Lower East Side. His parents had wanted David to become a rabbi, but Sarnoff's fortunes turned when he was able to get a job as a telegraph key operator at the Wall Street offices of the American Marconi Company. By chance he was able to meet Guglielmo Marconi, the inventor of the wireless telegraph-the precursor of radio.

Sarnoff curried favor with Marconi and soon became his office gofer. Marconi was a big hit with the ladies, and Sarnoff spent much of his time delivering chocolates and flowers to Marconi's female favorites.

It was on the fateful night of April 14, 1912, while continuing to work as a telegraph operator at American Marconi, that Sarnoff claimed he had heard over his earphones the first distress signal from the sinking and doomed luxury liner Titanic. An RCA biography later boasted that Sarnoff stayed at his telegraph position for 72 straight hours (critics have argued that both claims were apocryphal, knowing that Sarnoff was a relentless self-promoter).

Amid the madcap race for radio broadcast rights, the Radio Corporation of America was founded in 1919. David Sarnoff continued to climb the corporate ladder, becoming RCA's patent policeman. Sarnoff made sure that it would be against the law for anyone without a license from RCA to build a radio or sell one without paying royalties to his company.

One day in 1928, in his RCA headquarters in New York, 37-year-old David Sarnoff was reading an article in the *San Francisco Chronicle* about a young independent scientist named Philo Farnsworth who had set up a laboratory in a drafty loft on Green Street at the base of Telegraph Hill in San Francisco.

Sarnoff coveted the patent on television and he was determined to bully his way toward that goal. He decided to go to San Francisco and meet his rival. Accompanying Sarnoff was Vladimir Zwyorkin, a Russian expatriate engineer who was hired by Sarnoff to develop a television system for RCA. Zwyorkin was well aware of Farnsworth and his work, and he had been developing his own system that he called an "image orthicon," which was based largely on Farnsworth's principles.

SARNOFF COVETED THE PATENT ON TELEVISION AND HE WAS DETERMINED TO BULLY HIS WAY TOWARD THAT GOAL.

Sarnoff believed that Farnsworth was basically a simple boy genius who—like others under Sarnoff's command—could be easily controlled and bought out cheaply. It was truly David versus Goliath in the battle over a box with lights and wires that would eventually be found in more homes in this country than indoor plumbing.

Sarnoff swaggered into Farnsworth's San Francisco laboratory swinging his ever-present oak walking stick, with Zwyorkin in tow. Zwyorkin complimented Farnsworth on his accomplishments and Sarnoff immediately offered Farnsworth

$100,000 for his system. Farnsworth turned him down.

From that point it became a litigation battle between Farnsworth's image dissector and Zwyorkin image orthicon. The war began and litigation over which side would win the patent raged on for six years. It was the modest resources of Farnsworth and his few investors against the massive fortune of RCA.

The battle took its toll on Farnsworth. Facing bankruptcy, Phil became depressed, his health began to fail, and his relationship with his devoted wife, Pam (Elma), deteriorated. Farnsworth began to drink heavily.

Finally, in 1936, the courts ruled that Philo Farnsworth was indeed the inventor of television, and he was issued a patent. RCA was ordered to pay Farnsworth royalties, which infuriated Sarnoff. "We don't pay royalties!" he fumed, "we collect them."

While Farnsworth continued his work in anonymity, and financial rewards were slow in coming, Sarnoff became a national figure, offering the services of RCA during the critical war years in the early 1940s. Sarnoff had been a member of the U.S. Army Reserves in the 1920s, and though he had no real military experience, his inside connections resulted in his being given the rank of lieutenant colonel.

Sarnoff had denounced his Russian heritage and declared himself a true patriot of his country. Following the Japanese attack on Pearl Harbor on December 7, 1941, he telegraphed President Franklin Roosevelt from RCA headquarters and pledged that "all our facilities are ready and at your instant service. We await your commands." RCA became an important military contractor during the war, providing radar tubes, sonar systems, and radio transmitters as well as research and development.

In 1944, with the D-day invasion at hand, Sarnoff was given active-duty status and he reported directly to General Eisenhower in London. The Allied Forces Network provided communications that were instrumental in coordinating the greatest military operation in history.

For his services President Roosevelt gave Sarnoff the rank of honorary brigadier general in the U.S. Army. Returning to his headquarters in New York, Sarnoff promptly informed RCA that he was no longer to be addressed as simply Mr. Sarnoff. He was to be called General Sarnoff, or General.

To validate David Sarnoff's colossal ego, in 1950 he asked the Radio and Television Manufacturers Association to bestow upon him the title of "Father of Television." Sarnoff received his self-proclaimed honor and all RCA employees were informed that the designation was official. Only he was to be so recognized.

Farnsworth, who sought no glory, finally won his first patent-licensing victory over RCA in 1939. It was in 1939 that Farnsworth was named—along with New York Yankee first baseman Lou Gehrig—as one of the "Outstanding Young Men" in the nation. This would be one of the few national honors he would receive. The last national recognition for Philo Farnsworth-while he was living-came in 1957 on the popular television show *What's My Line?* Panelists on the show were blindfolded as they asked questions of their mystery guest (the studio audience and television viewers could see the guest.) When panelist Jayne Meadows inquired, "Does what you do sometimes cause pain?" Farnsworth replied, "Sometimes it does. Yes."

None of the panelists was able to identify Farnsworth as the inventor of television. As a reward for his appearance, Philo Farnsworth was given a carton of Winston cigarettes and eighty dollars.

(Curiously, both Farnsworth and Zwyorkin lamented the poor quality of programming during the early years of television. Zworkin said the most important part of a television set was the switch that allowed you to turn it off. Farnsworth chided his son for watching too much TV and at one time none of the eight television sets in the Farnsworth home were working).

In 1989 elementary school students in Utah became aware of the importance of Philo Farnsworth. It was through their efforts that a statue in his honor is on display in our nation's capital. At the National Statuary Hall in Washington each state is represented by two figures. For the state of Utah there is Brigham Young, while alongside stands Philo Taylor Farnsworth. He is holding and gazing at an image dissector tube. At the base of his statue there is an inscription: FATHER OF TELEVISION.

While denied the wealth that such a monumental invention should have provided, Elma (Pam) Farnsworth, Phil's wife, was able to live out her 92 years in financial security following her husband's death at age 64 on March 11, 1971.

David Sarnoff, who became a multimillionaire while president of RCA, died in his sleep at age 80 in 1971.

Thank you, Phil Farnsworth, for allowing me to have a great career. ■

Almanac Puzzler

DRESS FOR THE WEATHER

BY TERRY OBLANDER

There's a secret about dapper Dick Goddard's wardrobe on his days off.

To find out what the well-dressed meteorologist wears when he's not on camera, unscramble the weather-related words below and insert them on the adjacent spaces. When you are done, read the letters in the boxes to discover our silly secret.

SO SANE ___ [ ] ___ [ ] ___ ___ ___

GLINT NIGH ___ ___ ___ ___ ___ [ ] ___ [ ] ___

FLING DOO ___ ___ [ ] ___ [ ] ___ ___ ___

WED PINTO (2 wds.) ___ ___ [ ] ___ ___ ___ ___ ___

ROB A WIN ___ ___ ___ ___ ___ [ ] ___ [ ]

WHOSE GRIN ___ ___ ___ ___ ___ [ ] ___ [ ] ___ ___

LION COG ___ ___ ___ ___ [ ] ___ [ ] ___

DIETS ___ ___ [ ] ___ ___ ___

SENT US ___ ___ ___ [ ] ___ ___

IQ OXEN U ___ ___ ___ [ ] ___ [ ] ___

SIC LICE ___ [ ] ___ [ ] ___ ___ ___

LUBE SIKES (2 wds.) ___ ___ ___ [ ] ___ [ ] ___ ___ ___

AS LEG ___ ___ ___ ___ [ ]

URCHINS ARE ___ ___ ___ ___ ___ [ ] ___ ___ ___ ___

TAN DOOR ___ ___ ___ ___ [ ] ___ ___

PR GINS ___ [ ] ___ ___ ___ ___

JULY STATISTICS

(recorded at Cleveland Hopkins Airport)

SUNSHINE %	67
DRIEST MONTH	0.74"/1930
WARMEST MONTH	79.1°/1955
COLDEST MONTH	67.6°/1960
LIQUID PCPN AVG.	3.52"
RAINIEST DAY	2.87"/1969
RAINIEST MONTH	9.12"/1992
THUNDERY DAYS	6
SNOWIEST DAY	NONE
DAYS ONE INCH SNOW	0

July can be a meteorological firecracker in Northeast Ohio. Lightning laces the sky more in this month than any other. The legendary dog days begin on July 3 and continue for 40 days. The ancient Egyptians came up with the canine idea because they believed that the dog star, Sirius (the brightest star in our skies), lent its heat to that of the sun. Sirius is unseen in our summer sky because of the brightness of our sun; indeed, Sirius comes over the eastern horizon each summer morning just ahead of the star we call our sun.

Our July atmosphere is often humid, and torrential rains can fall. On July 12, 1966, a state record 10.51 inches of rain fell in 24 hours at Sandusky. Even on a blistering July day, the raindrops will feel cold. That's because nearly all rainfall at Ohio's latitude begins as ice crystals and snow high above. On July 4, 1969, 12 hours of nearly continuous thunderstorms resulted in 42 deaths, most by drowning. Just northwest of Wooster, 14 inches of rain fell from the storms. On warm and sultry July nights heat lightning can be seen. The lightning is unaccompanied by thunder, since it is coming from a thunderstorm that may be a thousand miles away, in Oklahoma or southern Canada.

In this lush and verdant festival month the ubiquitous Queen Anne's lace will proliferate in unmowed fields. Katydids are fiddling away the nights.

JAN FEB MAR APR MAY JUN JUL AUG SEP OCT NOV DEC

DAILY DATA FOR JULY

Date	Day	Moon	Day of Year	Days Left	Sunrise	Sunset	Length of Day	Avg. Hi°	Avg. Lo°	Avg. Lake°
1	Fri		182	183	5:57	9:04	15:07	81	60	67
2	Sat		183	182	5:57	9:04	15:07	82	60	67
3	Sun		184	181	5:58	9:04	15:06	82	60	67
4	Mon		185	180	5:58	9:04	15:06	82	60	67
5	Tue		186	179	5:59	9:03	15:04	82	61	67
6	Wed	●	187	178	6:00	9:03	15:03	82	61	67
7	Thu		188	177	6:00	9:03	15:03	82	61	67
8	Fri		189	176	6:01	9:02	15:01	82	61	68
9	Sat		190	175	6:02	9:02	15:00	82	61	68
10	Sun		191	174	6:02	9:01	14:59	82	61	69
11	Mon		192	173	6:03	9:01	14:58	82	61	69
12	Tue		193	172	6:04	9:00	14:56	82	61	70
13	Wed		194	171	6:05	9:00	14:55	82	61	70
14	Thu	◐	195	170	6:05	8:59	14:54	82	61	70
15	Fri		196	169	6:06	8:59	14:53	82	61	71
16	Sat		197	168	6:07	8:58	14:51	82	62	71
17	Sun		198	167	6:08	8:57	14:49	83	62	71
18	Mon		199	166	6:09	8:57	14:48	83	62	71
19	Tue		200	165	6:09	8:56	14:47	83	62	72
20	Wed		201	164	6:10	8:55	14:45	83	62	72
21	Thu	○	202	163	6:11	8:54	14:43	83	62	72
22	Fri		203	162	6:12	8:54	14:42	83	62	72
23	Sat		204	161	6:13	8:53	14:40	83	62	72
24	Sun		205	160	6:14	8:52	14:38	83	62	72
25	Mon		206	159	6:15	8:51	14:36	83	62	72
26	Tue		207	158	6:16	8:50	14:34	83	62	73
27	Wed		208	157	6:17	8:49	14:32	83	62	73
28	Thu	◑	209	156	6:18	8:48	14:30	82	62	73
29	Fri		210	155	6:19	8:47	14:28	82	62	73
30	Sat		211	154	6:20	8:46	14:26	82	62	73
31	Sun		212	153	6:21	8:45	14:24	82	62	73

Rec. Hi°	Rec. Lo°	On This Date . . .
95/2002	45/1988	Cleveland Municipal Airport opened (1925)
97/1954	47/1943	James A. Garfield shot in Washington, D.C. by Charles J. Guiteau (1881)
98/1949	46/1907	U.S. Veterans Administration created (1930)
98/1990	41/1968	Marilyn Sheppard murdered in Bay Village (1954)
96/1911	48/1979	Larry Doby signs with Indians; 1st black player in AL (1947)
97/1988	45/1979	Congress resolves to name U.S. currency the "dollar" (1785)
99/1988	45/1968	Cleveland Indians sign Leroy Satchel Paige (1948)
99/1988	45/1984	Architect Philip Johnson born in Cleveland (1906)
97/1936	43/1961	Football coach Paul Brown born in Norwalk (1908)
97/1936	46/1963	Trumbull County incorporated (1800)
99/1936	48/1996	Actress Beverly Todd born in Ohio (1946)
95/1936	48/1978	10.51 inches of rainfall, Sandusky (state record) (1966)
95/1952	51/1976	Live Aid concert (1985)
99/1954	51/1888	Sportscaster Steve Stone born in Cleveland (1947)
97/1980	48/1960	Senator George Voinovich born in Cleveland (1936)
100/1988	50/1954	15 drown in Old Riverbed when commuter boat overturns (1896)
96/1942	49/1946	Comedienne Phyllis Diller born in Lima (1917)
96/1878	51/1971	Hough riots begin (1966)
95/1930	50/1979	Gov. Rhodes declares state of emergency in Cleveland race riot (1966)
98/1930	46/1965	Actress Lola Albright born in Akron (1924)
97/1952	46/1966	Poet Hart Crane born in Garretsville (1899)
99/1952	471966	Moses Cleaveland arrives at mouth of Cuyahoga River (1796)
96/1933	49/1981	National Inventors Hall of Fame opens in Akron (1995)
99/1934	50/2000	Writer Ambrose Bierce born in Ohio (1842)
99/1941	47/1953	Cavaliers' Nate Thurmond born in Ohio (1941)
99/1941	46/1946	1st electric streetcar in U.S. operates in Cleveland (1884)
103/1941	47/1946	Singer Maureen McGovern born in Youngstown (1949)
96/1993	52/1977	14th Amendment ratified (1968)
95/1941	50/1948	Jefferson County incorporated (1797)
96/1941	50/1981	U.S. motto "In God We Trust" authorized (1956)
97/1955	52/1960	1st Indians game at Municipal Stadium (1932)

Flora & Fauna JULY

WEEK 1 **BIRDS:** As pale-blue Canada thistles begin to go to seed, goldfinches gather the thistledown for nesting material. Wild turkeys and their young poults come out of hiding to find insects in open fields thought the area. Barred owls search woodlots for a nocturnal dinner, followed by their still-fuzzy offspring. **WILDFLOWERS:** Wild bergamot, sometimes called "bee balm," is in full lavender bloom this week. Many beekeepers say this flower produces the sweetest honey of all our native flowers. Canada lily and other lilies begin to bloom along roadsides this week. **INSECTS:** The first of our annual "dog day" cicadas begin to tune up their summer songs from treetops throughout our neighborhoods. Their 17-year relatives, last seen here in 1999, will not emerge until 2016.

WEEK 2 **BIRDS:** The bright colors of male mallards and wood ducks begin to fade as they go into their summer "eclipse" plumage. This is an especially wary time for them, as they are unable to fly for several weeks. Canada geese become flightless at this time too. **WILDFLOWERS:** Queen Anne's lace, yarrow, blue vervain, butter-and-eggs, evening primrose, and enchanter's nightshade should all be in full bloom by now. Teasel heads, looking like tall purple burrs, are beginning to bloom along roadsides and in sunny open meadows.

WEEK 3 **WILDFLOWERS:** Early goldenrod, first of many goldenrods to bloom, becomes a harbinger of autumn as it adds touches of bright yellow to shady open places along parkways. The tall lavender blossoms of Joe-Pye weed may stand six feet tall in low wet places. It was once considered to be a medicinal plant. Purple coneflower blooms this week. **SHRUBS:** Crab apples become ripe this week, much to the delight of white-tailed deer!

WEEK 4 **BIRDS:** Young house wrens should have fledged by this week. The days grow shorter, and grackles and blackbirds begin to flock together to prepare for the long journey south. Young killdeer chicks scamper around like fuzzy golf balls. **WILDFLOWERS:** The brilliant reds of cardinal flowers contrast with the golds and greens of cattails and sedges in wet meadows and woods this week. White boneset flowers and the rich purple of ironweed brighten marsh edges. **INSECTS:** Katydids and cicadas should be in full treetop chorus by the end of the week. **TREES:** Tulip trees are turning orange, black tupelo is turning crimson, and sassafras is turning orange. Can autumn be far away?

Adapted from the Nature Almanac by Robert Hinkle, with permission from Cleveland Metroparks.

NORTHEAST OHIO'S WETTEST AND DRIEST SUMMERS *(Rainfall)*

Wettest: Cleveland: 19.88" / 1972 • Akron/Canton: 20.28" / 1892

Driest: Cleveland: 3.63" / 1933 • Akron/Canton: 3.18" / 1991

YOU'D BE AMAZED AT WHAT YOU CAN SEE IN JULY

July 8, around 9:30, you'll see Jupiter in the south, Venus, Mercury, and a thin crescent moon in the west.

That very bright star in the east is Vega. Because of its brightness, it is often confused with the north star. Vega, the fifth-brightest star in our evening sky, is very blue. It is a part of the "Summer Triangle" of stars in our summer sky. Binoculars or a dark location will show more stars than you can count, as this is a part of our galaxy, the Milky Way.

Courtesy of Jay Reynolds, Schuele Planetarium director, Lake Erie Nature and Science Center.

DOING LIVE TELEVISION IS EASY, GOLF IS HARD

By Tim Taylor

The old saying is "Golf doesn't build character, it reveals it."

Well, I'd like to suggest it actually reveals "characters." People do wacky things on a golf course, me included. Just ask any pro athlete who's tried to emulate his pro golfer counterpart, and they'll tell you it may be the toughest game in the world. It turns levelheaded, good-natured people into towering infernos of frustration. People can't believe they have so little control over a tiny ball that sits motionless in front of them. Ever see a major-league baseball player who can hit a 98-mile-an-hour fastball flail helplessly at the little white ball? Over the years I've had the good fortune to play with lots of pros, male and female. In fact, one of my most embarrassing moments on the golf course, and there've been many, came during an LPGA pro-am at Shaker Country Club. Now you'd think that having appeared nightly for several decades in front of thousands of people might qualify me to handle my nerves reasonably well in front of only a few hundred spectators. Well, not exactly.

Even though I carry a fairly respectable 12 handicap, my swing tends to get fast and ugly when lots of people are watching. The gallery's obvious skepticism that I belonged on the same course with these talented lady pros was quickly justified.

In fact, my videographer told me my swing was so quick, he didn't think he captured it on videotape. All I know is I snap hooked my tee shot into a tree about 20 yards to the left of the tee. It glanced wildly off a thick limb and made a direct right turn, flying about 50 yards into Shaker's swimming pool. All without striking a single swimmer in the head. It was a long time before I put my swing on display again.

Many of those I've played with over the years seem to get a little crazy on the golf course, believing somehow that they should play like a pro, without practicing like one or having the talent of one.

Actually, I've always been a decent striker of the ball, but a balky putter has turned some very good rounds into just average ones. A weakness with the flat stick has also put me on a relentless pursuit of the perfect putter. I've spent a small fortune on putters, such as the stand-up putter that allows you to circle behind the putter and line up your stroke while it stands on its own. I've owned almost every conventional putter ever made, from Pings to Titlest blade putters, to my current belly putter. The one that got the most laughs from my buddies was one that had all sorts of dials and alignment gimmicks on it. The sort of thing you might see in the bowels of a submarine, used for lining up an enemy tanker.

I remember being even par through 14 at Astorhurst, a pretty little course adjacent to the Metroparks in Walton Hills. I hit the 15th green in regulation and then proceeded to do the impossible with this bombardier-like putter that had worked so well. I four jacked it from about 10 feet. I hate to admit ever having a temper on the golf course, but this miscue, during a tournament, was more than I could bear. I soon learned this putter could also fly. I planted it so deep into the woods behind the 15th green it wouldn't be found for several years. It was, however, so ridiculously distinctive, there was no doubt who it belonged to when a course cleanup crew found it years later. Still embarrassed, I denied it was mine. Do you notice how often the word "embarrass" comes up in relation to golf? So much opportunity for embarrassment, so little talent.

Another embarrassing moment occurred several years ago when my wife, Cathy, used an 8 iron to ace the par 3 third hole. It was just a few days earlier that Cathy had asked if I remembered to put her ten dollars into the club's cash pot for hole-in-one winners. I assured her I had. Well, I had forgotten. Thankfully, the golf gods smiled on both of us a month later when, during a couples event, Cathy aced number three again!! This time, I made sure we were both entered, and she happily bought beverages for the entire grill room.

The most recent source of embarrassment—there's that word again—was something that happened last summer at Barrington, during another couples event. My drive landed in a fairway bunker with a pretty good lip on it. Greed overcame good sense, and instead of just knocking it out with a wedge and then playing an easy third shot to the green, I decided to go for it. That, of course, meant using a longer iron with a straighter face, which promptly drove the ball straight into the rock-hard lip. My nearly perfect follow-through, with my belt buckle facing the target, left my midsection totally vulnerable to the misplayed shot. I crumpled in a heap as the ball ricocheted off my groin area and onto the fairway, just a few yards away. The pain wasn't nearly as bad as enduring the howls of laughter.

Embarrassing moments aside, there have been many wonderful moments on the golf course, most of them involving the companionship of my friends and family.

My dad taught me to play. Later, I introduced golf to my children and grandchildren. What other sport can you so fully enjoy either alone, as a couple, or as an entire family, from the time you pick up a cut-down club at the age of three until you're playing the back nine of life.

And in my case, the game of golf has also allowed me to help, in a small way, thousands of children afflicted with epilepsy in Northeast Ohio. In 13 years, we've raised over $800,000 for the Epilepsy Society, including this year's record of $80,000.

In a way, golf is a microcosm of life. It seems that those who see the alluring challenge and the ironic humor in the game, where the best intentions often receive the least rewards, actually enjoy golf the most.

Tim Taylor serves as the Chief Anchor of FOX8 NEWS at 6 and 10 p.m., Monday through Friday on WJW. He is a member of the prestigious "Silver Circle," honored for his more than a quarter of a century of contributions to Cleveland television by the National Academy of Television Arts and Sciences. He is also a longtime member of the Ohio Broadcasters Hall of Fame and is a charter member of the Bedford High School Hall of Fame. Tim was also voted "Favorite Male News Anchor" in polls conducted by both *Cleveland Magazine* and the *Akron Beacon Journal*.

WINNERS ~ OF ~ ANNUAL NORTHEAST OHIO AWARDS

2004 "Outstanding Community Leader" Honorees by the Leadership Academy Society of Cleveland State University's Maxine Goodman Levin College of Urban Affairs: **Bonita W. Caplan**, *Cleveland Heights councilwoman and Chair of the Cuyahoga County Mental Health Board*; **Dennis M. Clough**, *Mayor, Westlake*; **John Hosek**, *Northeast Ohio Areawide Coordinating Agency*; **Ann Marie Donnegan**, *Olmsted Falls councilwoman*

Eleanor Steigman, was one of twenty-five senior Americans to receive the 2004 MetLife Foundation Older Volunteers Enrich America Award, The National Association of Area Agencies on Aging, and she also received the Team Spirit Award.

The winners of the 11th annual Northeast Ohio Technology Coalition Innovation Awards:

A. Schulman Inc., *Akron*: water-soluble polymer and a laminate that mimics the appearance of a painted coating.

Audiopack Technologies, *Garfield Heights*: microphone that translates vibrations from a skull into a clear voice ideal for loud situations.

DataTrak International Inc., *Mayfield*: software that manages medical clinical trials.

Diebold Inc., *North Canton*: improved automated teller machine.

Eaton Corp., *Cleveland*: fuel-limit vent valve that works more efficiently and costs less.

Flight Options LLC, *Cleveland*: wireless communications system between flight personnel.

Goodyear Tire and Rubber Co., *Akron*: two-piece tire.

ICI Paints, *Cleveland*: ceiling paint that goes on pink and dries white.

Invacare Corp., *Elyria*: wheelchair that provides increased mobility.

Kinetico Inc., *Newbury*: compact, multi-functional water softener.

Lincoln Electric Co., *Cleveland*: powerful power inverter for the welding industry.

Mirifex Systems Corp., *Strongsville*: collaboration with Flight Options.

Nanofilm Ltd., *Valley View*: nanomanipulated film that keeps clear surfaces from fogging up.

NASA Glenn Research Center, *Cleveland*: environmentally friendly way of restoring the surface of paintings.

Noveon, *Brecksville* (now part of Lubrizol Corp.): streamlined Spandex manufacturing and a flexible pipe for plumbing systems.

Omnova Solutions Inc., *Fairlawn*: peel-and-stick roofing product.

Plasticolors Inc., *Ashtabula*: process that makes sheet molding compounds more efficient.

PolyOne Corp., *Avon Lake*: conductive polymer with anti-corrosion properties.

PreEmptive Solutions Inc., *Euclid*: software that protects software design.

Royal Appliance Manufacturing Co., *Glenwillow*: vacuum-mop.

Sherwin Williams Co., *Cleveland*: more efficient paint for plastics.

Steris Corp., *Mentor*: anti-contamination systems.

Swagelok Co., *Solon*: miniature sample-handling system for the oil, gas and chemical industries.

Thermagon Inc., *Cleveland*: alloy that cools microelectronic components.

Trek Diagnostic Systems Inc., *Cleveland*: test for microbacteria.

Tremco Inc., *Beachwood*: improved waterproofing sealant.

The Chilcote Co. in Cleveland was named the 2004 Employee Stock Ownership Plan (ESOP) Company of the Year by the ESOP Association in Washington. Chilcote, founded in 1906, employs 450 people. It makes packaging products, such as albums.

Eaton Corp. was honored with the Power Quality Company of the Year Award by Frost & Sullivan, a global consulting firm. The award recognizes worldwide leadership in power distribution, power protection and power equipment maintenance.

Cleveland's Hispanic Business Association Entrepreneur of the Year: **Adrian Ortega**, *owner of Adrian Michael Jewelers in Rocky River*; Businesswoman of the Year: **Margarita De Leon**.

2004 Time Warner Cable Northeast Ohio Division Community Pillar Award: **Mr. O.D. Leonard**, *a minister who has served Northeast Ohio for 35 years without salary*; employee winner is **Ms. Nichelle Moore**, *a member of the Time Warner Cable Northeast Ohio division staff who has been a long standing supporter of an organization for young people*.

2004 Time Warner Cable 15th Annual National Teacher Awards: **Marianne Goebel** and **Joyce Krusinski**, *Grill Elementary School, Clinton*; **Jacqueline Danko**, *St. Joan of Ark Catholic School, Canton;*

Northeast Ohio Nurse Practitioners of the Year: **Sandra Jorgensen**, *MSN, CNP*

Cleveland Journalism Hall of Fame 2003 Inductees:

Tom Brazaitis, *Plain Dealer*

Joe Tait, *Cleveland Cavaliers*

Leonard Will, *WERE, WCPN and WKSU radio*

Janet McCue, *Plain Dealer*

Virgil Dominic, *WKYC-TV3 and WJW-TV8*

American Cancer Society Cuyahoga Area Unit Advocacy Award: **Elizabeth Nolan**, *founder and president of the Women's Diagnostic Center in Cleveland Heights*

Cleveland Chapter of the National Association of the Remodeling Industry Northeast Ohio Contractor of the Year Award: **Russ Masetta**, *owner of Nature Stone*.

YWCA of Greater Cleveland Women of Achievement Award: **Hon. Patricia Ann Blackmon**, *Ohio Court of Appeals, Eighth Appellate District*; **Kathleen B. Burke**, *partner at Jones Day and President of the Ohio State Bar Association*; **Olga D. Gonzalez-Sanabria**, *Director of Engineering & Technical Services at the NASA Glenn Research Center*; **Joy A. Jordan, DDA**, *Dental Director for the Cleveland Job Corps and the Trumbull Correctional Institution*; **Helen Rowland Marter**, *Head of School at Laurel School*; **Sandra Pianalto**, *VP and COO of the Federal Reserve Bank of Cleveland*

Cleveland Association of Insurance and Financial Advisors 2003 Rookie of the Year: **Paul McCormack**, *a financial planner with Sagemark Consulting*

CitiSun of the Year Awards (outstanding citizens, representing each edition of Sun Newspapers, honored for contributions to their communities): **Joseph Behal**, *Broadview Hts.*, **John Piazza**, *Bedford*, **Tip Nichols**, *Nottingham*, **Theresa Markowitz**, *Solon*, **Keith Jenkins**, *Westlake*, **Nancy Karr**, *Shaker Hts.*, **Chuck Hawley**, *Medina*, **Norm And Ginger Hamm**, *Brunswick*, **Lois Gerstenmaier**, *Akron*, **Diane Gacom**, *Nordonia Hills*, **Ruth Freita**, *Parma*, **Mary Forsythe**, *Independence*, **Phyllis Cowles**, *Berea*, **Robert Cowie**, *Copley-Fairlawn*, **John Colombo**, *Cleveland*, **Dennis Berzinskas**, *Euclid*, **Tom Barnum**, *Strongsville*, **Dawn Powers**, *Wadsworth*, **Paula Reed**, *Lakewood*, **Walter And Rosella Schendel**, *Moreland Hills*, **Ken Roddie**, *Twinsburg*, **Marge Spatafore**, *Avon*, **Jim Spring**, *Mayfield Hts.*, **Sandy Verduin**, *South Russell*, **James Wallace**, *Brooklyn Hts.*

The Beckoning Cat

By Dick Goddard

There are few Japanese or Chinese restaurants or other businesses without either foo dogs (temple dogs) or a statue of a sitting cat with an upraised paw.

In Asian countries the cat symbolizes good luck, and the colorful feline is Maneki Neko (MAH-nee-key NAY-Ko), the Beckoning Cat. Either the right paw or left paw will be held up. The right paw is an outright invitation to both money and good fortune. The left paw held up signifies the business is warmly welcoming customers.

When in Hawaii I was told by a Japanese merchant that the Maneki Neko at one time was the mascot at—let's say—"houses of ill repute." The idea originated during the rule of Japan's shogun warriors in the 19th century. This ceramic greeter was a big improvement over the vulgar phallic symbols used previously, which were outlawed by the Japanese Meiji emperor in 1872. The Japanese government was trying to improve its image in the eyes of Western nations.

Legend says that Maneki Neko was made an icon in tribute to a 17th-century cat who lived with a Shinto priest in a shabby temple in Tokyo. The cat was named Tama, and his priestly owner chided him about not doing his part in temple duties.

Their fortunes suddenly changed on a very rainy day when a feudal warlord named

Naotaka was passing by and sought shelter under a tall tree near the temple. As Naotaka peered through the pouring rain he saw Tama sitting at the temple door with an upraised paw, as if beckoning him to come in.

The lord was intrigued and moved away from the tree and through the temple gate. At that moment a terrible lightning bolt struck the tree under which Naotaka had been standing.

Tama had saved his life!

In deep gratitude the warlord made the small temple his family's place of worship, and from that time on both Tama and his master wanted for nothing.

Tama lived for many years and was honored by being buried in the garden of what became known as Goutokjui temple.

Today at Goutokjui you will find countless statues dedicated to Tama, the lucky, beckoning cat.

Many Maneki Nekos are calico cats. I have three of the protective felines myself: one gold-colored and two multicolored (and my humble home has never been hit by lightning!).

A pink Maneki Neko is specifically in charge of warding off illness and evil spirits, while also bringing love and financial success—as well as good health. The higher the paw, the better the results.

Curiously, while lucky cats in the Orient show the palm of the paw, in America the back of the paw is shown, imitating the way we gesture to someone to "come in."

PLANET VISIBILITY

Planet	Morning Visibility	Evening Visibility
Mercury	Jan 1–Feb 1 Apr 6–May 27 Aug 13–Sep 9 Nov 30–Dec 31	Feb 25–Mar 23 Jun 11–Jul 30 Sep 30–Nov 19
Venus	Jan 1–Feb 19	May 9–Dec 31
Mars	Jan 1–Nov 7	Nov 7–Dec 31
Jupiter	Jan 1–Apr 3 Nov 5–Dec 31	Apr 3–Oct 9
Saturn	Jan 1–Jan 13 Aug 11–Dec 31	Jan 13–Jul 5

Source: Nautical Almanac Office, United States Naval Observatory

HOLLYWOOD ON THE CUYAHOGA

A NORTHEAST OHIO FILMOGRAPHY

Do they make movies in Cleveland? According to the Cleveland Media Development Corp. (Cleveland's Film Commission), more than 50 feature films have been shot in and around Cleveland since 1970. From St. Theodosius Russian Orthodox Cathedral in Tremont (featured in the Academy Award winner *The Deer Hunter*) to the old Higbee's department store on Public Square (featured in the Christmas classic *A Christmas Story*), Cleveland landmarks have shown up in some of Hollywood's best-loved films. Rent a movie from the list below and discover Cleveland on film.

2000s

Against the Ropes, Paramount Pictures

American Splendor, HBO Films/Good Machine

Antwone Fisher, Fox Searchlight

Bet Your Life, Silver Pictures

Miracle Dogs, TAG Entertainment

Night Owls of Coventry, Nightowl Productions

Proximity, Silver Pictures

The Year That Trembled, Novel City Pictures

Turn of Faith, Boom Boom Productions

Welcome to Collinwood, Warner Bros./Good Machine

1990s

Air Force One, Columbia Tri-Star Pictures

Anywhere But Here, Every Footstep Films

Chester & Irene, Chester & Irene Productions

Diary of a Hit Man, Continental Film Group

Double Dragon, Imperial Entertainment

Edge of Seventeen, Luna Pictures

Flattered, Silent H Films

House Arrest, Rysher Entertainment

Journey of Man, Sony Pictures Classics

Men In Black, Fallout Shelter Productions

My Summer Story, MGM Productions

Noises Off, Disney/Amblin Productions

Paradise, Buena Vista Pictures

Pieces, Russo Productions

Renegade Force, HBO/Triple Peak Productions, Inc.

Shooting Star, Whitely Productions

Slaughter of the Innocents, Shapiro Glickenhaus Entertainment

Telling Lies in America, Banner Entertainment

The Dead Matter, independent

The Rain Maker, Paramount Pictures

The Shawshank Redemption, Castle Rock Pictures

1980s

A Christmas Story, MGM/UA

All The Marbles, MGM/UA

An Innocent Man, Touchstone Pictures

An Unremarkable Life, Continental Film Group

Big Business, Touchstone Pictures

Light of Day, Taft Entertainment

Major League, Paramount Pictures

Planes, Trains & Automobiles, Paramount Pictures

Stranger Than Paradise, Samual Goldwin Company

Tango and Cash, Warner Bros.

The Escape Artist, Zoetrope

Tiger Warsaw, Continental Film Group

Welcome Home Roxy Carmichael, Paramount Pictures

1970s

Harry & Walter Go to New York, Columbia Pictures

One Trick Pony, Warner Bros.

The Deer Hunter, EMI/Universal

The Instructor, American Eagle Productions

The Second Degree, Aselin Organization

Those Eyes, Those Lips, United Artists

Courtesy of **Jim Gelardin**, *an art director who has worked on 11 of 50 recent films shot in Cleveland. Recently he blew Cleveland up in the NBC film You Bet Your Life.*

AUGUST STATISTICS

(recorded at Cleveland Hopkins Airport)

SUNSHINE %	63
DRIEST MONTH	0.17"/1881
WARMEST MONTH	77.8°/1995
COLDEST MONTH	65.4°/1927
LIQUID PCPN AVG.	3.40"
RAINIEST DAY	3.65"/1994
RAINIEST MONTH	8.96"/1975
THUNDERY DAYS	5
SNOWIEST DAY	NONE
DAYS ONE INCH SNOW	0

The Perseids are coming! One of the most reliable of the meteor showers, the Perseids are most frequent around the 11th night. These night lights of August may be no larger than a bean, or grain of sand, as they become super-heated after entering our atmosphere at about 65 miles up, traveling at 150,000 mph. Shooting stars that make it through the atmosphere and strike earth are called meteorites. An especially bright meteor, called a bolide, was seen blazing across the Northeast Ohio sky in October of 1992; the bolide eventually struck the trunk of a car in New York State.

While May is the month of woodland flowers, August is the month of field flowers. New England asters, with bright yellow centers and purple petals, adorn the untended countryside.

Creating a summertime symphony will be the stridulation of crickets and red-legged grasshoppers. Personally, I'll take the noise of summer over the silence of winter.

On extremely hot August afternoons the refraction of light over Lake Erie has created a mirage, allowing the Canadian shoreline to appear—upside down.

DAILY DATA FOR AUGUST

Date	Day	Moon	Day of Year	Days Left	Sunrise	Sunset	Length of Day	Avg. Hi°	Avg. Lo°	Avg. Lake°
1	Mon		213	152	6:22	8:44	14:22	82	62	73
2	Tue		214	151	6:23	8:43	14:20	82	62	73
3	Wed		215	150	6:24	8:41	14:17	82	62	73
4	Thu		216	149	6:25	8:40	14:15	82	62	74
5	Fri	●	217	148	6:26	8:39	14:13	82	61	74
6	Sat		218	147	6:27	8:38	14:11	82	61	74
7	Sun		219	146	6:28	8:36	14:08	82	61	74
8	Mon		220	145	6:29	8:35	14:06	82	61	74
9	Tue		221	144	6:30	8:34	14:04	82	61	74
10	Wed		222	143	6:31	8:33	14:02	82	61	74
11	Thu		223	142	6:32	8:31	13:59	81	61	74
12	Fri		224	141	6:33	8:30	13:57	81	61	74
13	Sat	◐	225	140	6:34	8:29	13:55	81	61	74
14	Sun		226	139	6:35	8:27	13:52	81	61	74
15	Mon		227	138	6:36	8:26	13:50	81	61	74
16	Tue		228	137	6:37	8:24	13:47	81	60	74
17	Wed		229	136	6:38	8:23	13:45	81	60	74
18	Thu		230	135	6:39	8:21	13:42	81	60	74
19	Fri	○	231	134	6:40	8:20	13:40	80	60	74
20	Sat		232	133	6:41	8:18	13:37	80	60	74
21	Sun		233	132	6:42	8:17	13:35	79	60	74
22	Mon		234	131	6:43	8:15	13:32	79	60	74
23	Tue		235	130	6:44	8:14	13:30	79	60	74
24	Wed		236	129	6:45	8:12	13:27	79	59	74
25	Thu		237	128	6:46	8:11	13:25	79	59	73
26	Fri	◑	238	127	6:47	8:09	13:22	79	59	73
27	Sat		239	126	6:48	8:07	13:19	79	59	73
28	Sun		240	125	6:49	8:06	13:17	79	59	73
29	Mon		241	124	6:50	8:04	13:14	79	59	73
30	Tue		242	123	6:51	8:03	13:12	76	58	73
31	Wed		243	122	6:52	8:01	13:09	78	58	73

Rec. Hi°	Rec. Lo°	On This Date . . .
95/1917	47/1960	1st U.S. census (population 3,939,214) (1790)
97/1988	50/1962	Horror movie director Wes Craven born in Cleveland (1939)
97/1944	58/1976	1st aerial cropdusting (Troy, Ohio) to kill caterpillars (1921)
97/1930	46/1966	Circus fire at E. 9th & Lakeside kills dozens of animals (1942)
94/1947	46/1972	Browns coach Paul Brown dies at 82 (1991)
100/1918	45/1997	Actor Dorian Harewood born in Dayton (1950)
95/1918	48/1997	Shotzie, Cincinnati Reds dog mascot, dies at age 9 (1991)
96/1941	47/1975	Actress Suzee Pai born in Toledo (1962)
96/1949	50/1972	Richard Nixon resigns presidency (1974)
97/1944	47/1972	Race riots in Cincinnati (1827)
96/1944	48/1965	Singer Eric Carmen born in Cleveland (1949)
99/1881	44/1967	Space shuttle Enterprise makes 1st atmospheric flight (1977)
95/2002	47/1982	Annie Oakley born in Drake Ohio (1860)
97/1944	46/1964	Actress Halle Berry born (1968)
96/1944	44/1962	Wayne County incorporated (1796)
96/1944	45/1979	Indians' Ray Chapman dies after being hit by pitch (1920)
99/1988	48/1971	World's 1st moon probe explodes (1958)
96/1947	46/1981	Actor Trey Ames born in Canton (1971)
100/1955	47/1964	Hurricane Diane kills 200 & 1st billion $ damage storm (N.E. US) (1955)
95/1947	46/1998	Benjamin Harrison born in North Bend, OH (1833)
96/1947	45/1950	Next total solar eclipse visible from North America (2017)
94/1936	45/1982	Hurricane Camille strikes U.S. Gulf Coast kills 255 (1969)
93/1914	48/1969	Mars's closest approach to Earth since the 10th century (1924)
94/1947	44/1952	-127 F (-88 C), Vostok, Antarctica (world record) (1960)
97/1948	45/1951	Voyager 2's closest approach to Saturn (1981)
97/1948	47/1958	19th Amendment adopted (1920)
102/1948	49/1963	Earliest recorded hurricane in U.S. (Jamestown, Virginia) (1667)
98/1953	42/1968	1st known photograph of a tornado made near Howard, SD (1884)
98/1953	38/1982	Inventor Charles F. Kettering born in Ohio (1876)
96/1953	45/1976	William H. Taft dies (1930)
99/1953	46/1890	Comet Howard-Koomur-Michels collides with the sun (1979)

Flora & Fauna AUGUST

WEEK 1 **BIRDS:** Juvenile hummingbirds and their parents begin to appear at local feeders as the young finally leave their thimble-sized nest. **WILDFLOWERS:** Evening primrose unfolds its pale-yellow petals at sunset to be pollinated by night-flying insects. Marsh mallow colors browning wetlands, and ironweed begins to offer its dark-blue flowers to frantic bees gathering the last of the season's pollen.

WEEK 2 **BIRDS:** Small flocks of American woodcocks begin to migrate toward America's southland. Green-wing teal and hooded merganser ducks begin to pass through northeastern Ohio and move south as well. **FLOWERING SHRUBS:** Staghorn sumac has set its ripened fuzzy red fruits. Native inhabitants and the pioneers that followed steeped a lemony tea rich in vitamin C from the fruits. Today, robins, thrashers, and other seed-eating birds take advantage of the bounty.

WEEK 3 **MAMMALS:** Coyotes and red foxes shift their diet to fresh fruits and insects as the richness of the season comes forth. Do field mice breathe a sigh of relief? **WILDFLOWERS:** New England aster, perhaps the most attractive of the fall asters, begins to bloom this week and continues through September. Its purple flowers with bright yellow centers set it apart from all others. Wingstem, a seven-foot-tall plant with a ragged yellow flower, begins to bloom in open fields and low wet places. When it has "set seed," the seeds contain a two-pronged spear. The seeds latch on to an animal host and travel far away from the parent plant.

WEEK 4 **BIRDS:** Nighthawks form "staging" flocks to prepare for their autumn migration. By Labor Day, most nighthawks will be gone from our skies. Migrants this week include Cape May, Tennessee, magnolia, and blackburnian warblers on their way to the tropics. Migrating shorebirds at Baldwin Lake's mudflats may include Caspian terns, dowitchers, semipalmated and pectoral sandpipers, and lesser yellowlegs. **WILDFLOWERS:** Poison ivy and deadly nightshade set fruit this week. Chickadees, not affected by the oils, eagerly search for the white poison ivy berries as they ripen. Bottle gentian, an extremely rare and protected plant, begins to bloom at protected places near water.

Adapted from the Nature Almanac by Robert Hinkle, with permission from Cleveland Metroparks.

YOU'D BE AMAZED AT WHAT YOU CAN SEE IN AUGUST

August 12 and 13 bring the Perseids meteor shower. It is best viewed at a dark location. Ttake a friend and a lounge chair, face toward the northeast, and just look up. You will see the oldest rocks in our solar system burning from their high-speed entry into Earth's protective atmosphere (without it, not only could we not breathe, but Earth would resemble our pock-marked moon). Best viewed late in the evening.

Late August gives us a stellar treat that is easy to find. After the sun has set, wait till ten o'clock, face directly south, and, with binoculars, look a quarter of the way up from the horizon (25 degrees), and there you should see stars and clouds. Be patient, pan around, and you will see them. These are the stars and nebulas of the Milky Way.

Courtesy of Jay Reynolds, Schuele Planetarium director, Lake Erie Nature and Science Center.

Racing Cows

by Neil Zurcher

They call horse racing the Sport of Kings, but what do they call cow racing? That's right, cow racing. It happens every year at the Great Geauga County Fair in Burton, Ohio.

I have seen dog races, sheep races, even pig races, but cow races?

Cows don't run, you say? If you have ever been on a farm trying to round up a young heifer who doesn't want to leave the pasture, you know that cows can not only run, they can usually outrun a human.

There are a few rules. First, no bull. I mean it—they do not allow bulls in their races, only female cows are permitted. The race is on a one-mile course, but there doesn't seem to be any penalty if the cow, during the race, stops to graze or should wander into the infield. The cows must cross the finish line. Now this may sound easy, but most of the entrants just don't get the idea of going through a line of cones that mark the finish line. In fact, several usually have to be led through.

Cows seem to have a mind of their own when it comes to racing. Some lope along in a fairly straight line and then get distracted and head for the fence or for a nearby watering trough, despite the urging of the farmer-jockey on their back. Others just don t like to be told where to go. If the rider wants to go north, the cow will often decide it wants to go south. Cows are also not accustomed to having saddles on their backs and have been known to leave the race, find a fence post, and try to rub off the saddle and anything that might be sitting in the saddle.

But if the race does go well and the cows stay reasonably on the track, or at least within the park itself, the big finale of the contest can also be a problem. I speak of crossing the finish line.

Now if you have ever spent any time around dairy cattle you probably know that when they get frisky and start running, you can usually stop or at least redirect them by stepping into their path. Cows, unlike bulls, buffalo, horses, goats, and even small children, won't try to run you down. They will usually turn away. Which may explain some of the problems they have getting the cows to finally cross a finish line. Because that is the place where there are people milling around—judges, photographers with cameras flashing, and of course, the crowd, cheering. It s enough to make the poor cow turn around and run back to the barn. (Which some of them have been known to do.)

Watching a cow race is what you might call an udderly mooving experience. The couple that started the whole thing has a motto, "Don't milk them, race them."

Pete Ondrus and his wife, Barb Lambert, of Carson City, Michigan, sold their 500-head dairy farm herd in 1996 when they decided to retire from farming. They were looking for something fun to do that would include their knowledge of dairy cows. They decided that racing cows might be just what they were looking for and at the same time would promote agriculture. So they founded the Mid-Michigan Cow Racing Association, known as the MMCRA, and they also organized the World-Wide Cow Racing Association, or the WWCRA. (You know, everybody goes by initials these days, the NFL, the NBA the WWA, so why not the WWCRA?) They declared they would sponsor the "Udder Race."

In 2003, the Udder Race was won by a Vermont heifer by the name of Little Witch. She crossed the finish line in a blazing 7:31:54.

By the way, Dusty Roads, owned by Ondrus and Lambert, came in a distant fifth in the race with a speed of 13:57:61. The jockey could have probably walked faster. In fact, that speed sounds a bit like the times turned in at Dick Goddard's annual Woollybear Festival races in Vermilion. Which is about as fast as watching paint dry.

Cow racing may not compete with the Kentucky Derby or even Woollybear Racing, but it does attract crowds. Geauga County Fair officials said that on the day of the cow races several thousand people line up starting in the afternoon to get the available seats in the grandstands. Usually the crowd spills over all along the racetrack.

The jockeys are mostly area farmers who don't usually ride their cows. Perhaps that explains an apparent lack of control over the bovines. The breed seems to make little difference. Everything from a black-and-white Holstein to a buttermilk-colored Jersey heifer has been entered in the race. Size also doesn't seem to matter. Dusty Roads, the huge Holstein owned by Ondrus and Lambert, has won her share of races, but at the event we witnessed Dusty Roads was left in the Geauga County dust by a smallish Guernsey heifer by the name of Starlite. And, as one jockey-farmer put it, even if the cow doesn't win you can still milk her or even eat her. Try doing that with a woollybear caterpillar.

THE GREAT GEAUGA COUNTY FAIR
PO Box 402
Burton, Ohio 44021
440-834-1846
www.geaugafair.com

THE WORLD WIDE COW-RACING ASSOCIATION
Pete Ondrus & Barb Lambert
9517 South Warner Road
Carson City, Michigan 48611
989-584-6286
www.cowrace.com

Neil Zurcher was the longtime host of "One Tank Trips" on FOX 8 and is the author of four books: *One Tank Trips, More One Tank Trips, One Tank Trips Road Food*, and *Ohio Oddities*.

Observed the 3rd Saturday in October, **Sweetest Day originated in Cleveland in 1922**. Herbert Birch Kingston, a philanthropist and candy company employee, wanted to bring happiness into the lives of orphans, shut-ins, and others who were forgotten. With the help of friends, he distributed candy and small gifts to the underprivileged.

Source: www.theromantic.com/sweetestday.htm

The Job of Being God

By Dick Goddard

With the world population now around 6.4 billion and growing every day, the percentage of ne'er-do-wells and sinners must be rising exponentially. This makes the job of being God tougher and tougher.

The wisdom of children can never be underestimated, and when third graders in California were asked to explain the job of being God, the results were heavenly:

One of God's main jobs is making people. He makes them to replace the ones that die so there will be enough people to take care of things on earth.

He doesn't make grown-ups, just babies. I think that's because they are smaller and easier to make. That way he doesn't have to take up his valuable time teaching them to walk and talk. He can just leave that to mothers and fathers.

God's second most important job is listening to prayers. An awful lot of this goes on, since some people, like preachers and things, pray at times beside bedtime.

God doesn't have time to listen to the radio or TV because of this.

Because he hears everything there must be a terrible lot of noise in his ears, unless he has thought of a way to turn it off.

God sees everything and hears everything and is everywhere, which keeps him pretty busy. So you shouldn't go wasting his time by going over your mom and dad's head asking for something they said you couldn't have.

Atheists are people who don't believe in God. I don't think there are any in Chula Vista. At least there aren't any who come to our church.

Jesus is God's son. He used to do all the hard work like walking on water and performing miracles and trying to teach the people who didn't want to learn about God. They finally got tired of him preaching to them and they crucified him.

But he was good and kind like his father and he told his father they didn't know what they were doing and to forgive them and God said, "OK."

His dad (God) appreciated everything that he had done and all his hard work on earth so he told him he didn't have to go out on the road anymore. He could stay in heaven. So he did. And now he helps his dad out by listening to prayers and seeing which things are important for God to take care of and which ones he can take care of himself without having to bother God. Like a secretary, only more important.

You can pray anytime you want and they are sure to hear you because they got it worked out so one of them is on duty all the time.

You should always go to church on Sunday because it makes God happy, and if there's anybody you want to make happy it's God.

Don't skip church to do something you think will be more fun like going to the beach. This is wrong! And, besides, the sun doesn't come out at the beach until noon anyway.

If you don't believe in God, besides being an atheist, you will be very lonely, because your parents can't go everywhere with you, like to camp, but God can.

It's good to know that he's around you when you're scared in the dark or when you can't swim very good and you get thrown into real deep water by the big kids.

But you shouldn't just always think of what God can do for you. I figure God put me here and he can take me back anytime he pleases.

And that's why I believe in God.

If I have any beliefs about immortality it is that certain dogs I have known will go to heaven, and very, very few persons.

— James Thurber

A man content to go to heaven alone will never go to heaven.

— Boethius

You must believe in God in spite of what the clergy say.

— Benjamin Jowett

THE HEAT INDEX

The Heat Index serves as a diagnostic measure of the combination of temperature and relative humidity. The resulting "apparent" temperature (when the meteorologist says "it feels like . . .") gives an estimation of what the hot, humid air feels like to the average person.

Exceptional heat indices (which can endanger your life) occur mostly during the muggy summer months. The abundance of moisture and increased heat keeps you perspiring, which is your body's involuntary attempt to cool itself. Those with health concerns should keep a close eye on the heat index during prolonged spells of hot weather, as dehydration and heat exhaustion are very serious matters.

APPARENT TEMPERATURE READINGS

Caution: 85° to 94° F
Physical activity can cause fatigue.

Extreme Caution: 95° to 105° F
Possible heat cramps and/or heat exhaustion with lengthy exposure to the heat.

Danger: Above 105° F
Conditions for heat stroke if exposure to heat is prolonged; heat exhaustion and heat cramps likely.

DATES WHEN CLEVELAND'S TEMPERATURE REACHED 100°

June 25, 1988 (104°)
July 27, 1941 (103°)
August 27, 1948 (102°)
September 1–3, 1953 (101°)
June 28, 1944 (101°)
July 16, 1988 (100°)
August 19, 1955 (100°)
June 28, 1934 (100°)
August 6, 1918 (100°)

HEAT INDEX CHART

Temp	Relative Humidity (%)								
(°F)	90.0	80.0	70.0	60.0	50.0	40.0	30.0	20.0	10.0
65	65.6	64.7	63.8	62.8	61.9	60.9	60.0	59.1	58.1
70	71.6	70.7	69.8	68.8	67.9	66.9	66.0	65.1	64.1
75	79.7	76.7	75.8	74.8	73.9	72.9	72.0	71.1	70.1
80	88.2	85.9	84.2	82.8	81.6	80.4	79.0	77.4	76.1
85	101.4	97.0	93.3	90.3	87.7	85.5	83.5	81.6	79.6
90	119.3	112.0	105.8	100.5	96.1	92.3	89.2	86.5	84.2
95	141.8	131.1	121.7	113.6	106.7	100.9	96.1	92.2	89.2
100	168.7	154.0	140.9	129.5	119.6	111.2	104.2	98.7	94.4
105	200.0	180.7	163.4	148.1	134.7	123.2	113.6	105.8	100.0

Source: National Oceanic and Atmosphere Agency

{DICK'S PET OF THE YEAR}

JESSIE

BY JOY WALTERS

In her brief life, Jessie, a year-old shepherd-husky mix, has had to deal with trauma that would be hard for the most stoic human being to endure. When she was barely six months old, Jessie tried to cross Euclid Avenue with two other dogs. A motorist slowed to let the other dogs cross, but for some reason, when Jessie passed in front of the car, the driver sped up and hit her. Even though her left leg was badly shattered, Jessie managed to pull herself out from under the car before the driver sped away. She dragged herself down to Wade Lagoon, where she hid under a bush. Luckily, a Good Samaritan saw Jessie get hit and followed her down the hill to the pond. At great peril to her own safety, Bonnie Goddin brought Jessie back up and from there tried to find someone to care for the badly injured animal. Frustrated at repeated refusals of help from other humane organizations, Ms. Goddin called PAWS (Public Animal Welfare Society) and finally found the help she needed. She was told to take the dog to Gateway Animal Clinic, where she named the dog "Maverick" and through media exposure was able to collect enough money to facilitate medical care. Joy Walters, a member of PAWS, spotted the injured dog on local television and contacted the organization with an offer to foster and rehabilitate her. Although never a believer in love at first sight, Joy says, "As soon as I saw Maverick at Gateway I knew I'd never be able to give her up. It was almost like she was meant to be mine."

"It's been a process," Joy says. "The vet at Gateway told me the dog's leg looked like someone hit a chicken bone with a hammer." Joy took the dog home, renamed her Jessie, and began the long road of rehabilitating Jessie and teaching her to trust that not everyone possessed the mentality of the person who deliberately ran her over. Joy and her family officially adopted Jessie in January, and Joy continues to volunteer for PAWS.

"Jessie is a quiet, calm dog," Joy continues. "She is highly protective of me, but enjoys playing with her two canine sisters, a golden retriever named Mollie and an energetic springer named Cady. She also has made a few appearances for PAWS at PetSmart Adoptathons and at rescue/humane organization gatherings."

Jessie had more surgery to reconstruct her leg in July of 2004. The veterinarian who performed the surgery, Dr. Jeff Fogle of Richfield Animal Care, has hopes that Jessie will be able to use the leg almost normally, even if she never challenges a greyhound to a footrace. Donations through PAWS for Jessie's care have made her surgeries possible and have given her a chance at a normal life that she would otherwise not have had.

"If we were going to take a stray dog into our home," Joy says, "we were very lucky it was Jessie. She gets along with our other dogs and has become a trusting, almost friendly animal. Through our travels, she's met small children, other dogs, and even cats and has never shown any aggressive or undesirable tendencies. I wouldn't hesitate to take her anywhere. I love her with all my heart and I thank God that Bonnie was there to put the chain of events into motion that saved Jessie's life and bought her to us." ■

STORM SAFETY Lightning

Lightning kills more people in the U.S. each year than hurricanes and tornadoes combined. Eighty percent of those struck by lightning are male. Two of every three live to tell their story. Victims often recall these sensations just prior to the strike: a tingling sensation in the hands and feet, hair standing on end, and a pungent smell of sulfur. If you realize that you have suddenly become a human lightning rod, immediately drop to your knees, cover your head with your hands, and curl up into a tight ball.

Many victims who have been struck and appear to be dead can be revived with artificial respiration (CPR). The body does not carry an electric charge after being struck. If the victim is not breathing and has no pulse, CPR must be given within four to six minutes in order to prevent irreversible brain damage.

LIGHTNING SAFETY RULES:

1. A home or large building offers good protection. Avoid using the telephone and stay away from open doors, windows, and all plugged-in electrical appliances.
2. Automobiles (but not convertibles) with windows rolled up offer good protection. Stay off of and away from lawn mowers, tractors, motorcycles, scooters, bicycles, and golf carts.
3. Avoid wide-open areas such as beaches, football and baseball fields, and golf courses. Avoid hilltops and high ground; seek out a ravine or low ground. Avoid isolated tall objects such as trees and poles. In a heavily wooded area, seek shelter on low ground under a thick growth of small trees. Stay away from wire fences, railroad tracks, and all metal objects.
4. Swimmers should immediately leave the water. Boats should be taken ashore. If you are caught far from shore in an electrical storm, curl into a ball and stay low in the boat.

NORTHEAST OHIO RECORDS
listed in *Guinness World Records*

CUYAHOGA COUNTY

Longest Dance Party: The "Heart Health Hop," a dance party marathon organized by St. Joseph Aspirin and held at the Rock and Roll Hall of Fame and Museum in Cleveland, Ohio, USA, began on July 29, 2003, with 42 dancers—41 of which completed the marathon after 52 hours 3 minutes on July 31, 2003.

Greatest Winning Margin In An NBA Game: The greatest winning margin in a National Basketball Association (NBA) game is 68 points, when the Cleveland Cavaliers beat the Miami Heat, 148-80 on December 17, 1991.

Longest Car Ownership From New: Eugene Stenger of Orange Village near Cleveland, Ohio, USA, bought his white 1954 Chevrolet Corvette on April 5, 1954, and has owned it ever since. The original price was $3,577.85.

Oldest Person To Perform A Solo Skydive: The oldest solo skydiver is retired pilot Herb Tanner, of Mayfield Heights, Ohio, USA. On June 19, 1998, aged 92, he jumped unassisted from a single-engined plane above Cleveland, Ohio, USA. It had been a lifelong ambition of Tanner's to complete a parachute jump, but his wife had always discouraged it. She died two years prior to Tanner's jump.

ERIE COUNTY

Fastest Roller Coaster: The world's fastest roller coaster is Top Thrill Dragster, a hydraulically launched 'strata-coaster' at Cedar Point, Sandusky, Ohio, USA, which reaches its maximum speed of 193 km/h (120 mph) just four seconds after launch. The ride, which opened in May 2003, is 128 m (420 ft) tall, 853 m (2,800 ft) long, and cost $25 million to build.

HURON COUNTY

Largest Free-Standing Illuminated Star

Dale Gasteier built a 15.8-m (52-ft) long star structure which stands 23.16 m (76 ft) on its support tower, illuminated with 1,000 lights to celebrate American Thanksgiving holiday in Bellevue, Ohio, on June 20, 1998.

MAHONING COUNTY

Largest Chicken Dance: Organizers of the Canfield Fair in Ohio, USA, hatched a plan. At 3 p.m. on September 1, 1996, rides were paused and vendors stopped business. Then a record-breaking crowd of 72,000 did their thing. "It seems to be a tradition in this area of Ohio to chicken dance at weddings," laughs William J. Kish, who's the attorney for the Canfield fairground. The Canfield Fair's mascot also happens to be a rooster! One fanatic even turned up in a chicken suit!

Largest Irish Dance: A total of 6,971 people danced a ceilidh (a traditional Irish dance, pronounced kay-lay) for five minutes at the Dublin Irish Festival, Dublin, Ohio, USA, on August 1, 1998. Participants were led in the dance by professional ceilidh callers, and Irish bands played traditional jigs.

SUMMIT COUNTY

Heaviest Bed Of Nails: Lee Graber of Tallmadge, Ohio, USA, endured the weight of the heaviest bed of nails on his body. He was sandwiched between two beds of nails, with a weight of 752.5 kg (1,659 lb) placed on top for a total of 10 seconds on June 24, 2000. The weight was loaded on top of him using a crane. The most difficult aspect was controlling his breathing as he had a lot of weight on his chest and he needed to relax to avoid bursting a blood vessel in his head.

Source: www.guinnessworldrecords.com

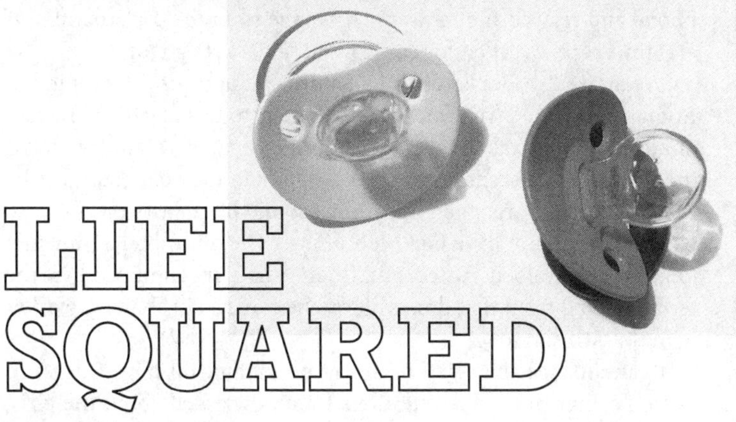

LIFE SQUARED

By Bill Martin

Humorist and author Sam Levenson (1911–1980) once wrote, "Somewhere on this globe, every ten seconds there is a woman giving birth to a child. She must be found and stopped."

I have twins. Twin girls to be exact. You see, twins are not just two little people (the girls are almost seven), but in point of fact, twins are very much like a nuclear blast, an exploding volcano, a tidal wave. That's why Sam Levenson got it right.

Now, don't get me wrong, I love my girls, but twins are just different. That's why we have Twins Days in Twinsburg to celebrate life squared.

The odd part in this equation is that my wife and I adopted the girls from Romania. Adoption is a wonderful process that allows the man to experience the pain of childbirth. Anyone who's ever dealt with the INS knows what I mean. You fill out a form, write a check, and wait for some bureaucrat to stamp the form. Then you start all over again. INS might stand for "I Know Saints"—they are the people who are called to adoption.

I remember the day our caseworker called and said, "We have twin girls. Are you interested?" I called my wife, Judy, on the cell phone and relayed the message. After she spun the car around several times and wrestled for control she said, "Let's go for it."

We arrived in Bucharest on a Saturday. Bucharest, the capital of Romania, is an old worn-out city with scars to this day from the revolution. We were taken to the train station very early Sunday morning. It was like a scene from an old Bergman movie, except for the McDonald's. A burger and fries didn't sound like a tasty meal at 7:30 a.m. (They did not have Egg McMuffins.) The trains had a romantic look to them, albeit rusted out. There was a morning mist in the terminal, and from that dreamlike scene came an orphanage worker with the twins in tow.

I can still see that picture in my mind, and I'll never forget it. Which brings me to the questions I am now asked about the girls, who are identical, by the way. "Do they ever get themselves mixed up?" "Are they the same age?" "Were they born on the same day?" In an article from a 1908 *New York Times*, Mark Twain wrote, "What a fine thing it is to have an intellect, and room enough in the seat of your breeches to hold it."

If you are a twin, apologize to your parents. Please go say you're sorry. Buy them some flowers or a nice dinner. Better yet, a nice, quiet getaway. If you're considering adopting a child, there is no more incredible gift—go for it. If you have adopted a child, thank you.

My house is filled with noise, a wonderful noise. I forgot to mention we also have a dog, cat, rabbit, turtle, and two horses. The horses, by the way, are not twins.

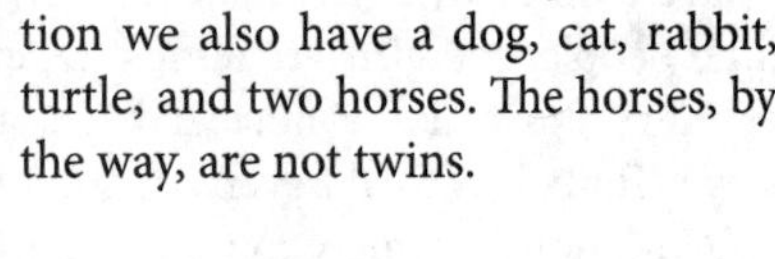

Bill Martin is the co-anchor of FOX 8 News at Noon and FOX 8 News at Five. Martin is a multiple winner of Emmy and Associated Press awards for excellence in broadcast journalism, and was inducted into the Ohio Television/Radio Hall of Fame in 1999. Martin lives in North Olmsted with his wife Judy and daughters Katie, Ibolya, and Otilia.

SEPTEMBER STATISTICS

(recorded at Cleveland Hopkins Airport)

SUNSHINE %	60
DRIEST MONTH	0.48"/1908
WARMEST MONTH	72.4°/1881
COLDEST MONTH	58.2°/1918
LIQUID PCPN AVG.	3.44"
RAINIEST DAY	5.24"/1996
RAINIEST MONTH	11.05"/1996
THUNDERY DAYS	3
SNOWIEST DAY	TRACE/1993
DAYS ONE INCH SNOW	0

A magnificent, yet melancholy, sight as this month goes by is the southward migration of those big and beautiful orange, black, and white monarch butterflies. One of the few insects to migrate (Ohio's green darner dragonfly is another), the fragile monarchs are known to fly 50 miles every day, sometimes up to 200 miles if a blustery cold front cooperates. This incredible odyssey will take the butterflies some 3,000 miles from Ohio, to such exotic places as Mexico's Quintana Roo (on the Yucatan Peninsula), a place they have never been. The departure of the monarch and the green darner, as much as the migration of birds, foretells the early-morning frosts that are just ahead.

The autumnal equinox (from Latin meaning "equal night") occurs around the 22nd. At the equinox each place on earth shares in 12 hours of darkness and 12 hours of light, and with the diminishing duration of sunlight, temperatures of 85° are seldom experienced after the 15th of the month. September did establish a Cleveland benchmark for extreme heat in 1953, when the high temperature on each of the first three days of the month hit a sizzling 101°F.

September 24, 1950, will forever be remembered as Dark Sunday throughout Ohio. The cause was ash and smoke from a major forest fire in Canada's Alberta province. September 29th is St. Michael's Day; folklore says that if there has been a heavy fall of acorns (mast), a very hard, cold winter is ahead.

JAN FEB MAR APR MAY JUN JUL AUG SEP OCT NOV DEC

DAILY DATA FOR SEPTEMBER

Date	Day	Moon	Day of Year	Days Left	Sunrise	Sunset	Length of Day	Avg. Hi°	Avg. Lo°	Avg. Lake°
1	Thu		244	121	6:53	7:59	13:06	78	58	73
2	Fri		245	120	6:54	7:58	13:04	78	58	73
3	Sat	●	246	119	6:55	7:56	13:01	77	58	73
4	Sun		247	118	6:56	7:54	12:58	77	57	72
5	Mon		248	117	6:57	7:53	12:56	77	57	72
6	Tue		249	116	6:58	7:51	12:53	77	57	72
7	Wed		250	115	6:59	7:49	12:50	76	57	72
8	Thu		251	114	7:00	7:48	12:48	76	57	72
9	Fri		252	113	7:01	7:46	12:45	76	56	72
10	Sat		253	112	7:02	7:44	12:42	75	56	72
11	Sun	◐	254	111	7:03	7:42	12:39	75	56	72
12	Mon		255	110	7:04	7:41	12:37	75	56	72
13	Tue		256	109	7:05	7:39	12:34	75	55	72
14	Wed		257	108	7:06	7:37	12:31	74	55	71
15	Thu		258	107	7:07	7:36	12:29	74	55	71
16	Fri		259	106	7:08	7:34	12:26	74	54	71
17	Sat		260	105	7:09	7:32	12:23	73	54	70
18	Sun	○	261	104	7:10	7:30	12:20	73	54	70
19	Mon		262	103	7:11	7:29	12:18	73	53	70
20	Tue		263	102	7:12	7:27	12:15	72	53	70
21	Wed		264	101	7:13	7:25	12:12	72	53	69
22	Thu		265	100	7:14	7:24	12:10	72	52	69
23	Fri		266	99	7:15	7:22	12:07	71	52	69
24	Sat		267	98	7:16	7:20	12:04	71	52	69
25	Sun	◑	268	97	7:17	7:18	12:01	70	51	68
26	Mon		269	96	7:18	7:17	11:59	70	51	68
27	Tue		270	95	7:19	7:15	11:56	70	51	68
28	Wed		271	94	7:20	7:13	11:53	69	50	68
29	Thu		272	93	7:21	7:11	11:50	69	50	67
30	Fri		273	92	7:23	7:10	11:47	69	49	67

Rec. Hi°	Rec. Lo°	On This Date . . .
101/1953	42/1970	Baseball season ends due to WW I (1918)
101/1953	45/1970	Rock and Roll Hall of Fame opens (1995)
101/1953	44/1976	Dirigible Shenandoah crashed near Caldwell Ohio, 13 die (1925)
95/1953	41/1946	U.S. authorizes Agency for International Development (1961)
99/1954	44/1974	Indians stage 1st "I hate the Yankee Hanky Night" (1977)
98/1954	40/1976	Actor Otto Kruger born in Toledo (1885)
94/1939	43/1962	Severance Hall dedicated (1931)
95/1978	41/1951	Ohio Senator Robert A. Taft born (1889)
94/1959	44/1986	Musician Macy Gray born in Canton (1970)
93/1964	39/1883	W. 117th St. sewer explosion (1953)
92/1952	42/1995	World Trade Center disaster (2001)
98/1952	40/1943	Indians sweep Yanks at Muni. Stad; largest AL crowd: 86,563 (1954)
96/1952	38/1964	Author Sherwood Anderson born in Camden, Ohio (1876)
94/1939	37/1975	President William McKinley dies in Buffalo (1901)
93/1991	37/1871	Mayflower departs from Plymouth, England (1620)
96/1944	45/1979	Cleveland Rams play 1st NFL game, beat Phila. 35-10 (1650)
95/1955	37/1984	19 students attend opening class at OSU (1873)
94/1955	39/1959	Indians clinch AL pennant, beat Tigers (3-2) (1954)
93/1955	40/1973	James A. Garfield dies (1881)
92/1978	40/1956	Washington D.C. abolishes slave trade (1850)
90/1931	35/1956	Sandra Day O'Connor 1st female Supreme Court Justice (1981)
92/1895	36/1904	Indians pitcher Bob Lemon born (1920)
88/1936	36/1995	1st female pres. candiate Victoria Chaflin Woodhull born in Ohio (1838)
87/1941	36/1995	1st Supreme Court of the U.S. established (1789)
88/1900	35/1976	Columbus sails on 2nd voyage to America (1493)
89/1908	37/1947	FCC formed (1914)
88/1946	33/1947	Actor Greg Morris born in Cleveland (1934)
89/1949	34/1984	Euclid Beach Park closes forever (1969)
95/1953	32/1942	1st congress adjourns (1789)
86/1881	35/1963	Ohio Turnpike opens (1955)

Flora & Fauna SEPTEMBER

WEEK 1 **BIRDS:** Shortly behind the nighthawk migration the chimney swifts also leave. Among September stopovers, look for large, orange-billed Caspian terns, semipalmated plovers, greater and lesser yellowlegs, great egrets, and hundreds of killdeers. Small sandpipers, called "peeps," are difficult to identify, but fun to watch as they probe the soft mud in search of tiny invertebrates. **INSECTS:** The fall monarch butterfly migration will sweep through the North Coast sometime in the next three weeks. These migrants make their way to mountaintop retreats in central Mexico each fall, then return in the spring. Check New England aster stems for preying mantises, waiting for unwary butterflies and bees.

WEEK 2 **BIRDS:** Although most warblers are in their confusing fall colors, watch for blackburnian, hooded, Tennessee, Cape May, and magnolia warblers in forested areas. They feed and rest by day and migrate south by night all the way to Central and South America. **WILDFLOWERS:** Cardinal flowers reach the peak of bloom this week. The vibrant red flowers dot many marshes and river edges. A stroll through any unmowed meadow reveals the beauties of gray goldenrod, gentians, great lobelia, and turtlehead. **TREES:** Ohio buckeye nuts are ripe! Can you find them before the squirrels do? Look for the polished-looking "buck's eye" beneath the tough green husk. A good crop of hickory nuts, acorns, and other "mast" may take the squirrels away from your bird feeders starting this week. To your delight (or dismay) they will soon return!

WEEK 3 **BIRDS:** Hummingbirds may still be flitting around your flower garden if the days have not grown too cold, but most will be gone by the end of this month. Their migration includes a nonstop trip of over 500 miles across the Gulf of Mexico! Our winter "snow birds," dark-eyed juncos, begin to appear at many feeders beginning this week. Legend says that they appear just before the first snow of winter and leave after the last snow of spring. Their timing is considerably off, fortunately. Flocks of robins increase their numbers daily as they prepare for migration. Fall-ripened crab apples are a favorite high-energy food. **WILDFLOWERS:** New England aster, perhaps the most beautiful of all fall asters, begins to bloom this week. The bright yellow center is surrounded by deep-purple petals, making a lovely contrast of colors in the fall landscape. Ironweed's bright indigo flowers top its stems at heights of five feet or more in fields and meadows. Look for it among the bright yellows of goldenrods blooming nearby. **TREES AND SHRUBS:** The first blush of autumn colors is now found on sumacs, sassafras, red and sugar maples, tulip trees, ashes, and dogwoods.

WEEK 4 **BIRDS:** Grackles gather in flocks numbering in the thousands as they prepare for migration. They may be joined by cowbirds and red-winged blackbirds as well. The woods grow silent as most nonresident songbirds leave for warmer climates. Cardinals and robins still serenade the dawn. White-throated sparrows begin to appear this week on their annual migration from Canada to warmer climates. Listen to their half-hearted "old Sam Peabody-Peabody-Peabody" calls.

Adapted from the Nature Almanac by Robert Hinkle, with permission from Cleveland Metroparks.

YOU'D BE AMAZED AT WHAT YOU CAN SEE IN SEPTEMBER

September 10 has a first quarter next to a very orange star called Antares, which is the heart of the constellation Scorpio. Antares is associated with the planet Mars because they are both about the same color and the same brightness, so it is easy to get them confused. Scorpio (Scorpius) is a late-summer constellation, but the beautiful tall trees of our area tend to cover up Scorpio's long tail. A clear view to the south makes Scorpio plainly visible.

Courtesy of Jay Reynolds, Schuele Planetarium director, Lake Erie Nature and Science Center.

Clifford (l) and Clarence (r)

My Two Boys: Brotherly Love

BY WILMA SMITH

Be still, my heart! What a delightful duo. Their full given names are Clifford Huntington and Clarence Charleston—Cliffy and Clary to those who love them. Frankly, to know them is to love them.

Where do I begin their story? How about with their arrival into our lives? Actually, my husband, Tom, was the one who delivered our first "baby." It was painless, and seems like it was just yesterday. I actually wish it were just yesterday so that we could have their friendship and companionship even longer. This is how those fateful days evolved for us and our babies . . . our little guys!

It began, actually, on a Friday night on my arrival home after the ten o'clock news. Tom was sitting in a chair at the end of a long hallway that I could see as I entered our home.

"Hi, honey, welcome home," he said. "Wilma, you have to come in here right away. I have a little job for this weekend."

As I walked toward him I thought I noticed an extra pair of eyes sheepishly looking at me. I was curious now.

As I stood there in front of him I remember hearing a long, "Ahaaaaa" come out of my mouth.

"Who is that?" I asked.

"Well, he's just visiting us for the weekend," he said. But I knew better than that and I knew that my husband did too!

As the puppy slowly and sadly, as if on cue, looked at me, I thought that with those long ears he certainly did not look like a sheltie.

"Honey, I think that's a beagle, not a sheltie!"

"Well, this guy was rescued, and that's what I was told," Tom answered laughingly.

You see, dear reader, a friend of his had driven through a neighboring state, where she found the little guy abandoned. She knew we were possibly looking for a sheltie puppy and that we loved animals, so that's how she baited the trap.

I say that thankfully now. She cleverly knew all along, of course, that the dog was a beagle but thought that the other description would get Tom to come and see him at her home on that Friday evening.

So, that's how our new little friend came to "visit" for the weekend.

Clifford was very ill when we first got him. We found out that he had received no care after he was born.

The next day we took him to the vet and discovered a number of ailments, poor little guy. I'll tell you, I remember that as the vet handed him over to me in his carrier, he looked at me through the cage door with such sad but thankful eyes. They seemed to say in soft, soulful tones, "thank you for helping me."

It's difficult to believe that was eight years ago. Needless to say, he won our hearts that weekend and continues to share their lives to this day.

Clifford Huntington is his name and now you know why. Huntington, West Virginia, as you may know, is a nice place, and he sounds very distinguished with that middle name, don't you think? Little "Cliffy," a gentle, sweet soul who never wants to do anything at all wrong. His job is to please and love. What a guy! My baby!

Fast forward to a few months later. The scene: Fox 8. The time: Between newscasts. The situation: another arrival . . . a little brother!!

"Wilma, your husband is downstairs and needs to speak with you," I was told in the newsroom.

Isn't it funny how when the phone rings unexpectedly late at night or if someone comes to your door unexpectedly, for a second or two you get a sinking feeling that something may be wrong? Well, as I went down the steps to meet Tom, I remember hoping everything was fine.

My, Tom looked like he was wearing a really big padded jacket. Turns out, he had another little friend with him for me to meet. Peeking out of his jacket were two little eyes. He put the puppy (you knew it was one) on the ground, and I'll tell you I have never seen such a rotund puppy. He had no visible personality, just stood there and it seemed he had absolutely no curiosity about people. He just waddled around the area.

"He was abandoned too, and the person who found him thought that since we loved Cliffy so much maybe we could find a good home for this one too."

"He's coming home for the weekend," Tom told me.

You found him a home? I thought. Would someone think even for a moment that we would actually consider giving him to someone else?

I wasn't sure, since at that point we had two cats and Clifford. These were all animals that held a prominent place inside our home and our hearts. They have so much to add to our lives. They help in so many ways to make a house a home. I hope *you* know that too, firsthand, or that you will one day soon.

Well, our chubby but still so little fellow "came home for the weekend." That was about seven years ago.

It turns out this little guy was found abandoned outside in the cold winter weather and his siblings were frozen. He was our sweet and so-frightened survivor. Thus, the birth of Clarence Charleston. As it turns out, he became a survivor yet another time in his journey through our lives. You may remember a few years ago when I reported a news story on Fox 8 about a coyote attacking my dog. That truly was one momentous day in my life and in the life of my little guy, Clarence.

It was a sunny January Sunday, about one o'clock in the afternoon. Who would have known what waited outside our door?

The dogs had to go out for a visit to their "bathroom." Nothing seemed unusual, that is, until they went outside. Maybe it was the beagle in them and their natural instinct toward hunting. Usually they stayed right by the door, but this time Clifford and Clarence ran to the side of the house, out of my sight, to the garage side of our home. By the time I could get there, even though I rushed as quickly as I could, it seemed like an eternity had passed. Actually, it was probably less than a minute. When I got to the other side of the house, where they had run in a frenzy, they were already out of sight, down a ravine but still within sight when I peered over. There was loud, extensive barking and fighting, and I could see that there were three animals involved. One of the animals was a tawny, long-haired, skinny street-fighter-type dog with its tail down, and very aggressive.

I screamed for what seemed like endless minutes, to little avail.

Then there was a quick visit up the ravine from Clifford, who barked and looked at me as if to say, "Help!! Do something else, Mom."

I screamed for what seemed like endless minutes, to little avail.

Clifford ran back down to his brother and the angry visitor.

I threw stones, wood . . . whatever I could find, without really thinking. I didn't want to hit my babies but I was at my wit's end, with my heart beating overtime as I desperately kept yelling. As I went back looking for something else to throw, there was silence.

Now I was really afraid.

Clifford came back and I remember saying, "Good boy. Where's your brother?" Then a few moments later, Clarence began walking toward me. "Clarence, baby . . . Thank God," I said.

His eyes looked glassy, and as he walked by me as if in a trance, I was startled to see, as he passed me, that his backside was all bloody.

I got a towel. I wrapped him up, and though my hands were shaking and I couldn't think straight, I somehow found my vet's phone number. Thank God she was home that Sunday afternoon and said she would meet me at her office.

Clarence was so docile. He sat on the passenger seat wrapped in extra towels. He seemed like a shell-shocked little soldier . . . so afraid but trying to be brave. **Continued on page 172**

{DICK'S **ANIMAL** OF THE YEAR}

THE BLACK SQUIRREL

BY DICK GODDARD

Over the years I have had more and more calls at Fox 8 about black squirrels.

When they first appeared in Northeast Ohio in February of 1961 many thought that they were a species of skunk that had somehow lost their distinctive white stripes. The blacks have continued to thrive, overrunning and driving out the red, gray, and fox squirrels.

Our black squirrels were brought to the campus of Kent State University from Canada 44 years ago by Larry Woodell, the KSU superintendent of grounds and M. W. Staples, a retired executive from the Davey Tree Company. Since then the black squirrels have taken over the Kent campus, and the Black Squirrel Festival, which began in 1981, is an annual daylong event held at the Student Center Plaza. There's a barbeque bash, along with live bands and local artisans.

The Erie Islands are rife with black squirrels, no doubt arriving as stowaways on recreational craft from Canada.

Black is considered the "normal" color of squirrels in the Canadian provinces of both Ontario and Quebec.

Black squirrels have moved steadily southward in the United States and are now found in Florida.

At Syracuse University in New York the coal-colored bushy-tails have grown fat and feisty on a menu of college students' castoffs from Taco Bells and McDonalds.

An Albion, Indiana, fan of the dark squirrels says that he has found them to be friendlier than the others, and more likely to feed out of your hand (be careful, since squirrels have four self-sharpening incisors, along with from 16 to 18 other teeth).

Few can deny that squirrels are cute and comical, but they are considered to be harmful nuisances to farmers and gardeners. I confess to putting out field corn for the bushy-tailed bandits. As we all have learned, squirrels will drain a bird feeder in a short time, and putting up baffles and obstacles only slows them down. Squirrels need to eat about one pound of food every week.

Red squirrels are often heard, if not seen. They sit on a tree branch about 10 to 20 feet above the ground, chattering away at you.

Black squirrels appear not to interbreed with the red, fox, or gray. Squirrels mate in midwinter and the furless, blind babies are born about eight weeks later. The deadbeat daddy disappears, while mom nurses the little ones until they are weaned about six weeks later.

While squirrels may live from two to three years in the wild, I know several people who have taken in injured baby squirrels and they have survived from 10 to 15 years (although Ohio state law makes it illegal to keep wild animals as pets).

To power companies, squirrels are miniature saber-toothed tigers, notorious for gnawing through electrical wires and frying themselves at substation transformers. In 1993 a squirrel took down the multimillion-dollar ASR-9 jetliner guidance system at Cleveland Hopkins International Airport. A backup system was quickly turned on, but it was almost a week until the primary system was back online.

My dad, who grew up in southern Ohio near Marietta, shot squirrels for both sport and food—like most of the gun-crazies down there (even so, he was a wonderful father).

Many American Indian tribes had superstitions about not eating squirrel meat.

Have you seen a white squirrel? White squirrels are not albinos, which have pink eyes. They are seen in many parts of the United States. Our squirrelly Canadian friends must have a bushy-tail production line going up there, with all models and colors.

The white squirrels are treasured at Exeter, Ontario, and there is an annual White Squirrel Festival and parade.

Olney, Illinois, has claimed white squirrels since 1902, and the city was recognized nationally for this in October of 2002. The white squirrels are protected and given abundant food and fresh water in Olney City Park. A monument to the whites has been erected in the park, which is located on Route 130. Early morning is the best time for viewing the squirrels.

Have you ever seen a flying squirrel in Northeast Ohio? Probably not, since these small squirrels are active only at night. They don't actually fly, but use winglike skin flaps on either side of their bodies below their front and back legs.

The name "squirrel" is from the French word *esquirel*, which is derived from the Greek words *skia* and *oura*, meaning "sits in the shade of its tail."

The Ohio Division of Wildlife has put Ohio's autumn squirrel population (of all colors) at nearly 4 million. It is also estimated that (incredibly) nearly one-half of Ohio's squirrels meet their end on highways.

The squirrel family is large, including chipmunks, woodchucks, and prairie dogs, and they make up 40 percent of all mammals.

Perhaps in reciprocity for Canada bringing black squirrels into the United States, we are blamed for introducing gray squirrels into England in 1876. In Britain the gray squirrel has become so prevalent that a British lawmaker has proposed putting a one-pound ($1.80) bounty on a gray squirrel tail that is presented to authorities.

The smaller, native red squirrel has been diminishing (about 160,000) at the expense of the grays, whose population is estimated at 2.5 million.

AREA 2003–2004 STATE CHAMPIONS
OHIO HIGH SCHOOL ATHLETIC ASSOCIATION

Boys Cross Country, Division II:
Edgewood High School
Ashtabula

Boys Golf, Division I:
Copley School
Wadsworth

Boys Golf, Division II:
University School
Hunting Valley

Girls Soccer, Division II:
Bay High School
Bay Village

Boys Baseball, Division II:
Walsh Jesuit High School
Cuyahoga Falls

Girls Softball, Division II:
Walsh Jesuit High School
Cuyahoga Falls

Boys Track and Field, DVN I:
Glenville High School
Cleveland

Boys Track and Field, DVN II:
Shelby High School

Girls Track and Field, DVN I:
Elyria High School

Girls Track and Field, DVN II:
Shelby High School

2004 Girls Basketball, DVN II:
Beloit West Branch

2004 Girls Basketball, DVN III:
Youngstown Ursuline

2004 Girls Gymnastics:
Brecksville-Broadview Heights

2004 Ice Hockey:
Lakewood St. Edward

2004 Wrestling, DVN I:
Lakewood St. Edward

2004 Wrestling, DVN III:
St. Mary C.C.

Football, Division II:
Avon Lake High School

Football, Division III:
Cleveland Benedictine High School

2004 OHSAAA SCHOLAR-ATHLETE SCHOLARSHIP RECIPIENTS

www.ohsaa.org/news/misc/news061404.htm

Northeast District (12)

- Russell Chappell, *Warren Howland High School*
- Colin Clemente, *Warren John F. Kennedy High School*
- Alyson Cotter, *Salem High School* (*)
- Zach Dennis, *Jefferson Area High School*
- Sarah Feagles, *Canton Central Catholic High School*
- Jan Kehres, *Alliance High School* (*)
- Ryan Maxwell, *North Lima South Range High School*
- Ashley Sandella, *Ashtabula Sts. John and Paul High School*
- David Scarpitti, *Sebring McKinley High School*
- Ryan Shingleton, *Wooster Wooster High School*
- Laura Skeeles, *Amherst Steele High School*
- Joseph Spain, *Warren G. Harding High School* (*)

(*) indicates OHSAA Foundation $2,000 scholarship recipient

OTHER SCHOOL ATHLETIC ACHIEVEMENTS

Northeast Ohio Chess Champions from www.ohiochess.org/
www.ohiochess.org/Results/
2004 Ohio Elementary Championships
K-3 Open Championship
Clearmount Elementary
N. Canton

2003 Ohio K-12 Grade Champions
Grade 8 Team Champion
Solon Middle School

Endangered babies born at Cleveland Metroparks' Zoo in the last 10 years include an orangutan, a Francois' monkey, 3 species of tamarin (small South American monkeys), a small clawed otter, an ocelot, a fishing cat, and a retriculated python. *Source: cleveland.about.com*

OCTOBER STATISTICS

SUNSHINE % 62
DRIEST MONTH .... 0.47"/1886
WARMEST MONTH .... 61.4°/1947
COLDEST MONTH............. 45.2°/1925
LIQUID PCPN AVG. .... 2.54"
RAINIEST DAY................ 3.44"/1954
RAINIEST MONTH .... 9.50"/1954
THUNDERY DAYS....................... 2
SNOWIEST DAY................ 6.7"/1962
LEAST SNOWFALL................ TRACE
(most recently in 1997)
DAYS ONE INCH SNOW 0

October's arrival means that the season of the sun is gone in Northeast Ohio. The first three weeks of the month are usually very pleasant with comfortably mild days and cool nights. It'll turn frosty by midmonth in many nooks and crannies, and the arrival of steadily colder air over the still-warm waters of Lake Erie will often cause waterspouts and cold-air funnels to develop over the lake.

Leaf color often peaks in Northeast Ohio during the third week, but it can vary if the growing season has been very wet or very dry. Most Ohioans are not aware of how lucky we are to be treated to the flaming foliage. More than 90 percent of earth's inhabitants, and three-quarters of the United States, never see the dazzling colors of autumn.

October is the Woollybear Festival and the Pumpkin Festival and apple cider. Ohio groundhogs are growing fat on clover and alfalfa as they prepare to enter their winter hibernation chambers. Turtles and frogs are likewise burying themselves in muddy pond and river bottoms. Hornets will be killed by the frosts of late October, but the queens are checking out attics for the long winter to come.

The return to Standard Time the last Sunday in October means we'll regain the hour of sleep we lost in early April.

DAILY DATA FOR OCTOBER

Date	Day	Moon	Day of Year	Days Left	Sunrise	Sunset	Length of Day	Avg. Hi°	Avg. Lo°	Avg. Lake°
1	Sat		274	91	7:24	7:08	11:44	68	49	66
2	Sun		275	90	7:25	7:06	11:41	68	48	66
3	Mon	●	276	89	7:26	7:05	11:39	67	48	66
4	Tue		277	88	7:27	7:03	11:36	67	48	66
5	Wed		278	87	7:28	7:01	11:33	66	47	65
6	Thu		279	86	7:29	7:00	11:31	66	47	65
7	Fri		280	85	7:30	6:58	11:28	66	46	65
8	Sat		281	84	7:31	6:56	11:25	65	46	64
9	Sun		282	83	7:32	6:55	11:23	65	46	64
10	Mon	◐	283	82	7:33	6:53	11:20	65	45	63
11	Tue		284	81	7:34	6:52	11:18	64	45	63
12	Wed		285	80	7:35	6:50	11:15	64	45	63
13	Thu		286	79	7:37	6:48	11:11	63	44	63
14	Fri		287	78	7:38	6:47	11:09	63	44	62
15	Sat		288	77	7:39	6:45	11:06	62	43	62
16	Sun		289	76	7:40	6:44	11:04	62	43	61
17	Mon	○	290	75	7:41	6:42	11:01	62	43	61
18	Tue		291	74	7:42	6:41	10:59	61	43	61
19	Wed		292	73	7:43	6:39	10:56	61	42	60
20	Thu		293	72	7:44	6:38	10:54	61	42	60
21	Fri		294	71	7:46	6:36	10:50	60	42	60
22	Sat		295	70	7:47	6:35	10:48	60	41	59
23	Sun		296	69	7:48	6:33	10:45	59	41	59
24	Mon		297	68	7:49	6:32	10:43	59	41	59
25	Tue	◑	298	67	7:50	6:31	10:41	59	41	59
26	Wed		299	66	7:51	6:29	10:38	58	40	58
27	Thu		300	65	7:53	6:28	10:35	58	40	58
28	Fri		301	64	7:54	6:26	10:32	57	40	58
29	Sat		302	63	7:55	6:25	10:30	57	40	57
30	Sun		303	62	7:56	6:24	10:28	57	39	57
31	Mon		304	61	6:57	5:23	10:26	56	39	56

Rec. Hi°	Rec. Lo°	On This Date . . .
87/1952	34/1947	Bob Feller 348th strikeout of the season (1946)
86/1919	32/1975	Bob Feller strikes out 18 Detroit Tigers (1938)
89/1953	29/1975	Indians' Frank Robinson becomes baseball's 1st black mgr (1974)
88/1952	33/1981	1st AL playoff game, Indians beat Red Sox, 8-0 (1948)
88/1951	32/1980	Browns' guard Bill Willis born (1921)
90/1946	34/2003	1st train robbery in US (1866)
88/1946	30/1964	Far side of moon seen for 1st time (1959)
88/1939	31/1952	U.S. Rep. Dennis Kucinich born in Cleveland (1946)
86/1947	30/1876	American Humane Association organized in Cleveland (1877)
86/1949	30/1895	Great Hurricane of 1780 kills 20,000–30,000 in Caribbean (1780)
86/1928	25/1964	Actor Luke Perry born in Mansfield (1966)
85/1893	26/1876	City Club of Cleveland incorporated (1912)
82/1969	29/1875	White House cornerstone laid (1792)
84/1989	30/1988	Cavs lose to Buffalo Braves in their 1st game 107-92 (1970)
86/1947	29/1876	Clarence Thomas confirmed as Supreme Court Justice (1991)
83/1962	29/1944	Disney Company founded (1923)
82/1953	32/1981	Actor Tom Poston born in Columbus (1921)
84/1950	28/1876	Hurricane Hazel (3rd of 1954) becomes most severe to hit U.S. (1954)
84/1953	29/1986	Actress LaWanda Page born in Cleveland (1920)
83/1953	27/1992	East Ohio Gas Co. explosion and fire (1944)
83/1953	26/1952	1st recorded total eclipse of the sun (2137 B.C.)
81/1947	27/1976	NFL Hall of Famer Joe Carr born in Ohio (1880)
80/1963	25/1976	Football legend John William Heisman born in Cleveland (1869)
80/1920	22/1969	1st telegram sent; Pony Express ends (1861)
80/1963	28/1982	Postcards 1st used in U.S. (1870)
81/1963	24/1976	Cleveland Coliseum opens (1974)
78/1927	23/1962	Actress Ruby Dee born in Cleveland (1924)
81/1927	24/1976	Coach Lenny Wilkens born (1937)
78/1946	24/1980	William Walker, publisher of the Cleveland Call & Post, dies at 85 (1981)
79/1950	23/1980	"War of the Worlds" broadcast (1938)
82/1950	19/1988	Conjuror/magician Harry Houdini dies (1926)

Flora & Fauna OCTOBER

WEEK 1

BIRDS: The first of the golden-crowned kinglets, residents of Canada's boreal forests, begin to appear. Chickadees at your feeders will now be wearing sharp new winter feather coats. The fall migration continues, with yellow-rumped warblers becoming common. Nearly all chimney swifts are gone. **MAMMALS:** Ever wary of winter, portly skunks intently prowl open grassy fields in search of their fall diet of insect larvae. Their nocturnal digging often damages carefully tended lawns. They grow ever rounder as the month passes and will be in winter sleep by late November. **WILDFLOWERS:** September is the month of asters. Most are at their peak of blooming this week and will quickly decline after mid-month. Jewelweed is in seed. Touch the cigar-shaped green seed pods and find out why they're called "touch-me-nots"!

WEEK 2

BIRDS: Wood ducks begin their migration southward in earnest. A few may stay the winter but most migrate farther south. Ruby-crowned kinglets follow in their golden-crowned relatives' migration paths this week. The peak of the invasion of white-throated sparrows has begun. They kick and shuffle through the underbrush in small flocks looking for insects and seeds, making a great deal of noise for such small birds. **TREES:** The peak of fall color usually arrives this week, generally between the 10th and 20th of the month. Due to local variations in climate, moisture, and "lake effect," different parts of the North Coast may offer views of peak color at different times.

WEEK 3

BIRDS: The ducks with long, pointed bills appearing at inland lakes and along the Lake Erie shoreline are mergansers, sometimes called "fish ducks." They may gather off the Lake Erie shoreline in rafts numbering in the thousands and stay most of the winter. **MAMMALS:** Woodchucks wax fat on the last of the green grasses. Some are seen feeding far into the night, preparing for their long hibernation to come. Surprisingly, they will also climb small trees and shrubs for ripe fruit. Most will disappear into their wintering forest burrows by late November. **INSECTS:** Crickets may still call on warm autumn nights before the first hard frost. **WILDFLOWERS:** New England aster and small white aster, the last of the autumn wildflowers, should be at their peak of bloom by now. They will quickly decline and leave the meadows a gentle brown haze of stems and seeds. **REPTILES:** Small and gentle DeKay's snakes can often be found sunning themselves along earthen trails this week as they prepare for a long winter hibernation.

WEEK 4

BIRDS: Whistling (now called tundra) swans begin to cross Lake Erie shorelines as winter begins in the far north. Flocks of over 300 have been counted as they head south. Red-bellied and downy woodpeckers return to feeders in earnest as cooler weather approaches. **MAMMALS:** Deer begin their fall breeding season, which will last until January. If you see a female deer, stand quietly and watch for a buck to follow shortly in her tracks. Does are often still in families of two to four, so where you see one, there may be more. **WILDFLOWERS:** Milkweed pods open and fill the air with their fluffy parachute seeds this week. **TREES:** By month's end, the appearance of flowers on witch hazel announces the final act of the plant world's play for the year.

Adapted from the Nature Almanac by Robert Hinkle, with permission from Cleveland Metroparks.

In the early 1800s, **Amish Mennonites** from eastern Pennsylvania crossed the Alleghenies and started the first settlement of people of their faith in Ohio near the present village of Sugarcreek in Tuscarawas County near the Holmes County line. This modest beginning has grown into the largest settlement of Amish people in the world.

THE CTS CAPER

By Chuck Schodowski

It was late summer, 1964. Cleveland television was right smack in the middle of the Ghoulardi era . . . an era that still holds all the Neilsen reocords.

Ernie Anderson was Ghoulardi. He was also TV 8's booth announcer. I first met Ernie in 1960, when I began my TV career as a summer replacement engineer at the old KYW-TV, Channel 3. In the fall of 1960 I got an engineering job at WJW-TV, Channel 8. Ernie and his good friend Tim Conway came over to Channel 8 about a year or so later. In 1962, Conway began doing comedy segments on the very popular Steve Allen show late nights on NBC. He then moved on to Hollywood and the *McHale's Navy* TV series. By then, Ernie and I had become close friends.

In February of 1963, Ernie began to host a new late-night show at TV 8 called *Shock Theater*. He did this as a character he called "Ghoulardi," and he made Cleveland TV history. In a short time, Ghoulardi had become a household word. No Cleveland TV personality was as popular before or since. Ernie was in demand—do a gig here, a gig there, record this promo, record that PSA (public service announcement), do celebrity sports events, you name it!

Besides being the busiest, most popular personality in Cleveland TV history, Ernie was the most in-demand voice-over commercial

announcer. He owned the Cleveland voice-over commercial market (later he would become the highest-paid, most famous announcer and commercial voice in the history of national television).

On a Friday afternoon in September of 1964, I came to work a bit early to help Ernie prepare for that night's show. Ernie said, "Before we get started, come on with me, I have to record a radio spot." (Ernie always wanted me to go places with him.)

The recording studio was several blocks east of our station, at about East 55th and Euclid Avenue. Ernie had a little two-seat sports car, an A.C. Ace convertible. It was a hot day, so he had the top down. As we drove east on Euclid, he startled me by yelling, "Holy _ _ _ _! There it is!" and pointing to a Cleveland Transit System bus going west on Euclid. He made a wild U-turn, yelling, "There it is! I got to have it for tonight's show!"

"You gotta have a bus?" I asked.

"No!" he said. "Look at the sides."

The sides of the bus, where advertising posters usually were, had big green public service posters from the mayor's traffic safety education committee that read: "Don't jaywalk . . . live longer," with a drawing of Ghoulardi on them.

"I forgot to tell you they were going to do that," Ernie said as he pulled directly behind the bus. "When the bus stops," he said, "jump out on the curb and see if you can get the poster off."

"How?" I said. "What if I get caught?"

"Don't worry, trust me!" he said (a favorite expression of his). "Just do it. I'll keep the bus driver occupied. He won't notice you."

He then pulled his car slightly to the left, behind the bus, so the driver could see him and not me. He waved to the driver; the driver went NUTS (as everyone did when they saw Ghoulardi in person). The driver was so excited and laughing so hard, he almost passed up a stop.

When the bus stopped to pick up people, the driver stuck his head out the window, looked back at Ernie, and said, "Ghoulardi! I watch you every night, man."

While he and Ernie talked, I jumped over the door of the car and surveyed the poster. It was enclosed in a metal frame with a lock on it. The frame was tight against the poster. I couldn't get my fingers in to pull at it. The bus started up, and I jumped back over the door into the car as Ernie followed the bus.

"It's not going to work," I said, "I can't pry it loose. The metal frame is too tight."

"Look in the glove compartment," he said. "There's a screwdriver in there, I think."

There was a screwdriver—a little three-inch one, very old and rusty, with a wooden handle that was split.

The bus stopped. The driver stuck his head out the window and excitedly continued flattering Ernie. Out I went, knowing I only had about 15 seconds of time to work. I slammed the screwdriver into the corner of the frame, and pulled down on it hard. I heard a snap. I hoped it was the posterboard popping out of the frame—no luck! It was the screwdriver busting in half and the handle cracking off.

The bus started. I jumped into the now-moving car.

"Well?" said Ernie.

I just held up half of the screwdriver and a piece of the handle. "The other half is stuck in the frame," I said, now noticing that my thumb was bleeding.

Ernie scooted towards me. "Here, in my pocket," he said. "A knife." (Did you ever try to put your hand in someone's pants pocket when they're sitting down?) "Here, you steer," Ernie said, twisting himself the opposite way and almost standing up. He managed to pop the knife out of his pocket, along with some coins, bills, and business cards. The knife was a tiny pocketknife about two inches long, but it was very sharp.

The bus stopped. Out I popped, and began jabbing away at the bottom left-hand corner of the poster, finding that it was made of some very tough material.

Bus starts. Back in the car I go, telling Ernie my strategy of digging a hole in the corner of the poster so I could get a couple of fingers under it to pry it out of the frame.

For the next two stops, I put my plan into action. We were now back in front of TV 8, where we first started. I figured it would take at least five more stops before I dug a hole big enough to get my fingers in. Ernie told me he thought the bus driver was getting a little suspicious. So, the next stop I tried very hard . . . and jammed one finger into the hole, getting a little ways under the corner of the poster.

The bus started. I tried to pull my finger out—it was stuck under the poster! I started running with my finger under the poster.

I jerked my arm back as fast as I could. My finger popped out, raking my knuckles against the edge of the frame. I jumped into the car. Ernie was laughing hysterically. Now both of my hands were bleeding. I told Ernie I didn't think it was so funny. My aching hands made me more determined now than Ernie was to get that poster out. I was MAD! Which, of course, made Ernie laugh even harder.

We had now traveled through Public Square and on to the Near West Side. The bus driver's fascination with Ghoulardi following his bus seemed to be fading a bit, as he was now probably wondering why Ernie was following the bus.

Ernie kept smiling, shouting wisecracks, and waving, but we knew the next couple of stops would be critical. A few stops later, I had most of the corner of the poster out of a slightly bent frame. We were well into the West Side now.

The bus stopped. I was pumped. Now, with a huge surge of adrenaline, I jammed my whole left palm under the poster, bent down, and pushed up until my whole hand was in up to my wrist. I reached my right hand over, grabbing the corner, and with both hands made a superhuman effort to pull the poster out.

I could feel the frame bending as the thick, sturdy poster board was forced out with a big pop. I fell backwards against the curb—the people getting on and off the bus were now telling the driver that some "nut" took the poster off his bus.

Holding the prize under my arm, I jumped into the car. Ernie let out a triumphant cheer, laughed, and pulled up along the side of the bus. He waved to the driver and said, "Thanks, man, be cool," made another frantic U-turn, and headed back to TV 8.

We had gone all the way to Lakewood. We had been gone for over an hour, Ernie had missed his voice-over gig, and I was late for my engineering shift. It was worth it, because in the car we had our subject for the content of the entire show that night. Then a worry crossed my mind.

I said, "What if the bus driver sees the show and tells the cops what happened?"

"Rat on Ghoulardi?" Ernie scoffed. "It'll never happen. Don't worry, trust me."

He was right. We pulled into the alley behind the station and hurriedly walked in the back door. We apologized for being late, and I started for the men's room to wash my hands.

"Hey!" Ernie said, "When you're done, bring in the show mail from the lobby so we can go through it."

The show mail was all in one box. As I started to go back with it, our receptionist, Marge, said "Here! This came in for Ernie too." She handed me a three-by-two-foot, half-inch-thick package, wrapped in shipping paper. The writing on the outside read, "Ernie, thanks for everything. Maybe you can use this on your show. The signs will be on the buses today!"

Ernie and I must have laughed for an hour after we had unwrapped the "Ghoulardi—Don't jaywalk" poster from the mayor's traffic safety education committee.

Ernie had a great show that night, and the poster became a permanent fixture on his set. And I still have the one I took off the bus—it's a permanent fixture in my rec room.

Even today, exactly 40 years later, each time I see it, it reminds me of how Ernie and I both enjoyed telling the story of how we got it.

And I really enjoyed telling it to you. Thanks for your time.

Love ya, Big Chuck.

"Big Chuck" Schodowski is the popular co-host of the Emmy Award-winning Big Chuck & Lil John Show seen Fridays at 11:30 p.m. and Saturday afternoons on FOX 8. For more than 35 years, he has written, produced, and starred in hundreds of comedy skits that remain local television favorites.

YOU'D BE AMAZED AT WHAT YOU CAN SEE IN

The morning of October 17 will have a lunar eclipse. Look toward the west, starting at 5:51 a.m. Over the next 30 minutes, you may begin to notice Earth's shadow slowly moving into the lower-right corner of our moon, causing a lunar eclipse. Unfortunately, we will see less than half of this event, because the moon sets at 7:45 a.m.

Autumn sees the return of the "angry red planet" Mars. [Mars really isn't red, it's more of a rusty orange, and Mars has nothing to be angry about!] The week of October 29 it will be at its closest and offer some of the best telescopic views. I urge everyone to see Mars in a telescope at least once in their lives.

Courtesy of Jay Reynolds, Schuele Planetarium director, Lake Erie Nature and Science Center.

CAPTION CONTEST

I'm sorry, Dick, but we just can't raise the age limit THAT far past 28!

Winning entry submitted by **Cheryl Nash** of Madison, Ohio.
Thanks for entering this year's caption contest on the FOX 8 web site.

WOOLLYBEAR RACE WINNERS

YEAR, NAME, HIGHLIGHTS

2003, "BOB," the great-great-great-great grandson of B-O-B (black-orange-black), won in 21 seconds! Skelaton came in 2nd, and Alley Dog finished 3rd.

2002, Fast'n Furrious, in 19 seconds, beat Patrick by one full length.

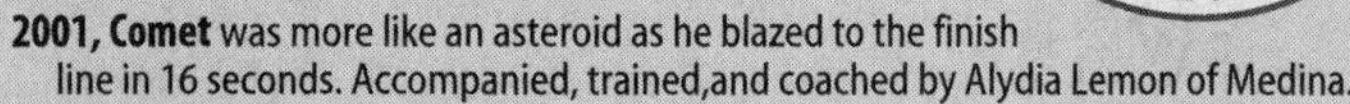

2001, Comet was more like an asteroid as he blazed to the finish line in 16 seconds. Accompanied, trained,and coached by Alydia Lemon of Medina.

2000, Gump On the coldest day since 1977 Gump took 26 seconds to dump Maisy and Rolly Polly.

1999, Hayden II On a wet track with wind chills in the 30s Hayden the deuce outslogged Cater P and Roadrunner.

1998, Skeeter Thousands cheered as this fellow (who trained on dandelion juice exclusively) beat out Lightning II and Woobie.

{DICK'S PLANT OF THE YEAR}

The Delectable Dandelion

Dick Goddard

Behold the lowly dandelion, my plant of the year.

Although it's the bane of greenskeepers and those who try to keep their lawns an unblemished, velvety green, I've always had (mostly) nice things to say about these saffron flowers that announce that spring is here. Benjamin Franklin wanted the ubiquitous dandelion to be our national flower (he also pushed the wild turkey for our national birds in place of the regal eagle . . . close call).

The dandelion is the Rodney Dangerfield of wildflowers and about the only place it gets respect is in England, where—believe it or not—it is a protected, endangered species.

The name *dandelion* comes from the French, "dent de lion," meaning "lion's tooth." Indeed, the jagged leaves of this cosmopolitan weed resemble the teeth of a lion.

Growing up in the Depression years of the 1930s, many families—ours included—used the dandelion in salad. I suggest that you find young plants, since the older they are the more bitter they taste. And don't spare the salad dressing.

The flower stem of the common dandelion is hollow with a milky juice, and all parts are edible. The root of the dandelion is used medicinally, primarily as a diuretic for kidney and bladder ailments. Liver and gallbladder diseases can also be treated.

Dandelion leaves have been used as a laxative. My granddad, Jessie, made dandelion wine. (That explains the results.)

There are a number of dandelion types: common, red-seeded, fall (autumn), and dwarf. They range in height from 2 to 18 inches.

I'm sure you also know that closing your eyes, making a wish, and then blowing away the puffy dandelion head can make you rich. Try it!

The word *dandelion*, by the way, is both singular and plural, the same as in deer and bluegill. There are no dandelions, deers, or bluegills.

STORM SAFETY Flash Flood

The flash flood has become this nation's deadliest weather event. The average annual death toll is 160, with yearly property losses of more than $1 billion. The reasons: denuding of the landscape by developers and the general public; more people setting up home sites in floodplains; more vacationers camping in flood-prone areas; more mobile home parks locating near rivers and streams.

The National Weather Service is responsible for issuing flash flood watches and warnings, based on current and past rainfall amounts, land configuration, and drainage potential. It is vital that communities set up local "river watches." The NWS, aided by ham radio and CB operators, will help establish that network.

FLOOD SAFETY RULES:

1. Never attempt to drive across a flooded area, since just two feet of water can float an automobile.
2. Never try to walk across a rapidly moving stream if the water is above your knees.
3. Never allow children to play near drainage ditches during or after heavy rains.

The Cleveland Metroparks's RainForest opened November 19, 1992, and has been host to more than 6.6 million visitors. The first animal to call the RainForest home was "Dreadnought" the American Crocodile, and you can still visit him! *Source: cleveland.about.com*

JAN FEB MAR APR MAY JUN JUL AUG SEP OCT NOV DEC

NOVEMBER STATISTICS

(recorded at Cleveland Hopkins Airport)

SUNSHINE %	31
DRIEST MONTH	0.41"/1904
WARMEST MONTH	51.2°/1931
COLDEST MONTH	31.3°/1880
LIQUID PCPN AVG.	3.17"
RAINIEST DAY	2.73"/1985
RAINIEST MONTH	8.80"/1985
THUNDERY DAYS	1
SNOWIEST DAY	15.0"/1950
SNOWIEST MONTH	23.4"/1996
LEAST SNOWFALL	TRACE *(most recently in 1994)*
DAYS ONE INCH SNOW	2

One of the electrifying sounds of November is the gabbling of Canada geese as they wing their way southward. The geese fly in their classic V formation for a reason. As each bird flaps its wings, it creates uplift for the bird immediately behind, thus allowing the flock to expand its flying range by about 70 percent. As the bird at the point of the V tires, it will drop back into the flock and another bird will become the leader. If the point bird is so worn out that it falls to the ground to rest, other birds will join their leader until he is able to return to the flock.

Ohio's state animal, the white-tailed deer, is now rutting and can be very dangerous to unwary woodsmen and hunters. Motorists need to be especially alert for the next three months since deer will be constantly crossing the highways. If one deer crosses in front of you, you can expect another close behind. Lake-effect snows can be expected before the month is over. The Thanksgiving week snowstorm of 1950 dumped record amounts of snowfall around the state of Ohio, with upwards of 20 to 40 inches around Greater Cleveland and Northeast Ohio. In November of 1996, 69 inches of snow fell on Chardon in the heart of the Northeast Ohio snowbelt in Geauga County—in only five days. It was Ohio's greatest single storm snowfall. Great Lakes seamen fear the west-to-northwest gale wind of November, the "Witch."

DAILY DATA FOR NOVEMBER

Date	Day	Moon	Day of Year	Days Left	Sunrise	Sunset	Length of Day	Avg. Hi°	Avg. Lo°	Avg. Lake°
1	Tue		305	60	6:59	5:21	10:22	56	39	56
2	Wed	●	306	59	7:00	5:20	10:20	55	38	56
3	Thu		307	58	7:01	5:19	10:18	55	38	55
4	Fri		308	57	7:02	5:18	10:16	54	38	55
5	Sat		309	56	7:03	5:17	10:14	54	37	55
6	Sun		310	55	7:05	5:15	10:10	53	37	55
7	Mon		311	54	7:06	5:14	10:08	53	37	54
8	Tue		312	53	7:07	5:13	10:06	53	37	54
9	Wed	◐	313	52	7:08	5:12	10:04	52	36	54
10	Thu		314	51	7:09	5:11	10:02	52	36	53
11	Fri		315	50	7:11	5:10	9:59	51	36	53
12	Sat		316	49	7:12	5:09	9:57	51	35	53
13	Sun		317	48	7:13	5:08	9:55	50	35	52
14	Mon		318	47	7:14	5:08	9:54	50	35	52
15	Tue		319	46	7:16	5:07	9:51	50	35	51
16	Wed	○	320	45	7:17	5:06	9:49	49	34	51
17	Thu		321	44	7:18	5:05	9:47	49	34	51
18	Fri		322	43	7:19	5:04	9:45	48	34	50
19	Sat		323	42	7:20	5:04	9:44	48	33	50
20	Sun		324	41	7:21	5:03	9:42	47	33	50
21	Mon		325	40	7:23	5:02	9:39	47	32	49
22	Tue		326	39	7:24	5:02	9:38	46	32	49
23	Wed	◑	327	38	7:25	5:01	9:36	46	32	49
24	Thu		328	37	7:26	5:00	9:34	46	32	48
25	Fri		329	36	7:27	5:00	9:33	45	31	48
26	Sat		330	35	7:28	4:59	9:31	45	31	47
27	Sun		331	34	7:29	4:59	9:30	44	31	47
28	Mon		332	33	7:31	4:59	9:28	44	30	47
29	Tue		333	32	7:32	4:58	9:26	43	30	47
30	Wed		334	31	7:33	4:58	9:25	43	30	46

Rec. Hi°	Rec. Lo°	On This Date . . .
82/1950	25/1988	1st President to live in White House (John Adams) (1800)
77/2003	25/1895	James A. Garfield elected president (1880)
79/1961	19/1951	Bob Feller born (1918)
77/2003	16/1991	First uniform election day (1845)
75/1948	16/1991	Roy Rogers born in Cincinnati (1911)
76/1977	17/1951	President William McKinley re-elected (1900)
79/1938	23/1971	Carl Stokes elected first black mayor of Cleveland (1967)
72/1945	19/1976	Actor Joe Flynn born in Youngstown (1924)
74/1975	22/1976	Actress Dorothy Dandridge born in Cleveland (1922)
70/1991	19/1991	TV host Jack McCoy born in Akron (1918)
73/1915	21/1957	Comedian Jonathan Winters born in Dayton (1925)
74/1949	18/1911	Criminal Charles Manson born in Cincinnati (1934)
72/1989	15/1911	Mariner 9, 1st spacecraft to orbit another planet (Mars) (1971)
72/1994	13/1986	Herman Melville's Moby Dick published (1851)
72/1931	14/1996	Detroit-Superior Bridge opens to traffic (1917)
72/1931	12/1933	Actor Burgess Meredith born in Cleveland (1907)
72/1954	14/1959	Congress holds 1st session in D.C. (1800)
71/1954	10/1959	Time zones established by railroads in U.S. & Canada (1883)
72/1908	4/1880	James A. Garfield born in log cabin in Orange Twp. (1803)
73/1931	15/1951	Actress/comedienne Kaye Ballard born in Cleveland (1926)
70/1930	3/1880	1st U.S. postage stamp in 2 colors (1952)
73/1934	0/1880	Ernie "Ghoulardi" Anderson born, in Massachusetts (1923)
75/1931	7/1880	1st issue of Life magazine
70/1931	7/1950	Browns receiver Dante Lavelli born (1930)
67/1906	15/1950	Former Browns quarterback Bernie Kosar born in Youngstown (1963)
70/1896	9/1880	1st national Thanksgiving (1789)
71/1990	7/1880	Earliest photo of a meteor shower made (1885)
68/1990	8/1955	Paul Warfield born (1942)
67/1933	6/1976	Mercury-Atlas 5 carries chimp (Enos) to orbit (1961)
71/1934	3/1976	Baseball's Negro National League disbands (1948)

Flora & Fauna NOVEMBER

WEEK 1 **BIRDS:** Canada geese by the hundreds stop by local refuges to rest and refuel on their way south. Common songbird migrants might include tree sparrows (light breast with a single spot), fox sparrows (larger than most sparrows, with a rusty red color), and juncos, sometimes called snowbirds. Among the rarest migrants are northern harriers or marsh hawks. Look for these long-tailed predators hunting over open fields, lofting their long wings like butterflies. Mice, small birds, and even migrating ducks sometimes fall prey to harriers. **MAMMALS:** November marks the peak of the white-tailed deer's breeding season. Adult bucks polish their antlers on small trees and shrubs to tell the world that this part of your world is theirs! Does crossing parkways are often followed by one or more bucks, so take care driving this month.

WEEK 2 **BIRDS:** Purple finches and pine siskins, visitors from Canada, reappear throughout the area. Look closely at the reddish-colored house finches you have seen all summer and watch for a slightly larger bird, more purple than red, without stripes on its breast to identify the rarer purple finch. **MAMMALS:** New beaver cuttings mark the last month of frenzied activity by these industrious creatures. They must set aside enough tender branches beneath the water's surface to provide an entire winter's food supply for a family of six or more.

WEEK 3 **BIRDS:** Rufus-sided towhees, singing "drink-your-tea," can still be found occasionally where crab apple trees and high-bush cranberry bear fruit. Dark-eyed juncos, apparently sensing the same day length as spring, begin their spring songs each morning. As the days shorten, the songs will cease. **MAMMALS:** Fox, gray, black, and tiny flying squirrels are busy adding insulation to their winter tree dens before the icy blasts of winter arrive. Unfortunate is the squirrel who may have to spend the winter in his drafty leaf nest, which may not provide enough insulation for his survival. Chipmunks return to bird feeders as their autumn crop of nuts has been eaten or carefully stored in snug burrows for the winter.

WEEK 4 **BIRDS:** The last of the autumn waterfowl move through. Look for hooded mergansers, buffleheads, and goldeneye ducks. Shoveler ducks with their attractive bright-green heads and large, scoop-shaped bills graze among the shallow water plants. **MAMMALS:** Hardy woodchucks still browse among the frost-laden grasses, storing up a few more days of food for their long winter hibernation. Most will enter hibernation between now and mid-December.

Adapted from the Nature Almanac by Robert Hinkle, with permission from Cleveland Metroparks.

2005 HURRICANE NAMES

Arlene, Bret, Cindy, Dennis, Emily, Franklin, Gert, Harvey, Irene, Jose, Katrina, Lee, Maria, Nate, Ophelia, Phillipe, Rita, Stan, Tammy, Vince, Wilma

YOU'D BE AMAZED AT WHAT YOU CAN SEE IN NOVEMBER

The evening of November 14, the bright orange planet Mars will have the full moon glide by it.

The period from November 13 through the 20th may be chilly but usually offers the consistently best meteor shower of them all, the Leonids. Even from the city, you usually can see the meteor streaks, but darker locations will offer better viewing. Late-night viewing, after mid-night, is best. However, some streaks can be seen at any time, even during the day!

Courtesy of Jay Reynolds, Schuele Planetarium director, Lake Erie Nature and Science Center.

THE IMPORTANCE OF YOU

By Bill Sheil

To start with, let me say that this essay has an agenda. And it asks a lot of questions on the subject of importance. The importance of what? The importance of you.

Importance seems so relative. What's important to me may not be important to you. And how do you measure a concept as amorphous as "importance" anyway? In one corner of life, there is a way. But that corner doesn't come to you; you have to go to it.

If you did pursue it, your mere presence could change a life for the better—and the difference you would make could be measured. All you'd have to do is be yourself. Interested?

So what do you have to do? You have to spend a couple hours a week—here's the big catch—doing whatever you want. Go to a ballgame. Go out to eat. Talk with a friend about anything. Spend a lot of money, or a little, or none at all.

Do you know where I'm going with this yet? Think of spending time doing almost anything that could fit under the broad definition of the word "fun." That's what you'd have to do to make that difference. Because that's what it's like to be a Big Brother or Big Sister.

Now, this is definitely not about volunteering your life away. This is about sharing a small piece of the best of you with someone who will appreciate you just for who you are.

We rightly have set aside Mother's Day and Father's Day to celebrate our parents. For those of us fortunate enough to come from solid two-parent homes, our childhood environment underpins our sense of self-worth.

Our parents proved our worthiness to us because, whatever we did, they loved us, and we knew it, and we could feel it, and every day their love silently gave us faith in ourselves. It still does to this day.

Many children, for many reasons, don't have that same opportunity. They are just as worthy of love as you or anyone else, but it is missing. A missing parent leaves a hole. Tomorrow, you can fill a small piece of that hole for a child—and you may change a life.

Let me be clear: this is not about being a substitute parent, about raising a child that's not your own, about getting bogged down in other people's problems. This is about bringing a little joy into a child's life. That's all it's about. Funny—turns out a little joy pays large dividends. Those dividends are important—and they can be measured.

Several years ago, almost a thousand boys and girls took part in a national research project conducted by Public/Private Ventures of Philadelphia. Half the children were matched with a Big Brother or Big Sister; the other half was assigned to waiting lists. On average, the matched children met with their "Bigs" three times a month for an average of one year. After eighteen months, researchers found the matched children were:

- 46 percent less likely to begin using illegal drugs
- 27 percent less likely to begin using alcohol
- 52 percent less likely to skip school
- 37 percent less likely to skip a class
- more confident in their schoolwork
- getting along better with their families

Simply put, Big Brothers/Big Sisters works. And its importance in children's lives can be measured. When an adult, one who doesn't have to, shows up for the sole purpose of spending time with a child, what do you think that does for a child's sense of self-worth? The power of the program is just that simple.

Now, here's the secret: you actually get as much out of the experience as your "little" does. I entered the program years ago, somewhat unsure of what I was getting myself into. The commitment was to see a boy once a week for a year. We saw each other regularly for almost ten years, Jamie was the ring bearer in my wedding, and we are still friends today.

Jamie had an all-too-typical relationship with men early his life. At four, he was physically abused after standing up to a jerk who was threatening his mother. But you could never imagine he'd lived through such pain when he smiled in a way that lit up his whole face and called the world to him. It seems to me the way all children smile when they are truly happy.

And what does it take to make a child like this happy? The same as it does any child: a little attention, a little love. Whether we went for a burger or a baseball game, our goal was simply to have fun. And when two people from different backgrounds choose to spend time with one another, that choice fosters an appreciation for one another that is unique.

Even people I know who joined the program and later dropped out never regretted trying. And, for the time they were involved, they probably made some difference—and that impact may still be growing inside a child.

There is a sense of self-worth you have from helping a child that you can't find in making money for your company or for yourself. In this context, how important you are depends only on how important you want to be.

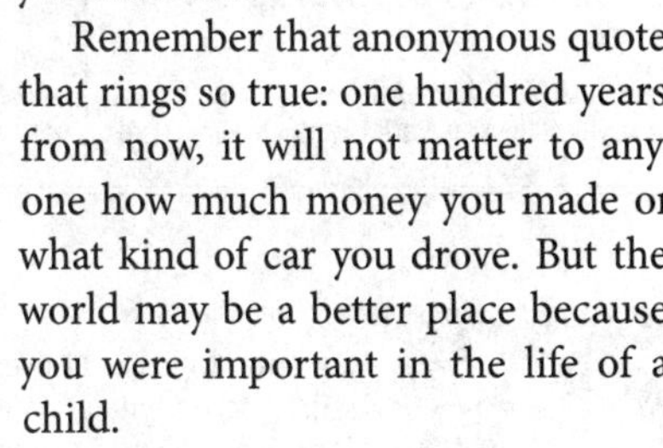

Remember that anonymous quote that rings so true: one hundred years from now, it will not matter to anyone how much money you made or what kind of car you drove. But the world may be a better place because you were important in the life of a child.

Bill Sheil is an I-Team reporter for FOX 8 NEWS. Bill has been honored by Big Brothers/Big Sisters of America as the Midwest Big Brother of the Year, and he serves on the Board of Directors of Big Brothers/Big Sisters in Cleveland.

NATIONAL OR INTERNATIONAL AWARD WINNERS FROM NORTHEAST OHIO

Tops Friendly Markets Armand J. Castellani Outstanding Achievement Award: **Joe Arcuri**, *perishable field specialist, Bedford*

2003 Great American Song Contest Outstanding Achievement In Songwriting Award: **James Pequignot**, *Macedonia, for his song* Insane.

Johnson & Wales second-annual Taste Down Under contest: **Bob Bebenroth**, *Strongsville, for pistachio-crusted lamb with sake corn stuffed bok choy*

National Forensic League Competition finalist: **Josh Marcin**, *junior at Firestone High School, Akron*

Horticulture magazine's "10 Gardens That Inspire Us": **Gardenview Horticultural Park**, *Strongsville*

Team USA, national roller hockey team: **Craig Frey**, *Solon*

One of 100 United States veterans honored in Paris on the 60th anniversary of D-Day and awarded the Legion of Honor: **Alvin Karges**, *Cleveland Heights*

2004 National Honor Society Scholarship Winners: **Benjamin Lee**, *Hudson High School, Hudson*; **Gina Moraco**, *Streetsboro High School*, **Streetsboro**; **Marie Strouse**, *West Holmes High School, Millersburg*; **Frank Yu**, *Mayfield High School, Cleveland*

ASCAP/American Symphony Orchestra League's annual Awards for Programming of Contemporary Music: **the Cleveland Orchestra and its music director, Franz Welser-Möst** *took 2nd place, Cleveland*

All-American Soap Box Derby: **RickiLea Murphy**, *Mantua.*

Agricultural Marketing Service's Small Business Contractor of the Year: **Park Farms**, *Canton*

American Society of Mechanical Engineers Pressure Vessel and Piping Medal: **Greg Hollinger**, *senior principal engineer at BWX Technologies, North Canton*

Selected for membership in the Royal Society, the United Kingdom's academy of science: **Dr. Frank Austen**, *graduate of Western Reserve Academy and Akron native*

Selected to participate in the National Young Leaders Conference in Washington, D.C.: **Jamelia Purdue**, *senior at McKinley High School, Canton*

The AMA Alliance Health Awareness Promotion Award: **Summit County Medical Alliance** *for its "No Bullies—No Victims" program.*

Leukemia & Lymphoma Society Service to Mankind Award: **Frederick R. Nance**, *managing partner of Squire, Sanders and Dempsey, LLP*.

Electrical Contracting and Engineering News Top 25 New Products of 2003: One product names was **Accessmount**, *a removable fixture-mounting system invented by Nelson Pitlor of Twinsburg*.

Screenprinting & Graphic Imaging Association International Golden Image Awards: **Forest Corp.**, *Twinsburg (Honorable Mention, single multi-color Banner category)*.

Convention Industry Council's Hall of Leaders, 2004 Class: **Bruce Harris**, *President of Conferon Global Services, Twinsburg (one of six inductees)*

Huntington's Disease Society of America Outstanding Educational Program: **Northeast Ohio Chapter** *won for the program, "Caring for the Individual with Huntington's Disease." The Chapter also won a Research Alliance Award.*

Currently, Ohio has 11 river systems (20 individual stream segments) designated as Wild and Scenic as part of ODNR's State Scenic Rivers Program. **Designated rivers in Northeast Ohio** include segments of Little Beaver Creek (Columbiana County), Grand River (Lake and Ashtabula counties), Upper Cuyahoga River (Geauga and Portage counties), and Chagrin River (Cuyahoga, Geauga, and Portage counties)

Source: www.ohiodnr.com

Gossip

By Dick Goddard

If you can't say anything nice about someone, come sit by me.

— Anne Roosevelt Whitney

It was early October in 1996 when I was finally able to return to my job as a weather forecaster at Fox 8 television. It followed the most devastating and depressing event in my life.

In a period of only 12 hours, I had lost not only my beloved mother, Doris, but my wonderful soulmate of 24 years, Julie Ann.

On my first day back on the air, I had just struggled through the evening news, when the telephone call came. The woman on the other end said, sarcastically, "I hear you killed your mother and your lady." It was so cruel and stunning that I don't remember if I said anything or just hung up. (Until this writing I had only told my friend and colleague Tim Taylor about the unbelievably inhumane call.)

THE REASON A DOG HAS SO MANY FRIENDS IS BECAUSE HE WAGS HIS TAIL INSTEAD OF HIS TONGUE

— Common Wisdom

That first week I was back on the air the television critic at the *Plain Dealer* complained that I was showing no energy on my weather programs (he was later removed from his job). Being a weather forecaster in Northeast Ohio guarantees that you need to have a thick epidermis, but I still regarded this as the epitome of the mean-spiritedness that has taken over our society.

People have been overwhelmingly nice to me since I first climbed into that lighted metal box some 44 years ago. Those who are in the public eye, be they entertainers, politicians, or whatever, are juicy and easy targets for the diaper-mouths. It simply goes with the territory.

Gossip has always been a titillating hobby for humans, even though the male of the species would probably deny any involvement. That, of course, is not true.

The word "gossip" comes from the root word "godsub," which meant "related" (as in family). From there the word mutated into "talk about those related to us," and eventually into "one who delights in idle talk." Simple, idle talk has since morphed into words that can psychologically maim and destroy.

No one is immune from gossip. Even though it is often totally false, once it has been passed on it is embellished and often develops a life of its own. Gossip is so frequently intriguing and delicious that people believe that it must be true.

I remember a player on the Cleveland Browns who was crucified and ridiculed—behind his back, of course—for his sexual preferences in the 1970s. The stories were fabrications, but it was terrific party talk. I'm sure it made the purveyors of thc fable feel so much better about themselves.

In the early 1980s, following painful root canal surgery, I was prescribed a pain reliever called zomax (which was subsequently banned by the FDA). Its effect could be seen in my breathing. I began to hyperventilate on television, and it was truly embarrassing. One day I was walking through a shopping mall when a mother and her child approached. As they passed, the little boy said, "My mom says that you're on drugs." Technically that may have been correct, but spreading mean-spirited assumptions like this is just one way that gossip is born.

LIVE SO THAT YOU WOULDN'T BE ASHAMED TO SELL THE FAMILY PARROT TO THE TOWN GOSSIP.

— Will Rogers

(For the diaper-mouths among us, I hate to spoil your favorite pastime, but I must tell you I have never taken drugs or nonprescribed medications, I have never been drunk, and no one can say I have a bad temper. I'm just a boring, carbon-based biped.)

It was gossip about his wife that caused a future president of the United States to shoot and kill a man. At the age of 24 Andrew Jackson married Rachel Donelson Robards. Because of a legal error, Rachel had technically not been divorced when she and Jackson exchanged vows in 1791. They rectified the problem when they exchanged vows again three years later.

Politics have seldom been honest or ethical, so the rivals of Jackson (known as Old Hickory) began a campaign against him and his wife prior to his election as president in 1828.

An early antagonist of the Jacksons had been Charles Dickinson. According to the code of chivalry followed in 1806, Jackson challenged Dickinson to a duel with pistols at eight paces. Dickinson shot first, with the bullet entering Jackson's breastbone, near his heart. It was not a fatal wound, but it was so close to his vital organs that doctors could not operate. Jackson carried the bullet in his body until his death.

The gentleman's code of the time also forbade returning fire if the opponent's shot was not fatal, but Jackson's fiery temperament ruled. He fired away, but the pistol's hammer failed. Jackson fired again, and the bullet hit Dickinson in the abdomen and went through his body, killing him.

Just before Jackson entered the White House as the seventh president of the United States, his wife—who had a history of heart problems—died of heart failure. The strain of being called a harlot, whore, and strumpet—even by ministers in the pulpit—finally took its toll on Rachel.

ONE OF THE MOST STRIKING DIFFERENCES BETWEEN A CAT AND A LIE IS THAT A CAT ONLY HAS NINE LIVES.

— Mark Twain

Whether we admit it or not, all of us gossip in some form. While gossip can be of the good-sport-only-kidding variety, too often it is malicious and harmful. While gossipers generally run little risk of retaliation or reprisal, they can be sued for libel or slander (discussed later in this book).

It is estimated that we utter an average of 33 words every minute that we are in conversation (although I know some who gust to 50).

We all know someone who is the "knife of the party," with a

great sense of rumor. We need to remember that thoughts can become words at any moment, and that talk is a verbal boomerang that often comes right back at us.

The exact contrary of what is generally believed is often the truth.

— Jean de la Bruyere

A harmful truth is better than a useful lie.

— Thomas Mann

My Name is Gossip

Remember Me?

My name is gossip. I have no respect for justice.

I maim without killing. I break hearts and ruin lives.

I am cunning and malicious and gather strength with age.

The more I am quoted, the more I am believed.

I flourish at every level of society.

My victims are helpless. They cannot protect themselves against me because I have no name and no face.

To track me down is impossible. The harder you try, the more elusive I become.

I am nobody's friend.

Once I tarnish a reputation, it is never quite the same.

I topple governments and wreck marriages.

I ruin careers and cause sleepless nights, heartache, and indigestion.

I spawn suspicion and generate grief.

I make innocent people cry in their pillows.

Even my name hisses. I am called gossip, office gossip, shop gossip, party gossip.

I make headlines and headaches.

Before you repeat a story, ask yourself, is it true? Is it fair? Is it necessary?

If not, then just keep your mouth shut. You could be next.

DECEMBER STATISTICS

(recorded at Cleveland Hopkins Airport)

SUNSHINE %	26
DRIEST MONTH	0.71"/1958
WARMEST MONTH	42.0°/1889
COLDEST MONTH	19.2°/1989
LIQUID PCPN AVG.	3.09"
RAINIEST DAY	2.81"/1992
RAINIEST MONTH	8.59"/1990
THUNDERY DAYS	0
SNOWIEST DAY	12.2"/1974
SNOWIEST MONTH	30.3"/1962
LEAST SNOWFALL	TRACE *(most recently in 1931)*
DAYS ONE INCH SNOW	4

Northeast Ohioans have now entered the dark weather tunnel from which we will not emerge for many months. In dark December Greater Clevelanders will experience only 26 percent of possible sunshine. From now through January, Cleveland will rank with such places as Seattle, Washington, Portland, Oregon, and Syracuse, New York, as the nation's cloudiest cities.

The sun (if seen) will reach its lowest point in the sky around December 21, the time of the winter solstice. It has taken 365 days for our small planet to complete its elliptical (not circular) orbit around the sun. Four hundred million years ago there were 400 days in a year, because our favorite planet was spinning much faster and days were shorter. It's been discovered that earth has nine separate movements as it wobbles, whirls, and nods while traveling at 1,100 miles per minute.

While many Ohio animals are in their deep winter snooze, raccoons, opossums, and skunks may awaken to forage for food. If you started to feed the birds in autumn you must keep it up, since they now depend on you for a handout.

Ohio's coldest Christmas was in 1983, with area high temperatures only around zero and a -50° wind chill; Ashtabula and Conneaut were snowbound.

DAILY DATA FOR DECEMBER

Date	Day	Moon	Day of Year	Days Left	Sunrise	Sunset	Length of Day	Avg. Hi°	Avg. Lo°	Avg. Lake°
1	Thu	●	335	30	7:34	4:58	9:24	43	29	45
2	Fri		336	29	7:35	4:57	9:22	42	29	45
3	Sat		337	28	7:36	4:57	9:21	42	28	45
4	Sun		338	27	7:37	4:57	9:20	41	28	44
5	Mon		339	26	7:38	4:57	9:19	41	28	44
6	Tue		340	25	7:39	4:57	9:18	40	27	44
7	Wed		341	24	7:40	4:57	9:17	40	27	43
8	Thu	◐	342	23	7:41	4:57	9:16	40	27	43
9	Fri		343	22	7:41	4:57	9:16	39	27	43
10	Sat		344	21	7:42	4:57	9:15	39	26	42
11	Sun		345	20	7:43	4:57	9:14	39	26	42
12	Mon		346	19	7:44	4:57	9:13	38	26	41
13	Tue		347	18	7:45	4:57	9:12	38	25	41
14	Wed		348	17	7:45	4:57	9:12	38	25	41
15	Thu	○	349	16	7:46	4:58	9:12	37	25	40
16	Fri		350	15	7:47	4:58	9:11	37	24	40
17	Sat		351	14	7:47	4:58	9:11	37	24	40
18	Sun		352	13	7:48	4:59	9:11	37	24	39
19	Mon		353	12	7:49	4:59	9:10	36	24	39
20	Tue		354	11	7:49	5:00	9:11	36	23	38
21	Wed		355	10	7:50	5:00	9:10	36	23	38
22	Thu		356	9	7:50	5:01	9:11	36	23	37
23	Fri	◑	357	8	7:51	5:01	9:10	35	23	37
24	Sat		358	7	7:51	5:02	9:11	35	22	37
25	Sun		359	6	7:52	5:02	9:10	35	22	37
26	Mon		360	5	7:52	5:03	9:11	35	22	36
27	Tue		361	4	7:52	5:04	9:12	34	22	36
28	Wed		362	3	7:52	5:04	9:12	34	21	36
29	Thu		363	2	7:53	5:05	9:12	34	21	36
30	Fri		364	1	7:53	5:06	9:13	34	21	36
31	Sat	●	365	0	7:53	5:07	9:14	34	21	36

Rec. Hi°	Rec. Lo°	On This Date . . .
65/1970	7/1929	LPGA golfer Barb Mucha born in Parma (1961)
70/1982	-5/1976	Actor Robert F. Simon born in Mansfield (1908)
77/1982	-7/1976	77ºF highest temp ever recorded in Cleve in Dec (1982)
70/1982	8/1871	Cleveland Cavaliers retire jersey #7, Bingo Smith (1979)
71/2001	2/1871	George Armstrong Custer born in New Rumley (1839)
68/1956	7/1977	Browns quarterback Otto Graham born (1921)
66/1892	-5/1882	Pearl Harbor bombed (1941)
67/1966	-9/1882	John Lennon shot (1980)
62/1952	-5/1917	Cavs guard World B Free born (1953)
69/1971	-5/1958	WSTV (now WTOV) channel 9 in Steubenville begins (1953)
64/1931	-2/1977	"Mike Douglas Show" first airs in Cleveland (1961)
63/1949	-1/1962	Bank of the U.S. opens (1791)
65/1901	-3/1962	Indians' Larry Doby born (1st black in baseball's AL) (1924)
64/1901	0/1914	1st state road authorized, Frankfort KY to Cincinnati (1793)
67/1971	-1/1958	Actor Tim Conway born in Willoughby (1933)
64/1984	-9/1951	Cleveland Rams win NFL championship (1945)
61/1984	-7/1989	WEWS TV channel 5 in Cleve begins broadcasting (1947)
62/1939	-5/1989	Director Steven Spielberg born in Cincinnati (1947)
61/1939	-5/1884	WJW TV Channel 8 in Cleveland begins broadcasting (1949)
62/1895	-4/1963	Rockers' guard Jenny Boucek born (1973)
65/1967	-7/1972	TV host Phil Donahue born in Cleveland (1935)
64/1949	-15/1989	1st string of Christmas tree lights created by Edison (1882)
61/1933	-7/1960	Voyager completes global flight (1986)
65/1964	-10/1983	Luna 13 lands on Moon (1966)
66/1982	-10/1983	Centigrade temperature scale introduced (1741)
64/1875	-8/1983	Lorain County incorporated (1822)
64/1936	-5/1944	Writer Louis Bromfield born in Mansfield (1896)
68/1982	-3/1880	Newscaster Jack Perkins born in Cleveland (1933)
66/1889	-12/1880	U.S. patent for chewing gum granted to W. F. Semple of Mt. Vernon (1869)
63/1971	-12/1880	Actor Jack Riley born in Cleveland (1935)
68/1875	-11/1880	Toboggan Chutes begin operation in Cleveland Metroparks (1966)

Flora & Fauna DECEMBER

WEEK 1 **BIRDS:** As the last of the migrating Canada geese move south, they may be joined by snow geese, white geese with telltale black wing tips. Open water remains at most refuges and rivers until month's end. Great blue herons and kingfishers remain where open waters still offer fish to eat. **MAMMALS:** Bucks' antlers become brightly polished as the breeding season continues from October and November. Territorial battles are rare, but the rattling antlers of combatants can sometimes be heard. Most fawns have lost their camouflage spotted coats, but still stay close to their mothers. Later, herds of related does and their fawns spend the winter foraging for food, and most bucks become solitary or form small bachelor herds.

WEEK 2 **BIRDS:** If winter hasn't been too harsh thus far, some of Hinckley's buzzards may still be seen circling overhead at midday. As food becomes scarce, they will gradually drift to more southerly locations for the winter. Cedar waxwings begin to harvest the summer's crop of overripe berries. The fermented sugars in the berries turn to alcohol, and the happily inebriated little birds occasionally lose all sense of direction, propriety, and flight when the alcohol-laden berries warm their tiny stomachs. **TREES:** Many oaks and beeches will hold dead leaves on their branches all winter. Spring growth sheds the golden brown mantle of old leaves, thus allowing the forest to gain two layers of nutrients each year. The rustle of leaves in the winter wind is a sharp contrast to the quiet of snowy meadows.

WEEK 3 **BIRDS:** Each year at this time the National Audubon Society sponsors a nationwide "Christmas Count" of birds remaining on the wintering grounds. Contact a local nature or visitor center, or an Audubon group center, for information on this year's Christmas Count. You'll be surprised at how many species are still here along the North Coast! **MAMMALS:** Cold, snowy weather and limited food resources mean the temporary disappearance of winter-sleeping mammals like the raccoon, opossum, and skunk. They may awaken from time to time to feed as winter passes. This is the latest week that woodchucks have been seen in our region. Most have been in hibernation for several weeks and will sleep until February or March.

WEEK 4 **BIRDS:** Tufted titmice and chickadees may be willing to take sunflower seeds from friendly hands from now until the end of winter. Bring a pocketful of seeds and make a new bird friend this week! As winter begins officially this week, scan leafless trees in larger forests for barred and great horned owls. **MAMMALS:** Chipmunks have become scarce as they "hole up" for the winter. These farsighted little squirrels depend on acorns, seeds, and nuts carefully stored in underground caches for their winter food. They remain active underground until March. Flying squirrels, red squirrels, and the larger fox and gray squirrels move to winter den holes in trees and remain active all winter. Flying squirrels begin to use stored nuts cached during summer and fall.

Adapted from the Nature Almanac by Robert Hinkle, with permission from Cleveland Metroparks.

The world's **first Silver Screen was created at Akron's, Majestic Theatre** on South Main Street. In 1924, projectionist Harry C. Williams painted the existing white cloth screen silver to better reflect light. He also painted the screen of the Norka Theater on East Market Street. The practice caught on, and the phrase "silver screen" came to symbolize Hollywood movies. *Source: www.geocities.com/buslady43*

Photographing Squirrels Photographing Me...

By Scott Alan Johnson

Everyone needs a hobby. Some collect stamps; others paint birdhouses. My hobby is photographing rodents, but there is one difference between other animal photographers and me—I photograph only rodents who are photographing me.

Most of my pictures are of the wild squirrels and chipmunks living in, or around, the west side of the Cleveland Metroparks. It was there I first met Pops, the American fox squirrel.

Pops is one of the most curious and intelligent squirrels I have ever met. It was he who founded the photography club A.C.O.R.N., also known as the American Camera Organized Rodent Network, and he who started me on my hobby as one of the world's few Rodent Photographer Photographers.

I can imagine that most of you do not believe that these wild squirrels and chipmunks could ever start a photography club, let

alone take pictures with old film cameras. The fact is, they only use the old film cameras because they can't afford the cost of the new digital cameras and all the computer equipment that is needed to produce pictures. I have been told that collecting acorns for a living is not very profitable.

The story on Pops and the A.C.O.R.N. club began about a year ago when I was sitting at a picnic table reading a photography magazine. An American fox squirrel (scientific name *Sciurus niger*) hopped up on the table and started looking over my camera. I always have a camera with me and can often be seen hiking the trails of the park, shooting the local flora and fauna. The squirrel examined the camera just as if he was a teenager looking over the new sports cars on a showroom. I figured the little guy was just hungry and was looking for food. I grabbed the camera and hoped I could get a picture or two off before he ran away.

To my surprise the squirrel didn't run off; he actually posed for me. He literally sat up and smiled for the camera. I took five or six pictures, put down my camera and just gazed at him. I think I was in shock as he walked over to my magazine and started to read an article on macro insect photography (macrophotography is the art of super close-up camera work). This, I thought, was not an ordinary squirrel.

Just then my watch alarm went off. It was time for me to go back to work; my lunch hour was about over. As I packed up my camera and started to close up the magazine, I looked into the eyes of the squirrel. "Okay," I said, "I'll leave you the magazine, but I'll be back tomorrow and I'll want it back." Again the squirrel smiled, and I walked to the car. As I looked back at the picnic table, I saw two other squirrels and a chipmunk run out from the bushes and onto the table. I shook my head and told myself I was dreaming.

I'm not sure if I really believed what happened that day, but the next day I went back to the same picnic table. Again I brought my camera and a surprise for my little friend. I figured if this squirrel was as fascinated with photography as he looked, I would help him as much as I could.

I got to the table and found my magazine just where I had left it, except that it had two big acorns on top. I looked around and called out for my friend, "Hey little guy! Come out here. I have a gift for you." A moment later, from the bushes, came two squirrels, both of whom climbed to the top of the table.

"Is this your son?" I asked. He responded with a proud look. "Well, that makes you a father, so I'll start calling you 'Pops'! And you, little guy," I pointed to the smaller squirrel, "can be 'Buddy.'"

"Hey little guy! Come out here. I have a gift for you."

Both Pops and Buddy began looking over my camera and chatting back and forth to each other. I could have sworn they were discussing the finer points of my digital Nikon.

"Hey guys," I said, "I have something for you." I reached into my camera bag and pulled out an old box camera. The camera was about 40 years old and didn't have a lot of features, but I loaded it with film and added a little tripod to make it easy to set up and shoot with.

You should have seen the way the squirrels jumped around and screamed. It was as if they had just won the Mega Lotto. I spent a little time showing them the shutter and film rewind buttons, and explained that it was the smallest camera I could find. I watched Pops put the camera strap around his neck and then both squirrels ran back to the bushes. I wished someone else had been there to see this, because I knew no one would believe me. I called out for Pops again, and said I wanted to photograph him with his new camera. He set it up and smiled. I took a few pictures, then told him to have fun. I went off and did what I always do—hiked along the river. Some time later I walked back to my car and spotted Buddy running toward me. He had a finished roll of film in his mouth and dropped it at my feet. I said, "Okay," and he ran off. I should have figured that the squirrels had no way to develop the film.

I could hardly wait until the girl at the drugstore finished printing the film. I had to see what squirrels like to photograph. Still somewhat in shock with disbelief, I opened the prints and looked them over. The first four shots were blurry and hard to define. They looked just like the pictures I took with my first camera. Then I looked at the next photo and my eyes opened wide. The shot was of a chipmunk sitting in the grass. The picture was in perfect focus, shot at the chipmunk's eye level, and framed like a pro. I have to say it was one of the best chipmunk pictures I had ever seen.

Until I saw that picture I kept thinking that Pops was just curious, and I was playing a game with him. Now I know that Pops is more than just an average squirrel. Pops and Buddy are photographers and, with help from me, could become some of the best nature photographers around. Hey, why not? They are part of nature already.

The rest of the photos on the roll were of average quality. Considering that Pops shot these pictures with a 40-year-old box camera, has only four fingers on each hand, and the fact that he is a SQUIRREL, I would have to say Pops is as good a photographer as any I have ever met.

Over the next few months I worked with Pops and Buddy, going over their pictures, and letting them try different cameras from my collection. Sometimes other squirrels and chipmunks would join us, and I would photograph them as they went around shooting. I would bring the latest photography magazines (after I read them) for them to read. I started calling our meeting the Camera Club, until Pops gave me an acorn. From that day on the club would be called the A.C.O.R.N. Group, which stands for The American Camera Organized Rodent Network.

The A.C.O.R.N. Group has grown, and now boasts a membership of over 1,000 squirrels and chipmunks throughout the Metroparks and Cleveland backyards. You may not realize it, but someday, as you hike the trails, go fishing, or just relax in the park, you may be photographed by a bushy-tailed rodent with an old box camera. If you happen to spy a squirrel taking your picture, remember to smile and say, "Peanut!" They always like that.

Note: Photographs shown here were taken by nature photographer Scott Alan Johnson and are of wild fox squirrels and Eastern chipmunks living in the Cleveland Metroparks. There is no post-photography computer editing used. At no time were any of the squirrels trapped or harmed in any way. If you would like to see more of Scott's squirrel photographs you can go to his photography website, www.fstopnature.com, or see them at harphampix.com

Scott Alan Johnson is the assignment editor at FOX 8.

YOU'D BE AMAZED AT WHAT YOU CAN SEE IN DECEMBER

December 14 offers the Geminids meteor shower. This could be the best meteor activity of the year, as some astronomers are predicting one streak per minute. While the peak activity is centered around December 14, we can easily see bright streaks (shooting stars) a couple of days before and after the 14th. Be patient, give it 15 minutes, and you should see a few, even in the brightest areas of our city.

Until December 11, the planet Mars continues to shine bright in the south. The "Red Planet" will be close to a nearly full moon, while the planet Saturn begins to rise in the east.

Courtesy of Jay Reynolds, Schuele Planetarium director, Lake Erie Nature and Science Center.

A lie will travel halfway around the world while truth is still putting on its shoes.
— Mark Twain

Three decades of research by psychologists in the United States have suggested that men lie more often than women. (Could men who fish have skewed the results?) But the percentage difference is narrowing. A 1980 study of "who lies more often" concluded that males lied 10 times more often than females. The most recent study, however, suggests that men now lie only three times as often as women. (Way to go, girls!)

Psychologists have also determined that the classic accepted sign that someone is lying does not exist: Liars do not avert their eyes; they gaze directly ad unblinkingly at you.

While there is no one trait that reveals a Pinocchio among us, liars often move their arms, hands, and fingers much less than those who are telling the truth. A liar's voice will frequently become more high-pitched and strained, along with obvious pauses in their story telling. This indicates a need to concentrate on their fibs.

According to psychologists most people tell at least one lie during every 10 minutes of conversation. Many of these

untruths must be in the "little white lie" category, such as the almost automatic reply of "good" in response to the ubiquitous Jersey Guy's witty "How ya' doin'?"

The lies, whether white or any other color, are programmed into humans in childhood. Specialists in child behavior estimate that by age two and a half, 65 percent of children lie . . . and they do it well.

Seldom are the little con artists reprimanded, so they quickly learn it's not a big deal. Experts tell parents that this is wrong. They should not let the tykes off the hook. Researchers also tell us that the higher a child's IQ, the more likely they are to fib.

There is a difference in what females and males lie about. Women often lie to protect the feelings of others, or to protect the macho male's fragile ego. (I recently saw a woman in Cleveland driving by with an Ohio license plate that read: MEN LIE.)

Men frequently lie to boost their self-esteem. As an example, the majority of male golfers never break 100, but they often report their score using the Celsius scale.

While both sexes cheat in their relationships, men are the leaders in marital indiscretions. Women, however, are trying their best to catch up in illicit affairs. According to one estimate, there has been a 50 percent increase in female infidelity in the last decade.

As you can imagine, trying to find the truth about lying isn't easy (and that's the truth).

But how about that modern technological marvel called the "lie detector," or polygraph? The courts have decided—in spite of protests from those who manufacture the devices—that polygraphs are unreliable, and their results are not admissible in most states.

Polygraphs measure respiration (breathing), blood pressure, and pulse rate. As scientific as it is purported to be, the lie detector is only as accurate as the machine's operator says it is.

In terms of litigation, lies fall into two categories: libel and slander. Both relate to false defamation that can injure a person's good name and reputation. While libel can refer to something expressed either orally or in writing, slander is confined to the spoken word (although words spoken in a movie or television program are usually interpreted by the courts as being libelous, since they are more lasting than ordinary speech). ■

Continued from page 132

I was telling him; "You'll be alright, baby . . . we're going to see the doctor and she'll help you too."

The vet was already there upon our arrival at the animal hospital. She helped me get him out of the car and into the examining room. She cleaned the blood that was all over his backside. Once the wound was uncovered it took just moments before she said that Clarence had his groin bitten in what was an obvious attempt to eviscerate him. In other words, the attacker tried to disembowel Clarence, that is remove his lower organs. She added that the wounds from the bite mark were eye tooth marks spanning five inches, meaning the animal's mouth was that large. She said it was a classic coyote attack.

Now it all made perfect sense. The animal I saw was unusual to me and *did* completely fit the description of a coyote and its typical manner of attack.

Did we ever really think that coyotes lived in our urban, residential neighborhoods? We weren't out West, after all.

Well, dear reader, they *are* living here, struggling with the harsh reality of their own existence with little natural food available.

Even with what happened, I have a sense of sadness for the coyote trying to survive here with the extensive encroachments of civilization. These are not the plains or the prairies of the West, where they can more easily survive. These are highly populated areas. So . . . please do be aware, both for yourself and those you love!

Well, time has marched on and Clarence, thank God, has healed, at least physically. He is now my shadow. Where I go, he goes. If I look at something, he looks. I like to call him my little, constant helper. His confidence may have been altered by the attack but his loyalty is enormous. As I said, what I do and where I go are always a part of his agenda too.

When I brought him home from the vet the day of the attack our other animals knew something was terribly wrong with their buddy. At the time he had been heavily sedated and I laid him on a blanket on the floor. I put a heating pad beneath him, since he was shaking. Let me tell you something, although I'm sure if you're an animal lover you already know this: Never say animals don't know or aren't aware! Our cat, Romeo, and our other dog, Clifford, took turns staying next to him as if in a caring, loving vigil.

Interestingly, as I write this story to you, there is a major report out of Simi Valley, California, of coyote attacks on three children there. Admittedly, it is an extremely rare occurrence that a coyote would attack children. However, it should also be noted that in this California case as well, the attacks happened in afternoon daylight and very close to the children's homes. In one case, the female coyote attacked the little boy on his front porch.

So many people believe, as do I, that there is no such thing as coincidence. Hearing about these attacks as I write this means to me that I should tell you about them now to help make you aware. You may know the sage saying, "Knowledge is power"—now, my friend, you are even more powerful.

Well, that is a segment from the lives of my little guys. I love them very much, as you must love your "babies." They add so much to our daily lives. They teach us all so much about ourselves and about how people sometimes react to other people.

There is a sincere wisdom in animals. Our job, if we are lucky enough to be open to the opportunity, is to enjoy God's gift in our lives.

Animals have so much to share with us. They have so much love inside them. They are ready and eager to share, and to make our time on earth heavenly.

Enjoy your "babies" too. Remember something I was once told: "From what we get we can make a living. What we give, however, makes a life!!"

Our lives are so much richer with animals.

Wilma Smith is anchor of the 6 and 10 p.m. editions of FOX 8 NEWS. She is the recipient of 10 Emmy nominations and 10 Emmy Awards for excellence in her television work. She was voted "Anchor of Excellence" by the National Association of Career Women, "Newscaster of the Year," a Cleveland Pacesetter, and "Best Anchorperson" by Cleveland Magazine, and is a member of the Ohio Television/Radio Hall of Fame. She is also one of the few women to be named to the NATAS prestigious "Silver Circle."

Northeast Ohio COUNTY STATISTICS

ASHLAND

Name: Named for Henry Clay's Kentucky estate (a Whig presidential candidate)

Established: Feb 24, 1846

Size: 424.4 square miles

Population: 53,173

Projected population for 2015: 57,538

Persons under 5 years old: 6.6%

Persons 65 years old and over: 13.9%

Persons per square mile: 125.3

Average personal per capita income: $22,744

Mean travel time to work (minutes), workers age 16+: 20.3

County Seat: Ashland

House Districts: 90, 97

Senate Districts: 19, 22

ASHTABULA

Name: Named for the Ashtabula River, a Native American word meaning "River of Many Fish"

Established: June 7, 1807

Size: 702.7 square miles

Population: 102,985

Projected population for 2015: 102,985

Persons under 5 years old: 6.5%

Persons 65 years old and over: 14.7%

Persons per square mile: 146.6

Average personal per capita income: $23,335

Mean travel time to work (minutes), workers age 16+: 23.9

County Seat: Jefferson Village

House District: 99

Senate District: 32

CARROLL

Name: Named for Charles Carroll, last surviving signer of the Declaration of Independence

Established: Jan 1, 1833

Size: 394.7 square miles

Population: 29, 262

Projected population for 2015: 32,893

Persons under 5 years old: 6.0%

Persons 65 years old and over: 14.2%

Persons per square mile: 74.1

Average personal per capita income: $22,878

Mean travel time to work (minutes), workers age 16+: 27.5

County Seat: Carrollton Village

House District: 61

Senate District: 33

COLUMBIANA

Name: Named for Christopher Columbus and "Anna"

Established: May 1, 1803

Size: 532.5 square miles

Population: 111,571

Projected population for 2015: 111,868

Persons under 5 years old: 5.9%

Persons 65 years old and over: 15.0%

Persons per square mile: 209.5

Average personal per capita income: $22,771

Mean travel time to work (minutes), workers age 16+: 22.7

County Seat: Lisbon Village

House District: 1

Senate District: 30

COSHOCTON

Name: Named for a Delaware Native American word meaning "Black Bear Town"

Established: Jan 31, 1810

Size: 567.6 square miles

Population: 37,415

Projected population for 2015: 35,400

Persons under 5 years old: 6.4%

Persons 65 years old and over: 14.7%

Persons per square mile: 65.1

Average personal per capita income: $23,206

Mean travel time to work (minutes), workers age 16+: 22.4

County Seat: Coshocton

House District: 94

Senate District: 20

CUYAHOGA

Name: Named for the Cuyahoga River, a Native American word meaning "Crooked River"

Established: June 7, 1807

Size: 458.3 square miles

Population: 1,373,997

Projected population for 2015: 1,309,637

Persons under 5 years old: 6.5%

Persons 65 years old and over: 15.6%

Persons per square mile: 2,998.0

Average personal per capita income: $33,382

Mean travel time to work (minutes), workers age 16+: 24.4

County Seat: Cleveland

House Districts: 7, 8, 9, 10, 11, 12, 13, 14, 15, 16, 17, 18, 98

Senate Districts: 18, 21, 23, 24, 25

ERIE

Name: Named for Lake Erie and Erie Indians, a Native American word meaning "cat"

Established: March 16, 1838

Size: 245.5 square miles

Population: 78.868

Projected population for 2015: 82,264

Persons under 5 years old: 6.0%

Persons 65 years old and over: 15.6%

Persons per square mile: 321.3

Average personal per capita income: $30,155

Mean travel time to work (minutes), workers age 16+: 18.8

County Seat: Sandusky

House District: 80

Senate District: 2

GEAUGA

Name: Named for a Native American word meaning "raccoon"

Established: March 1, 1806

Size: 404.1 square miles

Population:92,617

Projected population for 2015: 101,286

Persons under 5 years old: 6.8%

Persons 65 years old and over: 12.0%

Persons per square mile: 229.2

Average personal per capita income: $37,868

Mean travel time to work (minutes), workers age 16+: 27

County Seat: Chardon

House District: 98

Senate District: 18

HARRISON

Name: Named for William Henry Harrison, 9th President of the U.S.

Established: Feb 1, 1813

Size: 403.6 square miles

Population: 15,866

Projected population for 2015: 15,607

Persons under 5 years old: 5.8%

Persons 65 years old and over: 17.7%

Persons per square mile: 39.3

Average personal per capita income: $22,312

Mean travel time to work (minutes), workers age 16+: 28.8

County Seat: Cadiz Village

House District: 96

Senate District: 30

HOLMES

Name: Named for Major Holmes from the War of 1812

Established: Jan 20, 1824

Size: 423.0 square miles

Population: 40,319

Projected population for 2015: 44,848

Persons under 5 years old: 10.3%

Persons 65 years old and over: 10.5%

Persons per square mile: 95.3

Average personal per capita income: $19,647

Mean travel time to work (minutes), workers age 16+: 21.6

County Seat: Millersburg Village

House District: 97

Senate District: 22

HURON

Name: Named for the Huron Indians

Established: March 7, 1809

Size: 493.1 square miles

Population: 59,922

Projected population for 2015: 62,613

Persons under 5 years old: 7.5%

Persons 65 years old and over: 12.4%

Persons per square mile: 121.5

Average personal per capita income: $24,234

Mean travel time to work (minutes), workers age 16+: 20.2

County Seat: Norwalk

House District: 58

Senate District: 13

JEFFERSON

Name: Named for Thomas Jefferson, 3rd President of the U.S.

Established: July 29, 1797

Size: 409.6 square miles

Population: 72,270

Projected population for 2015: 63,598

Persons under 5 years old: 5.2%

Persons 65 years old and over: 18.6%

Persons per square mile: 176.4

Average personal per capita income: $23,622

Mean travel time to work (minutes), workers age 16+: 22.2

County Seat: Steubenville

House District: 95

Senate District: 30

LAKE

Name: Named for Lake Erie

Established: March 6, 1840

Size: 228.2 square miles

Population: 228,746

Projected population for 2015: 233,764

Persons under 5 years old: 6.1%

Persons 65 years old and over: 14.1%

Persons per square mile: 1002.4

Average personal per capita income: $30,860

Mean travel time to work (minutes), workers age 16+: 22.9

County Seat: Painesville

House Districts: 62, 63

Senate District: 18

LORAIN

Name: From the French province of Lorraine

Established: December 26, 1822

Size: 492.6 square miles

Population: 288,075

Projected population for 2015: 233,764

Persons under 5 years old: 6.9%

Persons 65 years old and over: 12.5%

Persons per square mile: 584.8

Average personal per capita income: $26,964

Mean travel time to work (minutes), workers age 16+: 22.8

County Seat: Elyria

House Districts: 56, 57, 58

Senate District: 13

MAHONING

Name: Named for the Mahoning River, a Native American word meaning "at the salt licks"

Established: March 1, 1846

Size: 415.3 square miles

Population: 252,794

Projected population for 2015: 241,166

Persons under 5 years old: 6.0%

Persons 65 years old and over: 17.8%

Persons per square mile: 608.7

Average personal per capita income: $25,924

Mean travel time to work (minutes), workers age 16+: 21.5

County Seat: Youngstown

House Districts: 60, 61

Senate District: 33

MEDINA

Name: Named for the Arabian city where Mohammed is buried

Established: Feb 18,1812

Size: 421.6 square miles

Population: 158,367

Projected population for 2015: 175,920

Persons under 5 years old: 7.0%

Persons 65 years old and over: 10.5%

Persons per square mile: 375.6

Average personal per capita income: $30,685

Mean travel time to work (minutes), workers age 16+: 26.4

County Seat: Medina

House Districts: 69, 97

Senate District: 22

PORTAGE

Name: Named for a Native American word meaning "a carrying path"

Established: June 7,1807

Size: 492.4 square miles

Population: 153,955

Projected population for 2015: 160,600

Persons under 5 years old: 6.1%

Persons 65 years old and over: 11.0%

Persons per square mile: 312.7

Average personal per capita income: $26,834

Mean travel time to work (minutes), workers age 16+: 25.1

County Seat: Ravenna

House Districts: 43, 68

Senate District: 28

RICHLAND

Name: Named in honor of the county's rich soil

Established: March 1, 1808

Size: 497.0 square miles

Population: 128,380

Projected population for 2015: 121,200

Persons under 5 years old: 6.4%

Persons 65 years old and over: 14.2%

Persons per square mile: 258.3

Average personal per capita income: $25,098

Mean travel time to work (minutes), workers age 16+: 20.2

County Seat: Mansfield

House Districts: 73, 90

Senate District: 19

STARK

Name: Named for Revolutionary War hero General John Stark

Established: Feb 13, 1808

Size: 576.2 square miles

Population: 377,629

Projected population for 2015: 373,980

Persons under 5 years old: 6.4%

Persons 65 years old and over: 15.1%

Persons per square mile: 655.4

Average personal per capita income: $27,519

Mean travel time to work (minutes), workers age 16+: 21.3

County Seat: Canton

House Districts: 50, 51, 52, 61

Senate Districts: 29, 33

SUMMIT

Name: Named for the highest point of land along the Erie-Ohio Canal, Portage Summit

Established: March 3,1840

Size: 412.8 square miles

Population: 546,175

Projected population for 2015: 561,806

Persons under 5 years old: 6.6%

Persons 65 years old and over: 14.1%

Persons per square mile: 1,323.1

Average personal per capita income: $31,155

Mean travel time to work (minutes), workers age 16+: 22.4

County Seat: Akron

House Districts: 43, 44, 45

Senate Districts: 27, 28

TRUMBULL

Name: Named for Jonathan Trumbull, Governor of Connecticut

Established:July 10, 1800

Size: 615.8 square miles

Population: 223,168

Projected population for 2015: 215,994

Persons under 5 years old: 6.1%

Persons 65 years old and over: 15.7%

Persons per square mile: 362.4

Average personal per capita income: $25,156

Mean travel time to work (minutes), workers age 16+: 21

County Seat: Warren

House Districts: 64, 65, 99

Senate Districts: 32

TUSCARAWAS

Name: Native American word meaning "open mouth"

Established: March 15, 1808

Size: 567.6 square miles

Population: 91,599

Projected population for 2015: 93,991

Persons under 5 years old: 6.6%

Persons 65 years old and over: 15.0%

Persons per square mile: 161.4

Average personal per capita income: $23,029

Mean travel time to work (minutes), workers age 16+: 21.6

County Seat: New Philadelphia

House Districts: 61, 96

Senate Districts: 30, 33

WAYNE

Name: Named for Revolutionary War General "Mad" Anthony Wayne

Established: Aug 15, 1796

Size: 555.4 square miles

Population: 112,808

Projected population for 2015: 123,519

Persons under 5 years old: 7.0%

Persons 65 years old and over: 12.2%

Persons per square mile: 203.1

Average personal per capita income: $25,002

Mean travel time to work (minutes), workers age 16+: 19.4

County Seat: Wooster

House Districts: 3

Senate District: 22